UNIVERSITY OF CAMBRIDGE
ORIENTAL PUBLICATIONS

No. 19

A NESTORIAN COLLECTION OF CHRISTOLOGICAL TEXTS

II

UNIVERSITY OF CAMBRIDGE
ORIENTAL PUBLICATIONS PUBLISHED FOR THE
FACULTY OF ORIENTAL STUDIES

1 *Averroes' Commentary on Plato's Republic*, edited and translated by ERWIN
   I. J. ROSENTHAL
2 *FitzGerald's 'Salaman and Absal'*, edited by A. J. ARBERRY
3 *Ihara Saikaku: The Japanese Family Storehouse*, translated and edited by
   G. W. SARGENT
4 *The Avestan Hymn to Mithra*, edited and translated by ILYA GERSHEVITCH
5 *The Fusul al-Madanī of al-Fārābī*, edited and translated by D. M. DUNLOP
6 *Dun Karm, Poet of Malta*, texts chosen and translated by A. J. ARBERRY;
   introduction, notes and glossary by P. GRECH
7 *The Political Writings of Ogyū Sorai*, by J. R. MCEWAN
8 *Financial Administration under the T'ang Dynasty*, by D. C. TWITCHETT
9 *Neolithic Cattle-Keepers of South India: a Study of the Deccan Ashmounds*, by
   F. R. ALLCHIN
10 *The Japanese Enlightenment: a Study of the Writings of Fukuzawa Yukichi*, by
   CARMEN BLACKER
11 *Records of Han Administration*, vol. I, *Historical Assessment*, by MICHAEL
   LOEWE
12 *Records of Han Administration*, vol. II, *Documents*, by MICHAEL LOEWE
13 *The Language of Indrajit of Orchā*, by R. S. MCGREGOR
14 *Japan's First General Election, 1890*, by R. H. P. MASON
15 *A Collection of Tales from Uji*, by D. E. MILLS
16 *Studia Semitica*, vol. I, *Jewish Themes*, by ERWIN I. J. ROSENTHAL
17 *Studia Semitica*, vol. II, *Islamic Themes*, by ERWIN I. J. ROSENTHAL
18 *A Nestorian Collection of Christological Texts*, vol. I, *Syriac Text*, edited by
   L. ABRAMOWSKI and A. E. GOODMAN
19 *A Nestorian Collection of Christological Texts*, vol. II, *English Translation*, by
   L. ABRAMOWSKI and A. E. GOODMAN
20 *The Syriac Version of the Pseudo-Nonnos Mythological Scholia*, by SEBASTIAN
   BROCK
21 *Water Rights and Irrigation Practices in Laḥj*, by A. M. A. MAKTARI

A NESTORIAN COLLECTION OF CHRISTOLOGICAL TEXTS

CAMBRIDGE UNIVERSITY LIBRARY
MS. ORIENTAL 1319

EDITED AND TRANSLATED BY
LUISE ABRAMOWSKI

Professor of Church History
in the University of Bonn

AND

ALAN E. GOODMAN

Fellow of University College Cambridge
University Lecturer in Aramaic

VOLUME II

INTRODUCTION, TRANSLATION
INDEXES

CAMBRIDGE
AT THE UNIVERSITY PRESS
1972

Published by the Syndics of the Cambridge University Press
Bentley House, 200 Euston Road, London NW1 2DB
American Branch: 32 East 57th Street, New York, N.Y.10022

© Faculty of Oriental Studies, University of Cambridge 1972

Library of Congress Catalogue Card Number: 77–130904

ISBNS:
0 521 07578 5   vol. I
0 521 08126 2   vol. II

Printed in Great Britain
at the University Printing House, Cambridge
(Brooke Crutchley, University Printer)

CONTENTS

INTRODUCTION

The manuscript here edited, University Library, Cambridge, Or. 1319 (= C), is a late nineteenth-century transcript, belonging to a collection of Syriac mss. which had been acquired by the Reverend David Jenks, M.A., S.S.M., between the years 1892 and 1899, during which period he was a member of the Archbishop of Canterbury's Mission to the Assyrian Christians in Urmia, Persia. Jenks died in 1935, and these mss. were presented by the Society of the Sacred Mission to Pembroke College, Cambridge, who decided, with the Society's approval, to transfer the gift to the University Library,[1] keeping one ms. for itself as a souvenir of its alumnus.

It was Jenks' custom to have copies made of any ms. which he considered to be of importance, either in Urmia or elsewhere. Many such transcripts were collected by the Church of England Mission Station at Urmia, but unfortunately the whole of this library was looted in 1917, as was also the library of the American Presbyterian Mission. The catalogue of the latter, prepared by Dr J. H. Shedd and Oshana Sarau,[2] lists 232 Syriac mss., and it is apparent that at least four of Jenks' transcripts were copied from mss. in this collection, but not ours.

C is a transcription on ruled foolscap paper; 112 leaves; 10 quires, signed with letters, mostly of 12 leaves (ܐ and ܗ have 10, ܘ has 8); usually 23 lines to a page, pp. 150–204, 207, 208, 220–2 have 24, pp. 96, 207 have 25, pp. 56, 72 have 22, pp. 8, 54 have 21 lines. It is written in a clear Nestorian hand (though the writing sometimes becomes less legible through haste), is fully vocalized with Nestorian vowels, and is rubricated. As in the case of the other transcripts, the aim of the scribe has been to reproduce in every detail the ms. which was before him (= U, after Urmia). Lacunae are clearly indicated by spaces left blank in the text; readings he was not sure of (caused by the state of U) were put into brackets with a query; explanatory notes are sometimes added, either in Syriac or in English, the latter always by Jenks; marginal notes in U are reproduced as such, even when in cases of omission their correct place in the text is evident. The whole transcript was compared by Jenks with U, as his pencil notes testify.

[1] A. E. Goodman, 'The Jenks Collection of Syriac Manuscripts in the University Library, Cambridge', *Journal of the Royal Asiatic Society*, Oct. 1939, pp. 581–600.

[2] O. Sarau and W. A. Shedd, *Catalogue of Syriac mss. in the Library of the Museum association of Oroomiah College*, Oroomiah, Persia, 1898.

C was undoubtedly written during the same period (1892–9) as the other transcripts. There is no colophon, but a pencilled note by Jenks at the foot of p. 205 indicates that the name of the copyist was Daniel. That the latter is identical with 'Daniel, son of the deacon Saul', whose name appears in the colophon to Cambridge Or. 1312 ('The Treatise of Heraclides'), and who was the final copyist of that ms., is borne out by a comparison of the handwriting. But there is no indication where C was transcribed, and we cannot say whether U had been found at Urmia or at some other place.

On the reverse of p. 1, there are two inscriptions taken over from U in Jenks' hand which relate to the history of U from which C was copied. We here transcribe the whole of this page verbatim (the lines in English are remarks of Jenks'):

'Selections from the writings of the Fathers. This inscription is on the fly leaf of the book in a later handwritg'

'On a still earlier page is this inscription in red and black, which is possib contemp: with writ of the book'

We translate the first inscription as follows:

'This book was handed on, being a gift from the monks, disciples of the spiritual philosopher, Rabban and Mar Cyriacus, may he be preserved in life. For me Sabrisho did they make it, in the year 1645 of the Greeks.'

1645 Gr. is A.D. 1333/4. Rabban Mar Cyriacus may be the personage mentioned by Baumstark[1] and dated tentatively as a contemporary of Kamis[2] (who in his turn is 'ein offenbar wesentlich jüngerer Zeitgenosse' of Barhebraeus),[3] which would bring us to the end of the thirteenth or the beginning of the fourteenth century. That would indeed fit quite well, 'this book' being U. The 'making' of the book *could* then mean that the monks collected the large excerpts of which it consists, and so composed it, though much more probable is the simple explanation that they wrote, i.e. copied, it from a ms. in their possession (the root 'to make' having *inter alia* the meaning of 'to write' *sc.* a book). The ms. from which U was copied we will call Q (after the Syriac spelling of the name Cyriacus).

The name Sabrisho, however, appears again in the second inscription. This is at first glance confusing, particularly in view of the somewhat misleading notes added by Jenks. The second inscription is to be translated:

'This book is the property of the feeble Sabrisho, Metropolitan of Ḥisn Kef, son of the true believer, the priest Jacob. He purchased it from a priest, a certain Abdas of Mosul, in the presence of the priest Hormizd, and of the priest Joseph. And from now onwards, no person whatsoever has power over it, save its owner, namely the wretched Sabrisho. Yea and Amen.'

Unfortunately no date is given here. Ḥisn Kef, the modern Ḥisn Kaifa, was situated on the Tigris, north-west of Mosul. What is known about the bishops of the place has been collected by Le Quien, *Oriens Christianus* ii, cols. 1317–18, from Assemani's notices. Assemani knew of it as the seat of two bishops: Elias[4] in the time of Machicha II, and Emmanuel,[5] in the time of Jahballaha III (1244–1317), and as the seat of the metropolitan Gabriel,[6] under the catholicos Elia IV, in the year A.D. 1616. A metropolitan Sabrisho is not mentioned. Since the episcopal see of Ḥisn Kef was elevated to metropolitan honours somewhere between 1317 and 1616, there is every chance that the Sabrisho of the second inscription is younger than his namesake in the first inscription; he may even have lived after 1616. In any case his name is a welcome addition to the only too short list of holders of this bishopric.

[1] *Geschichte der syrischen Literatur*, p. 322.   [2] *Ibid.* p. 323.
[3] *Ibid.* p. 321. Barhebraeus lived 1225/6–86.
[4] *Bibliotheca Orientalis* ii, p. 455.   [5] *Ibid.* p. 456.
[6] *Bibl. Or.* i, p. 547; iii, p. 600.

One could not suppose the two Sabrisho's to be one and the same person in spite of their homonymity; the events related of them, together with the facts about the see of Ḥisn Kef, cannot concern the same man. Jenks' remarks show that he regarded the second inscription as the older, judging by the handwriting ('possib contemp: with writ of the book'). We think it justifiable to infer that the inscription of the metropolitan was in a better hand than that of 1645 Gr. The reason may well be that the metropolitan was a better educated man than his namesake, who perhaps was a layman. If we consider further the original order in which the inscriptions occurred in U, we find the one of 1645 Gr. nearer the text, while the other is 'on a still earlier page', that is to say, nearer the cover. One may conjecture that a new leaf was added to carry the inscription of the metropolitan.

When one examines the contents of the inscriptions, only one course of events seems possible. The monastery of Rabban Mar Cyriacus had in its library a volume containing our collection of texts (Q). This volume was copied by monks of the monastery and given as a present to Sabrisho in the year 1645 Gr. Contrary to the opinion of Jenks, this then is the inscription 'contemporary with the writing of the book'. From the possession of Sabrisho, U comes at a time and by means unknown to us, into the hands of Abdas of Mosul. The latter sells it to the metropolitan Sabrisho by a formal contract. It is very difficult to imagine how the sequence of these events should be reversed.

The most important fact for the history of the text of C to be gathered from the inscriptions is the year in which U was written according to the first inscription: 1645 Gr. = A.D. 1333/4. But there is another date contained in the ms. which raises a number of difficulties. It apears on p. 105 and belongs to the colophon at the end of the excerpt II*b* (Ps. Isaac). Perhaps the scribe noted the date after having completed, not only the longest excerpt, but also nearly half of the ms. (53 leaves out of 112 in C). Day and month are given, the year is written in numeral letters and the word 'year' is abbreviated to its first letter: ܩܡܗ : ܂ ܂ ܗ : ܂ ܐ : ܂ ܒ : ܝܐ : ܬ ܂ '2nd Iyor, y. 1545' (Gr.) = A.D. 1233/4. It is surely remarkable that there should be this difference of exactly 100 years between the colophon and the inscription. It could of course be purely accidental; but is that likely? If, however, we suppose an error to have taken place, and that colophon and inscription were in fact written in the same year, on whose side are we to locate the error? The Sabrisho of the first inscription may have been a layman, the 'later handwriting' commented on by Jenks, may in fact point to an imperfect acquaintance with the Syriac script, and the style of this inscription is, in part, suggestive of the Arabic idiom. But even when all this has been taken into account, it is difficult to see how Sabrisho, who has written out his date in full, could have made such an error. We should note that, if the error is in fact Sabrisho's, the connection with Baumstark's Cyriacus is severed, though in any case the time of this latter Cyriacus is only vaguely guessed. On the other hand, it may be that Sabrisho's date is the correct one, and that the error is to be found in the colophon. One would, however, have expected a copyist monk to be sure of his numbers. On the whole, we are inclined to the view that inscription and colophon were written in the same year, and that the year is that given in the inscription (A.D. 1333/4). The two alternatives (1233/4 *and* 1333/4, or 1233/4 *only*) cannot nevertheless be ruled out.

To gather from Scher's description of the ms. Séert No. 87,[1] this ms. (=S) had the same contents as C, but like U it is now lost. The colophon of S showed that it was written in 1920 Gr. = A.D. 1609.[2] In theory S could be a copy of Q or U, since it is later than them both. A criterion which would, if S were preserved, make it possible to define the relationship of S at least to U is the textual error at the beginning of ch. 35 in excerpt IX (p. 206). In C the first words of IX 35 do not make sense, and the meaning of what follows is obscure. One must assume a loss of text; the more so as immediately after the first word there is a stop (the equivalent of a comma). The scribe of C gives no indication of a lacuna in spite of his extreme care in reproducing every point of interest in U. Therefore he found the text in U already in this form. Fortunately we are able to fill the lacuna with the help of a witness for IX which has not yet been published. From the possession of J.-B. Chabot there have come into the hands of A. van Roey (Louvain) photostats of IX (=R), in which ch. 35 is complete. Thus R cannot be copied from U. A. van Roey remembers that Chabot had received R (in form of photostats?) from Father Giamil. Giamil is no doubt the 'chercheur des vieux livres', Samuel Giamil who collected Syriac mss. and books in the library of the Chaldean monastery Notre-

---

[1] A. Scher, *Catalogue des manuscrits syriaques et arabes conservés dans la bibliothèque épiscopale de Séert (Kurdistan)*, Mossoul 1905, p. 64.

[2] 'Le livre fut achevé le Jeudi 1er Juin 1920 (= 1609) dans le couvent de Mar Jacques-le-Reclus, au temps de métropolitain Elia; il est écrit par Thomas, fils du prêtre Joseph, de la ville de Gazarta.'

Dâme des Semences near Alqoš in Iraq. As Vosté's catalogue of this library informs us,[1] Giamil exerted himself a great deal on behalf of the library, buying or having copied mss. and books, writing prefaces and reports and putting his collection of sermons at the disposal of readers. Among the mss. he had copied were some from Séert. He himself was also on a mission in Kurdistan, where Séert is situated.[2] It seems to be within the realms of possibility that Giamil or one of his scribes excerpted the text IX from S (the interest of the 'chapters' was their attribution to Nestorius). Should S have contained IX in its complete form, it could not derive from U. The common ancestor of S and U could be Q, or alternatively some X farther back.

Another point in the history of the collection contained in C which could be cleared up with the help of S is 'the addition from another manuscript' found in excerpt VIII (Ḥenanisho') on pp. 178 and 179. As the things stand, we do not know when the 'addition' had been inserted. It is only certain that it was already to be found in U.

THE CONTENTS OF C

C consists of a collection of christological texts of varying length, most of which are unknown or unpublished. C begins (p. 1) : 'By the power of the Trinity I am collecting a little from the confession of the heretics from the writings of the fathers, and questions and responses against them.' Scher gives the lemma of S in Syriac; it is identical with ours except for the very beginning: 'Collection of a little from' etc. Perhaps Scher abbreviated the lemma for the catalogue.[3]

A division of the contents according to S is given by Scher; he makes it into 10 parts.[4] Goodman, in his description of C, numbers 23 parts.[5] The difference is due to the fact that for several authors there is more than one excerpt included. For this edition we have

---

[1] J. Vosté, *Catalogue de la bibliothèque syro-chaldéenne du couvent de Notre-Dame des Semences près d'Alqoš (Iraq)*, Rome/Paris 1929; for the Rev. Giamil, see index, p. 131.   [2] Vosté, p. 112.

[3] Scher's French rendering of the lemma is too general: 'Compilation des fragments de la religion des hérétiques extraits des livres des pères et controverses avec eux.'   [4] Scher, p. 64.

[5] Goodman, 'Jenks Collection', pp. 596–8. Here S is not yet taken into account. On the other hand, Goodman's description of the Jenks Collection is not used by I. Ortiz de Urbina, *Patrologia Syriaca*, Rome 1958, so that there Baumstark's references to ms. Séert 87 are not brought up to date.

combined and used more consistently Scher's method of division according to authors, and Goodman's enumeration of the single pieces. This results in twelve groups of texts (the symbolic number was perhaps intended by the collector). The compilation as a composition is suitably rounded off by texts of Ephrem. The contents of C are (page numbers are of the Syriac text):

I *a*,[1] p. 1 (Scher I, Goodman I): 'First from the *book* which the holy of memory, Mar *Shahdost*, bishop of *Tarihan*[2] composed, *why we Easterns have separated ourselves from the Westerns, and why we are called Nestorians.*'

I *b*, p. 3: 'The same'.

I *c*, p. 9: 'Against those who confess one hypostasis.'

I *d*, p. 34 (Goodman II): 'Again, another extract, also from the book of Mar *Eustathius* (sic) of Tarihan.'

At the end of I *d*, p. 57: 'Ended is the selection of the book of the holy Mar *Eustathius*, bishop of Tarihan. May his prayer be with us all. Amen.'

II *a*, p. 58 (Scher II, Goodman III–V): 'And now, of the holy of memory, Mar *Isaac*, bishop *of Nineveh*, true recluse, and orthodox in truth. May his prayer assist us. Amen.'

II *b*, p. 69 (Goodman VI): 'Again, from the same holy Mar Isaac, against those who confess that Christ is two natures (and) one hypostasis.'

At the end of II *b*, p. 105: 'Finished is the *tract concerning the orthodox confession* composed by the holy of memory Mar Isaac, bishop of Nineveh, the faithful and orthodox recluse, in truth. May his prayer succour us, and Iyor, in the year 1545.'

III *a*, p. 105 (Scher III, Goodman VII): 'Again, a *treatise of* Mar *Michael Malpana.*'

III *b*, p. 106: 'By the same.'[3]

---

[1] It is sometimes difficult to say (III especially is such a case) where we have a lemma indicating the beginning of a new excerpt, and where the author or somebody else has made an internal division of a continuous text with the help of headings. The use of small letters in our division is made for excerpts. In XII the four Ephrem texts are separate entities, so we have put small letters to each of them. XI, on the contrary, is one entity in spite of appearances.

[2] Tarihan, so vocalized in C, is the Tirhan of other sources; = modern Teheran.

[3] Here, and in the same way at the beginning of III *c* and *d*, there follow so many particulars about the refuted doctrines that we take them to have been said by the author and not by the compiler.

III*c*, p. 108: 'By the same.'

III*d*, p. 110 (Goodman VIII): 'By the same.'

At the end of III*d*, p. 113: 'Finished is the treatise of Mar *Michael Badoqa*, may his prayer succour us. Amen.'

IV, p. 113 (Scher IV, Goodman IX): *Anonymous*, 'Again, chapters of a *treatise* against those who confess Christ as one nature and hypostasis'.

(In fact, two excerpts from the document of 612, and so recurring in VII.)

At the end of IV, p. 116: 'Finis.'

V, p. 117 (Goodman X): *Anonymous*, 'Again, by the power of the Holy Trinity, we will set down a few words spoken in the holy scriptures by the Holy Spirit through the tongues of the blessed apostles concerning the dispensation which is in Christ our Lord and our God', etc.

(About the inadequacy of the lemma see below, the introduction to V; V is in fact an excerpt from an apology for Narsai.)

No colophon to V on p. 130.

VI, p. 130 (Goodman XI): *Anonymous* (in spite of the lemma), 'The chapters of Cyril' (quoted to be refuted by the 'orthodox').

No colophon to VI on p. 147.

Pp. 148 and 149 are blank on both sides, which according Jenks' notes corresponds to U. Since neither VI nor VII seem to be affected in their text this is not a lacuna.

VII*a*, p. 150 (Scher V, Goodman XII): 'Again, the *creed of the bishops of Persia which Kosroes requested from them.*'

VII*b*, p. 157 (Goodman XIII–XVII): '*Controversial chapters which the fathers drew up and affixed to the creed.*'

On p. 169 the text breaks off, because 10 leaves (one quire) have been lost in U. But no more than the rest of VII has disappeared.

VIII, p. 170 (Scher VI, Goodman XVIII): 'Again, chapters of *disputations* which are made in brief against those heretics who confess the unity of composition in Christ, *by* Rabban *Ḥenanisho' the monk*, sister's son to Mar Elijah who founded the monastery in Assyria.'

On pp. 178 and 179 is 'an addition which we found in another copy', according to a marginal note. To this refers the colophon on p. 179: 'Finished is the addition which we found afterwards in another manuscript.'

IX, p. 179 (Scher VII, Goodman XIX): 'Again, *various chapters and diverse questions of* the *holy Nestorius.*'

At the end of IX, p. 206: 'Finished are the chapters of the holy Mar Nestorius.'

X, p. 207 (Scher VIII, Goodman XX): '*From Mar Babai the Great.*'

No colophon at the end of p. 209, only a note of the scribe of C saying that p. 210 is blank, although nothing is missing.

XI, p. 211 (Scher IX, Goodman XXI and XXII): 'Again, the *kephalaia of Cyril.*' P. 214: 'Again, the *theses of Mar Nestorius.*'

(Of the connection of kephalaia and theses, see below in the introduction to XI.)

At the end of XI, p. 218: 'They are ended.'

XII*a*, p. 219 (Scher X, Goodman XXIII): 'Again, *from the sermons against Bar Daisan, of Mar Ephrem.*'

XII*b*, p. 221: 'Again, from the holy Mar Ephrem.'

XII*c*, p. 222: 'Again, from the holy Mar Ephrem, *in the fourth tone.*'

XII*d*, p. 222: 'Again, from the holy one.'

At the end of XII*d*, p. 223, there is no colophon, nor is there one for the whole ms. But the lines of Ephrem with their biblical admonition to wake and pray and to fall not into temptation form a worthy conclusion to the whole.

Has the collection of these texts grown gradually, or is it the work of one compiler? In the latter case one would have expected to find the Ps. Nestorius pieces, IX and XI, not separated by X, but listed one after the other. A strong argument for the assumption of an older form of the collection lies also in the fact that there is VII in spite of the existence of IV. The compiler does not seem to have noticed that IV is contained in VII (a later scribe has, however, noted in the margin of IV: 'This chapter is written in its place below'). The explanation is that the compiler found IV in its present short, excerpted and anonymous state elsewhere. There are some other texts maimed nearly out of recognition in C, viz. V and VI. Then there is X which has preserved the name of its author, but has no title. In matter of brevity these excerpts have competitors in III and VIII, and there too, the titles of the original writings are not mentioned. The brevity and (or) lopped appearance of III, IV, V, VI, VIII, X (and XI?) puts them in distinct opposition to the enormous length of I and II, which together fill half of the ms. and are well provided with lemmata.

So we assume that the compiler of the present collection used an earlier compilation of dogmatic excerpts which consisted of III, IV, V, VI, VIII, X, perhaps also XI (and even XII?), to which he added I, II, VII, IX (and XII if it did not derive from the earlier collection). Since none of the authors of this older collection is later than the seventh century, it may already have been in existence at that time.

The *terminus ad quem* for the whole collection is the year given in the colophon of II*b*, 1233/4 (if it should not be 1333/4, as we are inclined to think); the *terminus a quo* is the latest of the authors excerpted and mentioned by name, Shahdost (Eustathius) of Tarihan. This bishop was patriarchal vicar under the catholicos Mar Aba II who died in 751. Thus we get the great time span of 500 or 600 years, unless II has a later origin than I. But it does not seem necessary to keep the date of the origin of the compilation contained in C entirely open between the *termini* named. The turn of the eighth to the ninth century was a golden age for the Nestorian church. Baumstark emphasizes frequently that at the time of the catholicos Timotheus I (d. 823) the heretical trends going back to Ḥenana were finally dispelled. Timotheus 'stood up for the purity of the Nestorian creed at two general synods in the years 790/1 and 804'. He is the author of 'two series of answers to various questions apparently devoted to interconfessional polemic'; he also had a dispute with the Jacobite patriarch.[1] The theological, apologetic and antiheretical interests of the contemporaries of Timotheus are also well known. Might not the text ascribed to Isaac (II) have been written by one of these contemporaries? In any case we would like to place the compilation within this period.

THE INTENTION OF THE COMPILER

In the lemma of C, which serves as a kind of introduction to the collection of texts, the compiler says that he wants to present 'the confession of the heretics', as it is to be found in the 'writings of the fathers'. The purpose is of course the refutation of the heretics. The collector mentions the literary genre of 'questions and

[1] Baumstark, *Geschichte*, p. 217 with n. 10.

answers', although not all of the excerpts belong to this form. There is no mention in the lemma of the subject of the heresy; the texts themselves show sufficiently that it is christology. The excerpts from Shahdost (I) fulfil the function of a historical introduction, but theological argument is not neglected. Among the authors whose names are given, several belong to one important period: Michael Malpana (III), Ḥenanisho' the monk (VIII), Babai the Great (X) and the official document of the year 612 (VII, and accordingly IV), of which it has been assumed that Babai is the author. All these are pillars of Nestorian orthodoxy. That Nestorius himself appears as an authority is not surprising (though the texts attributed to him here are not genuine). Isaac of Nineveh is included as the alleged author of a long text, with the intention of making use of his spiritual authority, which was undisputed among both Nestorians and Jacobites. His authority gives weight to the position of the compiler, that is to say, to Nestorian orthodoxy. Its slogans are: two natures, *two hypostases* and one person in Christ. All the texts gathered together in C are witnesses to this christology.

The heretics refuted are not only the monophysites (sometimes distinguished according to their different schools), but also the 'Chalcedonians'. It is remarkable to see the dialectical powers of nearly all the authors (with the exception of II) directed against the 'one *composite* hypostasis'. It seems that 'the one composite hypostasis' was attacked not only as being the catchword of neo-Chalcedonism but also as that of the Ḥenana school. Otherwise it would be impossible to explain the important place occupied by the polemic against this term in our collection. In 612 the christology of two hypostases became the official doctrine of the Nestorian church. The above mentioned group of theologians of this period (Michael Malpana, Ḥenanisho' the monk, Babai the Great) were upholders of this doctrine. At the same time they were opponents of Ḥenana and his christology, presumably also of his exegesis. The texts of our collection witness to the Nestorian dogmatical war on two or three fronts within their own church and against the neighbouring churches.

PARTS OF THE COMPILATION IN SEPARATE TRADITION

Some texts of the collection in C are also preserved elsewhere. VII, the document of the year 612 (and accordingly IV) is edited in *Synodicon Orientale* as part of a ms. containing texts belonging to Nestorian canonical law. The compiler has certainly excerpted it from a similar collection of official documents (C has a better text which corrects a confusion in the *Synodicon Orientale,* and is therefore independent of the latter).

VIII (Ḥenanisho') offers more difficulties. It is preserved without the addition, and with curious theological differences, in a manuscript of mixed content formerly in Berlin. Did the Berlin parallel derive from our compilation, at a time when the addition to VIII was not yet made? And which side is responsible for the differences?

Three chapters from IX, arranged in a different order, are preserved together with the Ps. Nestorius part of XI in a Vatican ms. and have been published from it. The neighbourhood of the pieces there suggests that they are taken from a collection of our type.

About the separate tradition of IX in its entirety see above, pp. xiii f.

Of XII (Ephrem), one of the poems is to be found in two mss. and has been published from them. Since the manuscript tradition of Ephrem's works is so very rich, there need not necessarily be any connection with C, i.e. with its predecessors.

THE SYRIAC TRANSLATION OF
CYRIL'S ANATHEMATA IN C

The twelve anathemata (kephalaia, chapters) against Nestorius by Cyril of Alexandria are three times quoted and refuted in C: by Shahdost (I), by an anonymous refutation originally written in Greek (VI) and by the so-called Syriac counter-anathemata of Ps. Nestorius (XI). We have compared the three series of Cyril's anathemata in Syriac translation and have come to the following results.

First, the version used in I and XI is identical, the variants are quite unimportant, as this list shows.

I	anathema	XI
p. 49, 19 ܩ	I	p. 211, 3 om.
p. 51, 5 ܗܘ	8	p. 212, 17 om. (after ܕ)
p. 51, 14 ܐ	9	p. 213, 6 ܟܠܐ
p. 52, 5 lacuna (Jenks in marg. 'illegible')	10	p. 213, 22 ܘ
p. 52, 5 f. ܗܘ		p. 213, 23 ܗܝ
p. 52, 7 ܘ	11	p. 214, 2 om.
p. 52, 10 ܐ		p. 214, 5 ܘ
p. 52, 12 ܗܘ ܕ		p. 214, 8 ܕ

Secondly, there is quite another kind of relationship between the series I and XI on the one hand, and VI on the other. For the sake of simplicity a comparison is made here between VI and XI, I is only referred to when necessary; the same applies to the Greek (reference to the Greek is to Schwartz's edition of Cyril's letter with the anathemata in *Acta Conciliorum Oecumenicorum* I 1, 1; the anathemata are to be found on pp. 40, 22–42, 5). The three series of anathemata in C have one difference from the Greek in common: whereas the Greek starts each anathema with Εἴ the Syriac begins with ܡܢ = τίς. This regularly recurring variant is not included in the list below.

VI	anathema	XI	Greek
p. 130, 23 ܗܘ	1	p. 211, 2 ܐܠܗܘܬܗ	
p. 131, 1 ܩܕܝܫܬܐ (=I)		p. 211, 3 om.	p. 40, 23 ἁγίαν
p. 131, 2 ܠܐܠܗܐ		p. 211, 5+ ܐܒܐ	p. 40, 23=VI
p. 132, 14 ܕܩܢܘܡܐܝܬ (=I, XI)	2		p. 40, 25 καθ' ὑπόστασιν
p. 132, 15 ܘܕܚܕܘ		p. 211, 8 ܘܕܚܕ ܐܠܗܘܬܗ	
(p. 132, 16 ܐܒܐ sed delendum)			
p. 132, 16 ܐܟܚܕ		p. 211, 9 ܟܚܕ	p. 40, 26 ὁμοῦ
p. 133, 4–5 ܕܡܦܪܫ ܠܗ ܠܬܪܝܢ ܩܢܘ̈ܡܝܢ ܠܡܫܝܚܐ ܡܪܢ	3	p. 211, 11–12 ܕܠܐ ܚܕ ܡܫܝܚܐ ܡܦܪܫ ܠܗܘ ܠܩܢܘ̈ܡܐ ܡܢ	p. 40, 28 ἐπὶ τοῦ ἑνὸς Χριστοῦ διαιρεῖ τὰς ὑποστάσεις
p. 133, 6 ܠܚܘܕ		p. 211, 13 ܒܠܚܘܕ	
p. 133, 6 ܐܝܟ		p. 211, 13 ܗܝ	p. 40, 29 τῇ
p. 133, 8 ܕܝܢ ܡܠܟܘ		p. 211, 15 ܝܬܝܪܐܝܬ	p. 40, 29 f. δὴ μᾶλλον
p. 134, 18 ܦܪ̈ܨܘܦܝܢ	4	p. 211, 17 ܦܪ̈ܨܘܦܐ	
p. 134, 18 ܠܬܪܝܢ		p. 211, 17 ܬܪܝܢ	p. 41, 1 non habet
p. 134, 18 ܩܢܘ̈ܡܝܢ		p. 211, 17 ܩܢܘ̈ܡܐ	
p. 134, 19 ܡܦܠܓܝܢ		p. 211, 18+ ܠܗܘܢ	
p. 134, 19 ܩ̈ܠܐ		p. 211, 18+ ܕܐܡ̈ܪܝܢ	p. 41, 2 φωνάς
p. 134, 19 ܕܟܠ		p. 211, 18 ܟܠ	
p. 134, 17–20 ܕܒܐܘܢܓܠܝܘܢ ܘܫܠܝܚܐ		p. 211, 19 ܒܟܬܒܐ ܕܐܘܢܓܠܝܘܢ ܐܘ ܕܫܠܝܚܐ	p. 41, 1 f. ἐν τοῖς εὐαγγελικοῖς καὶ ἀποστολικοῖς συγγράμμασι

VI	anathema	XI	Greek
p. 134, 20–1 ܒܟܠܗܘܢ ܐܠܐ ܐܡܪ:	(4)	p. 211, 20 vice versa	
p. 134, 22 ܠܒܪ:		p. 211, 22 ܦܠܓ:	
p. 134, 23 ܡܟܢܗܢ ܕܝܢ ܐܝܟ ܕܠܒܢ̈ܬ ܩ̈ܠܐ		p. 211, 23 ܘܡܟܢܗܢ ܐܝܟ ܕܒܢ̈ܬ ܩ̈ܠܐ	p. 41, 4 τὰς δὲ ὡς
p. 135, 1 ܐܠܗܐ		p. 212, 2+ܐܒܐ	p. 41, 4 θεοῦ πατρός
p. 135, 1 ܡܠܟܘܬ		p. 212, 2 non habet	p. 41, 4 non habet
p. 135, 19 ܕܡܡܪܚ ܕܢܐܡܪ:	5	p. 212, 2 ܕܐܡܪ:	p. 41, 5 τολμᾷ λέγειν
p. 135, 20 ܠܒܝܫ ܐܠܗܐ		p. 212, 3–4 ܫܩܠ ܠܐܠܗܐ	p. 41, 5 θεοφόρον
p. 135, 20 ܘܠܘ		p. 212, 4 ܘܠܐ ܗܘܐ	
p. 135, 21 ܡܟܝܠ		p. 212, 4 ܝܬܝܪܐܝܬ	p. 41, 5 μᾶλλον
p. 135, 21 ܗܘ		p. 212, 5 ܐܝܬܘܗܝ	
p. 135, 22 ܕܒܟܝܢܐ (=I, XI)			p. 41, 6 καὶ φύσει
p. 135, 22 ܒܕܗܘܐ		p. 212, 6 ܒܗܝ ܕܗܘܐ	
p. 136, 11 ܡܠܬܐ ܐܠܗܐ	6	p. 212, 9 ܡܠܬܐ ܕܡܢ ܐܠܗܐ ܐܒܐ	p. 41, 8 τὸν ἐκ θεοῦ πατρὸς λόγον
p. 136, 11–12 ܡܘܕܐ ܡܟܝܠ ܕܗܘܝܘ ܐܠܗܐ ܐܟܚܕ		p. 212, 10–11 ܗܘܐ ܝܬܝܪܐܝܬ ܡܘܕܐ ܕܗܘܝܘ ܐܠܗܐ ܐܟܚܕ	p. 41, 9 δὴ μᾶλλον τὸν αὐτὸν ὁμολογεῖ θεὸν τε ὁμοῦ
p. 136, 12 ܒܕܗܘܐ		p. 212, 11 ܒܗܝ ܕܗܘܐ	
p. 136, 12–13 ܐܝܟ ܕܒܟܬܒܐ (=I, XI)			p. 41, 10 κατὰ τὰς γραφάς
p. 137, 23 ܐܬܚܛܦ ܝܫܘܥ ܘܐܣܬܥܪ:	7	p. 212, 13 ܐܣܬܥܪ: ܝܫܘܥ	p. 41, 11 ἐνηργῆσθαι …τὸν Ιησοῦν
p. 138, 1 ܐܬܥܛܦ		p. 212, 14–15 ܐܡܪ: ܕܡܣܒܗ ܒܟܠܗܘܢ	p. 41, 12 περιῆφθαι
p. 138, 1 ܗܘ (=I, XI)			p. 41, 12 ὑπάρχοντι
p. 138, 22 ܗܘ (=I)	8	p. 212, 17 om.	
pp. 138, 23–139, 1 ܘܡܟܗ ܠܡܫܒܚܘ		p. 212, 19 ܘܠܡܫܬܒܚܘ	p. 41, 13 συνδοξάζεσθαι
p. 139, 2 ܒܐܚܪܢܐ		p. 212, 21+ܐܝܬܘܗܝ	p. 41, 14 ἑτέρῳ
p. 139, 3 ܒܐܡܝܢܘ		p. 212, 22 ܐܡܝܢܐܝܬ	
p. 139, 3 ܡܣܒܪܐ ܠܝ		p. 212, 22–3 ܕܒܪܐ ܠܝ ܠܡܣܒܪܘ	p. 41, 15 νοεῖν ἀναγκάσει
p. 139, 3–4 ܘܠܘ ܡܟܝܠ		p. 212, 23 ܘܠܐ ܗܘܐ ܕܝܢ ܝܬܝܪܐܝܬ	p. 41, 15 καὶ οὐχὶ δὴ μᾶλλον

VI		anathema	XI		Greek
p. 139, 4 ܐܒܝܕ		(8)	p. 212, 23 ܐܒܝܕ		
p. 139, 4 ܘܝܟ̈ܐܠܕ ܗܕ			p. 213, 1 ܠܬܝܡܐ		p. 41, 15 τιμᾷ
p. 139, 5 ܐܢܩܡܘܩ			p. 213, 2 ܠܩܡܐ		p. 41, 16 ἀνάπτει
p. 139, 6 ܐܬܠܡ ܗܘܐ ܕܪ			p. 213, 2–3 ܐܬܠܡܗ		p. 41, 16 καθὸ γέγονε
ܪܡܒ			ܗܘܐ ܪܣܒ ܪ ܗܘ		σὰρξ ὁ λόγος
			ܐܬܠܡ		
p. 139, 16 ܡܚܝܘܢܝܗ		9	p. 213, 4 ܡܚܢܝ ܗܢܘܢ		p. 41, 17 κύριον
			ܡܫܝܚܐ		Ἰησοῦν Χριστόν
p. 139, 18 ܘܟܬܚܫܚܢܝܐ			p. 213, 6 ܘܟܬܚܫܚܢ		p. 41, 18 χρώμενον
			(I ܟܬܚܫܚܢܙ)		
p. 139, 18 ܕܡܥܒܕܘܬܐ ܕܒܝܕܗ			p. 213, 6–7 ܒܝܕ ܡܫܟܚܐ		p. 41, 18 τῇ δι᾽ αὐτοῦ
			ܕܡܥܒܕܘܬܐ		
p. 139, 19 ܢܡܫܟܚ			p. 213, 7 ܡܫܟܚ ܠܡܣܥܪ		p. 41, 18 τὸ ἐνεργεῖ
ܠܡܣܥܪܘ					δύνασθαι κατά
p. 139, 20 ܘܠܡܫܠܡܘ					p. 41, 19 καὶ τὸ
(= I, XI)					πληροῦν
p. 139, 20–1 ܘܠܐ ܕܝܢ ܣܟܠܘ			p. 213, 9 ܘܠܐ ܗܘܐ ܕܝܢ		p. 41, 19 f. καὶ οὐχὶ δὴ
			ܠܬܝܪܐܝܬ		μᾶλλον
p. 139, 21 ... ܕܝܠܝܗ ܗܘܝ			p. 213, 10 ܕܕܝܠܗ ܗܘ		p. 41, 20 ἴδιον
ܕܚܝܠܝܐܝܬ			ܚܝܠܬܐܝܬ ...		

(Greek ἰδίαν and ἰδία are again rendered by ܕܝܠ + this adverb[1] by all three Syriac
series in the translation of pp. 41, 28 and 42, 2.)

| p. 139, 22 ܕܢܚܐ | | | p. 213, 11 ܐܠܗ ܐܝܬ ܕܐܬܪܟܠ | | p. 41, 20 τὰς |
| | | | ܟܘܠܬܐ | | θεοσημείας |

(But τὰς θεοσημείας of Gr. p. 41, 19 is ܐܬܘܬ in I, VI, XI.)

p. 140, 13 ܗܟܝܠ		10	p. 213, 16 ܗܘܒܠ		p. 41, 23 τοίνυν
p. 140, 13 ܘܠܘ ܠܗ ܠܡܪܐ			p. 213, 16 ܘܕܕܠܡܪܐ		
p. 140, 14 ܠܘ ܗܘ ܒܪ ܗܘ			p. 213, 17 ܠܐ ܗܘ ܗܘܐ		p. 41, 23 οὐκ αὐτὸν τὸν
ܐܬܠܡ ...ܒܪܐܚ			ܐܬܠܡ ܕܠܗ ...ܒܪܐܚ		ἐκ θεοῦ λόγον, ὅτε
p. 140, 15 ܐܝܟܢ			p. 213, 18 ܕܐܝܟܢ		p. 41, 24 καθ᾽ ἡμᾶς
p. 140, 16 ܕܝܠܢ ܐܝܬܝ			p. 213, 19 ܕܐܝܬܘܗ ܕܝܠܢ		
ܕܐܝܬܘܗ			ܐܝܬܝ		
p. 140, 16 ܕܝܠܢܐܝܬ					p. 41, 24 ἰδικῶς
(= I, XI)					

The Syriac presupposes an itacistic εἰδικῶς which has been translated literally.

[1] ܕܝܠܗ can be used for Greek ἴδιος, and also for the possessive pronoun; to exclude
this ambiguity the translator has added the adverb.

VI	anathema	XI	Greek
p. 140, 17 ܩܪܒ (=I, XI)	(10)		p. 41, 25 προσενεγκεῖν αὐτὸν
p. 140, 18 ܘܠܘ ܕܝܢ ܡܠܘܢ ܕܚܠܦܝܢ		p. 213, 21–2 ܘܠܐ ܗܘܐ ܠܝܬܝܪܐܝܬ ܕܚܠܦܝܢ ܕܝܠܢ	p. 41, 25 f. καὶ οὐχὶ δὴ μᾶλλον ὑπερ μόνων ἡμῶν

(μόνων, which the Syriac does not have, is also missing in the Greek ms. S [=Coll. Seguierana=Paris. Coisl. 32] of the *ACO*; see Schwartz's apparatus.)

VI	anathema	XI	Greek
p. 140, 18 ܡܬܩܒܠܘ		p. 213, 22 ܡܬܩܒܠܘܢܐ	
p. 141, 13 ܕܦܓܪܗ (=I, XI)	11		p. 41, 28 σάρκα
p. 141, 13 ܕܡܪܢ		p. 214, 2+ ܡܫܝܚܐ (I+ ܝܫܘܥ ܡܫܝܚܐ)	p. 41, 28 τοῦ κυρίου
p. 141, 14 ܘܕܠܗ ܗܘ		p. 214, 2 ܘܕܠܗ ܗܘ	
p. 141, 14 ܐܒܐ		p. 214, 3 ܐܠܗܐ ܐܒܐ	p. 41, 29 θεοῦ πατρός
p. 141, 15 ܕܐܝܬ ܗܘ ܐܚܪܝܢ (=I, XI)			p. 41, 29 ἑτέρου τινὸς πὰρ' αὐτόν
p. 141, 16 ܕܐܠܗܘܬܐ (=XI)		(I ܕܐܠܗܐ)	p. 42, 1 θείαν
p. 141, 17 ܡܠܘܢ		p. 214, 6 ܠܝܬܝܪܐܝܬ	p. 42, 1 μᾶλλον
p. 141, 17 ܗܘ		p. 214, 7 ܐܬܘܗܝ	
p. 142, 11 ܕܡܠܬܐ ܐܠܗܐ		p. 214, 10 ܕܐܠܗܐ ܡܠܬܐ	p. 42, 3 τοῦ θεοῦ λόγου
p. 142, 13 ܗܘ		p. 214, 13 ܐܬܘܗܝ	
p. 142, 14 deest (=I, XI)			p. 42, 5 ὡς θεός

This long table of variants shows a considerable difference between the Syriac anathemata in VI and XI (and I). It is not, however, the kind of difference which results from a complete independence of Syriac translation on both sides, but from the revision of an already existing translation. Proof of this is to be seen, not only in the stretches of identical text in VI and XI, but also in the differences over against the Greek common to both. Such differences are (besides the already mentioned omission of the initial Εἴ):

(1) that comprehension is facilitated by the addition of words, mostly repeated from the context: Gr. p. 41, 1. 4. 18;

(2) some slight omissions over against the original, one of which (Gr. p. 41, 25–6) occurs also as a Greek variant: p. 41, 25. 25–6. 29; p. 42, 5;

(3) *kata* + acc. translated by an adverb (Gr. p. 40, 25) or by a short sentence (p. 41, 10);

(4) more generally, the same not quite literal translation of a Greek expression: Gr. p. 41, 18. 19. 28; p. 42, 1;

(5) the accentuating translation of ἴδιος Gr. p. 41, 20. 28; p. 42, 2;

(6) finally – proof enough in itself – Gr. p. 41, 24, where the Syriac ܠܐܝܕܝܥܐܝܬ presupposes εἰδικῶς in place of ἰδικῶς.

On this common basis the versions differ in this way:

(1) translator and revisor both have their peculiarities in using the possibilities the Syriac language affords for shorter and longer forms. While the version in VI prefers the shorter forms, that of I and XI keeps to the longer forms. So we have ܗܘ in VI, but ܐܝܬܘܗܝ in XI, the same applies to ܕܠܗ, and ܗܘ ܕܠܗ, again to ܥܠ and ܠܐ ܗܘܐ or ܒܐܝܕܗ and ܗܘܐ ܒܗ (see the table);

(2) another idiomatic peculiarity is that VI renders the Greek μᾶλλον with the borrowed word ܡܠܘܢ, while XI translates it properly with ܝܬܝܪܐܝܬ;

(3) the version of VI uses the status absolutus pluralis of the noun more often than the other version; this is one indication that the older unrevised form of the anathemata in Syriac is that of VI. But this argument has weight only in combination with others;

(4) at several points Greek expressions are translated differently, without its being possible to decide whether the one is nearer to the Greek than the other;

(5) there are a few cases where VI renders the Greek more exactly than XI: in anath. 1 and 2, and Gr. p. 41, 2. 5. 12. 13. 28;

(6) but far more frequent are the cases where XI is more exact than VI, not only in the words used, but also in their order: Gr. p. 40, 28. 29; p. 41, 4. 8. 9. 15 (νοεῖν..., though XI is here not absolutely literal either). 15 (τιμᾷ). 16 (ἀνάπτει). 16 (καθὸ...). 17. 20. 23 (again not quite literal). 29; p. 41, 3.

The last point is decisive for the conclusion that I and XI reproduce the revised form of the anathemata in Syriac, while VI uses the same translation in the older unrevised form. This is quite in harmony with the age of the whole text VI (see introduction to VI).

THE BIBLE TEXT USED IN C

True to the Antiochene tradition, biblical citations and arguments based on them play an important part in our collection. There are several long series of quotations arranged according to christological subjects. It seems certain that concordances were available to the authors. The number of biblical quotations or allusions in the whole collection is about 600. Generally the Syriac vulgate (Peshitta) is used; exceptions are noted in the apparatus and in the special introductions. The exceptions are often cases of agreement with the Greek bible text against Syr. vg. Evidently, knowledge of the Greek text could be drawn from Syriac translations of Greek commentaries.

1a–d: SHAHDOST (EUSTATHIUS) OF TARIHAN, PP. 1–57 (TEXT) 'SELECTION' OF HIS 'BOOK' ON THE 'SEPARATION BETWEEN ORIENTALS AND WESTERNS'

Shahdost is the author whose contribution to our collection is the largest, even though none of the four excerpts is as long as II*b* (Ps. Isaac). He is also the latest of the authors who can be dated with certainty and the only one to offer historical polemic as well as biblical and syllogistic arguments. Baumstark refers to our excerpts from Scher's description of S.[1] Since Scher does not mention the second form of Shahdost's name, 'Eustathius', Baumstark does not occupy himself with the problem of the identity of the two. For the compiler of our texts there is no doubting the fact that both names indicate the same person. As style and content of the excerpts do not demand the assumption of a second author, our only problem is whether the second name is the error of some scribe or whether Shahdost occasionally used the Greek name himself. Either case can be explained by a certain similarity of the consonants in the two names.

Shahdost's polemical attitude shows a remarkable mildness in his judgement of the synod of Chalcedon (p. 20 transl.), quite unlike Ps. Isaac.

Shahdost is also well-read, but in the interest of polemic makes reprehensible use of his knowledge (see the apparatus). In particular, Cyril of Alexandria and the emperor Justinian suffer from this treatment. Sources used by Shahdost are: (1) the acts of the Robber Synod (we gain in fact some unknown lines at the

---

[1] *Geschichte*, p. 215.

beginning of I*a* which unfortunately is damaged). (2) Some writing which contained quotations of Apollinarius; it is interesting to see that Shahdost's citations of Apollinarius appear also in neo-Chalcedonian florilegia. (3) It seems that Shahdost was acquainted with the *Apology for Diodorus and Theodorus* by Theodoret, though he mentions neither the title nor the author, for he uses an argument and quotations from Cyril apparently taken over from this source. The author's knowledge of Eustathius probably derives from one of Theodoret's florilegia. (4) Shahdost also knows several works of Cyril directly, and we hear from him for the first time that Cyril's *Contra Synousiastas* consisted of three books. The famous anathemata are quoted in full and refuted (for the Syriac version of the anathemata, see above). (5) Shahdost quotes Justinian, so he knows something of neo-Chalcedonian christology. (6) Shahdost has perhaps glanced at a work of Josephus and he knows the story of the translation of the Septuagint in the form given by Ps. Justin, *Cohortatio ad Graecos*. (7) He is able to cite a catchword from Basil the Great and two sayings of the desert fathers. (8) He has read Nestorius, making some unknown lines available, even the *Liber Heraclidis*, as is shown by some of Shahdost's expressions; in this he differs from the two Ps. Nestorii in C. (9) A passage of considerable length has been excerpted from the document of 612. The Syriac text agrees with that of *Synodicon Orientale* over against the parallel passage in VII*b* (see apparatus to Syriac text p. 14, 5. 8. 19. 21).

The author's historical argument is concerned in particular with the second half of the fifth and the beginning of the sixth centuries. Peter the Fuller is mentioned more than once. Shahdost knows, for instance, that the monophysite bishops of Alexandria ('the successors of Cyril') attacked Peter because of his moderate views (p. 19 transl.). We hear of the emperor Zenon and his Henotikon; the activities of the diophysite Syrians, Acacius and Barsauma, are touched upon. When Shahdost in this connection speaks of disputes about the correct biblical text, he may have in mind the exertions of Philoxenus in this field (p. 6, 8 ff. transl.). On p. 16, 15–31 there is a kind of salvation history of Oriental christendom, brought in for apologetic motives.

Clarity of thought and disposition are not among Shahdost's most marked characteristics. He frequently repeats his arguments: he refers to Peter the Fuller on pp. 6, 8 ff.; 19, 6 ff.; 22, 33–23, 3; to the origin of the Septuagint under Ptolemy on pp. 17, 39–41 and 35, 19 ff.; to Cyril's former diophysite utterances on pp. 5, 11 and 13, 5 f.; Cyril's writing against the emperor Julian is mentioned on pp. 18, 7–9; 33, 18 f.

His pleasure is in periodization of history: twice synchronistic tables of the Persian and Roman rulers occur, p. 18, 27–19, 3 for the second half of the fifth century, p. 23, 6–21 for the fourth century. Points of orientation for the synchronistic calculations are the various councils. Also the death of Nestorius is brought into a chronological relation with the council of Ephesus in 431: he died 22 years after it (p. 24, 6 f.).

It is noteworthy that the name 'Nestorian', which had originated as a term of abuse, had by the time of the author been taken over by the Oriental diophysite Christians themselves (p. 3, 7; 31, 8).

Shahdost's christology has nothing original about it, he is an orthodox Nestorian; it is only the use of the Nestorius expressions which is remarkable. Shahdost belongs to those authors of our compilation who attack the composite hypostasis.

The reasons which he gives for the separation of the Eastern diophysites from the West make it clear beyond all doubt that it was not so much Chalcedon as monophysite propaganda and imperial church politics (with the Henotikon as one of its results) that led to the division. For strict Antiochene diophysites, an agreement was no longer possible with neo-Chalcedonism which recognized Cyril's anathemata and condemned the Three Chapters, although until 612 the official doctrine of Eastern diophysitism was not yet two hypostases but rather two natures.

Since the section on the dogmatical alterations of the Bible text in I*a* (pp. 6, 8–8, 16) is particularly difficult and the necessary explanation too long for the apparatus, it must be discussed in greater detail here. P. 6, 8 ff. tells of the followers of Peter the Fuller who interpreted biblical sayings concerning the human nature of Christ as referring to his divinity. The procedure is compared with that adopted by the Jews. This argument of Shahdost's has its value only *e contrario*, since he maintains that the 'ancient Jews' 'corrupted' the sayings of scripture '*about God the Word* born from the Father' (p. 6, 23 ff.). Two examples of the Jewish interpretation are given: Matt. 22: 42 ff. (Ps. 110: 1) and Matt. 1: 23 (Isa. 7: 14). Isa. 7: 14 is an ancient bone of contention between Jews and Christians. Shahdost is acquainted with the argument that '*almah* means 'young woman' and not *parthenos*, and with the corresponding translations (p. 7, 12–15). His comments on the text of Ps. 110: 1 also have a long tradition behind them. Shahdost declares that the *ladoni* = 'to my lord' is the result of Jewish antichristian interpretation which had replaced (so he presupposes) an original tetragrammaton (=JHWH pronounced *adonai*), leaving 'the Lord' as the only tetragrammaton. But the reading the author denounces in this way is that of the traditional massoretic text. Included in the argument about the alleged replacement of one of the tetragrammata is a definition of the tetragrammaton itself and of its function (p. 7, 1–8 transl.), which is best understood with the help of two parallels. The parallels are both taken from the *argumentum* which in ancient commentaries on the Psalms preceded the exegesis proper. Essential for an *argumentum* concerning Ps. 110 is the declaration that this psalm refers to Christ. The first *argumentum* is that of Aḥob Qatraya (sixth century) :[1]

Ps. 110...prophecies about the dispensation of our saviour Christ, Aḥob: proclaiming in it the honour which happened to the manhood and indicating also the eternal generation of God the Word, and the high-priesthood of the humanity on the analogy of that of the Jews, and the judgement that will take place at his hands, and the honour that will be given to the saints. Now the stupid Jews take it as being [said] ex persona of the servant of Abraham, when he went to espouse Rebecca, as if these words were said by him. But they are refuted[2] by the very beginning of the Psalm, because it is confessed by them, *that there are four letters in the alphabet of their own scriptures, by which the name of God only is written, which are in the same way written for 'the Lord' and for 'my Lord', whenever one wishes to call God with the appellation 'the Lord' and 'my Lord';* just as also these tell who believe in the Lord[3] *that by those (four) letters these names, 'the Lord' and 'my Lord', are written here.*

Vandenhoff[4] compares with this a passage from the Latin commentary on the Psalms edited by Ascoli, where the same theory is put forward:

---

[1] *Ibid.* p. 132 with n. 1. The text quoted is edited from the transcription of a Mosul ms. by B. Vandenhoff, *Exegesis psalmorum imprimis messianicorum apud Syros nestorianos*, Rheine 1899, pp. 46 f., Latin transl., pp. 46 f. To the parallel mss. enumerated by Baumstark (*loc. cit.*) should be added Cambr. Or. 1318 (the quotation there on f. 123 r). Or. 1318 is described by Goodman, 'Jenks Collection', pp. 595 f. S. Brock refers us also to ms. Mingana Syr. 58; this ms. begins with two treatises on the Psalms by Aḥob. The first (f. 1–11 a) has the title 'A treatise on the cause of the psalms'; see Mingana's description of the ms. in his 'Syriac and Garshuni Manuscripts' (*Woodbrooke Catalogues*, vol. 1), Cambridge, 1933.

[2] 'these words...refuted' om. in Cambr. Or. 1318.

[3] Vandenhoff, p. 47 (transl.) n. 1, explains 'who believe in the Lord' as: 'qui linguae hebraicae periti sunt'.

[4] Vandenhoff, p. 47 (transl.) n. 2.

in ebreis voluminibus nomen quod dicitur tetragrammaton per quod divinitatis vocabulum
tantum scribitur in utroque loco similiter positum est et dominus scilicet et domino...unde
manifestum est, quod de homine quolibet non possit intelligi, sed de eo qui sit
et deus verus et omnium dominus qui christus est. cessant ergo falsae opiniones
iudeorum qui aut abrachae servi personam de domino suo loquentem introduci
putant...aut ipsum david quid deus abrachae in procinctu belli dixerit
describentem intelligi volunt...secundum divinitatem dominum suum pro-
pheta christum appellat quem sciebat secundum hominem de semine suo
nasciturum...pariter ergo in alterutra substantia filius eius dominusque
christus est.

Vandenhoff still takes the whole Ascoli commentary to be a
work of Theodore of Mopsuestia in an old Latin tradition. Since
then, Devreesse has demonstrated that only the beginning of the
commentary is by Theodore, while for the rest the question of
authorship is very complicated.[1] But there is a chance that a connection with Theodore still exists:

Je noterai qu'il faut encore, au dèbut de presque chacun des psaumes, laisser de
côtè deux éléments, l'inscription et l'argument – cette sorte de vue d'ensemble
sur le contenue du psaume; il est probable que ces entrées en matière, le plus
souvent des brefs résumés des prologues de Théodore, ont vécu assez longtemps
d'une façon de vie propre.[2]

Shahdost goes further than those parallels in showing some
knowledge of the *Hebrew*, where in fact two *different* words are used
for 'to my lord' and 'the Lord'. He tries to explain the difference
by Jewish polemical alteration of the text. Aḥob and the Latin
argumentum, on the other hand, argue without the least doubt from
Syr. vg. and Septuagint, where the words concerned are the *same*:
ὁ κύριος τῷ κυρίῳ μου and ܠܡܪܝ ܡܪܝܐ; *to this* they apply their
inherited knowledge of the qerē perpetuum *adonai* for JHWH.
The dogmatic interest is the same in both cases.

With the alleged machinations of the Jews are compared the
doings of the followers of Paul of Samosata, who are said to have
replaced expressions for the divine nature of Christ by expressions
for his human nature (p. 7, 17–21 transl.). The list collected by
Shahdost consists, curiously enough, with one single exception, of
variants of Syr. vg. over against the Greek text, or even of variants
between two forms of Syr. vg. text (which go back to Greek
variants). The biblical verses concerned are: Heb. 2: 9; Acts 20:
28; Heb. 2: 16; John 2: 19, 21; 1 Tim. 2: 5; Acts 2: 36; see the
apparatus. For the last two instances the author unfortunately does

[1] R. Devreesse, *Le commentaire de Théodore de Mopsueste sur les Psaumes* (*Studi e
Testi* **93**), Città del Vaticano 1939, pp. xxv ff.   [2] *Ibid.* p. xxvii with n. 1.

not quote what he calls the altered version. The exception just mentioned is the astonishing form of John 2: 21: 'but he spoke concerning the temple of his *church*'. It is perhaps possible to explain this remarkable 'reading' by reference to Origen's *Commentary on John*, where John 2: 21, 22 is interpreted in X 39. Origen commences ch. 39 with a reflection concerning the weight the exegete will accord to the identification of 'temple' and 'body': he may understand it 'more simply' (ἁπλούστερον), or he may 'aim higher' (φιλοτιμητέον); in the latter case he will 'apply' (ἀνάγειν) everything written about the temple to the body of Jesus, whether it be the body taken from the Virgin, or the church which is called his body, and of which body we are members, as the Apostle states (ed. E. Preuschen, *GCS* **10**, p. 215, 8–13). Origen's preference is of course for the 'anagogical' exegesis: ἕκαστον δὲ τῶν κατὰ τὸν ναὸν ἐπὶ τὴν ἐκκλησίαν ἀνάγειν πειρασόμεθα (*ibid.* p. 216, 3 f.), after having already decided to interpret 'body' as 'church' (*ibid.* p. 215, 30). Shahdost's 'reading' of John 2: 21 looks like the shortest possible compression of Origen's exegesis of this text. How then does this 'quotation' fit into the whole argument, the background of which we try to unravel below, and which side has provided it? Shahdost himself is not at all above the manufacturing of corrupted quotations. If he is responsible here, he has certainly not drawn from Theodore of Mopsuestia's *Commentary on John*, for Theodore makes no reference to Origen or his interpretation when commenting on this passage.

What has caused Shahdost to start this discussion? We can only think of the following explanation: Philoxenus of Mabbug undertook a 'new' Syriac translation of the New Testament (*ca.* A.D. 500–5), because he asserted that the Syr. vg. text had been 'falsified' by the Nestorians, i.e. he considered that Syrian diophysites had arguments in their favour from the Syriac bible which were somewhat too useful to them.[1] Perhaps he listed such biblical sayings and they were afterwards used by other monophysites against the Nestorians. Since the Nestorians like Nestorius himself and others before him were already suspected of being representatives of the ideas of Paul of Samosata, it was their apologetic practice to attack Paul themselves (therefore their polemic against the doctrine of the two sons). Thus Shahdost either attacks, as maliciously altered by 'followers of Paul', biblical sayings which Philoxenus had corrected for dogmatical reasons (and perhaps altered according to the Greek), or he uses his knowledge of the

[1] See A. de Halleux, *Philoxène de Mabbog*, Louvain 1963, pp. 117 ff.

Greek text to dissociate himself from the Syr. vg. text which was incriminated as 'Nestorian'. But the matter needs to be investigated in greater detail.

IIa, b: (PS.) ISAAC OF NINEVEH, PP. 58–105 (TEXT), 'TRACT CONCERNING THE ORTHODOX CONFESSION'

What we know of the literary activity of Isaac of Nineveh (second half of the seventh century) makes it appear highly improbable that he should have written a polemical christological treatise of the kind found in our text. Baumstark did not enter II into his paragraphs on Isaac, though he must have known of its existence from the description of S. But the popularity of the great spiritual writer with all Oriental Christian denominations makes it quite comprehensible that a writing refuting Chalcedonian and monophysite christologies should be put under the cover of his great authority. That IIa and IIb are by one and the same author is evident from the style – his predilection for long, complicated sentences and his flowery insults against opponents. In this he exhibits the greatest possible contrast to the terseness both of Michael Malpana (III) and Ḥenanisho' (VIII).

The colophon of IIb gives the title 'tract concerning the orthodox confession'. At the beginning of IIa it is said: 'For the confirmation of the orthodox faith which the holy church of the East has held, in accordance with the apostolic teaching, against the confession "God-bearer", and that of the one hypostasis, and the natural union and the rest.' It is evident from style and contents that the text which follows is the prooemium and the introduction to a whole writing, therefore IIa is the beginning of the 'tract' itself. The introduction speaks in a general manner of Cyril (it was he who brought impiety into the church) and the 'bad Synod of Chalcedon'. On p. 37 there is a subtitle saying that the next section refutes the confession of Chalcedon, on p. 39 another subtitle announces a section against 'theotokos'.

IIb has a lemma of the compiler announcing a refutation of the confession of two natures and one hypostasis, i.e. again against the creed of Chalcedon. This is conducted in a lengthy dissertation (IIb is the longest excerpt in the whole compilation). Then under the subheading 'Questions' (p. 48, 10 transl.), the 'theotokos' and the Chalcedonian dogmata are treated in the form of a dialogue with the 'heretic'. The dialogue is represented as having actually happened, p. 48, 10 f.: 'I asked the heretic on one occasion concerning his saying "God-bearer"'; p. 54, 13 ff.: 'And when he heard these things, he rose up...and went out.' After this the author goes on (pp. 54–61) with instructions on how to behave in a discussion with the followers of Severus and Jacob (Baradai) about one nature and one hypostasis. This section has accordingly the subheading 'And now, against the Severians'. So the lemma to II*b* should have indicated that not only the Chalcedonians but also the monophysites were subject to its attacks.

In contrast to Shahdost (I), the author of II disapproves completely of the council of Chalcedon ('the bad synod'). He concedes, however, that in 451 the properties of the natures were distinguished in the right way. He himself supports the doctrine of the two hypostases in Christ. He is even prepared to go so far as to assert that no heresy ever taught two hypostases; on the contrary it is characteristic for heretics of every kind to teach *one* hypostasis, and he gives the names of Mani, Marcion, Bar Daisan, Arius and Eunomius, Apollinarius, Paul of Samosata, Eutyches, Severus, Jacob of Sarug, Aksenaya of Garmek (Philoxenus) and Cyril (pp. 38 ff. transl.).

It is noteworthy that Ps. Isaac does not busy himself very much with the notion of composite hypostasis, this distinguishes II from most other authors in C. He knows the word, certainly, but it is not often used by him; he seems to take it as a matter of course that one hypostasis is always one *composite* hypostasis. One gains the impression that the fight against that notion is no more a matter of any interest. Is II therefore a late product?

Ps. Isaac makes use of the old expression *kyriakos anthropos* in its Syriac form (p. 45, 32 'lordly man'). He knows further the *Liber Heraclidis* of Nestorius, for he speaks (p. 47) of the two prosopa whose mutual ownership makes them one prosopon.[1] The expression 'prosopon of the union' is also taken from Nestorius (cp. also V, where sermons of Nestorius are quoted). The acquaintance with the *Liber Heraclidis* affords a clear *terminus a quo* for our pseudonymous text: 539/40, the year the *Lib. Her.* was translated into Syriac.

On p. 51, 19 ff. the relationship between the eucharistic bread as the body of Christ and of Christ himself is used as an illustration of Nestorian christology.

---

[1] This is in fact the idea of the *Ps. Nestorius* who wrote the dialogue at the beginning of the *Liber Heraclidis*, see L. Abramowski, 'Untersuchungen zum Liber Heraclidis des Nestorius' (*CSCO* **242**, Subs. 22), Louvain 1963, pp. 185 ff. The Nestorians of course took the whole *Lib. Her.* to be genuine.

The Bible text of Ps. Isaac is ordinarily taken from Syr. vg. There are slight variants, most of them due no doubt to his quoting from memory. Exceptions are 2 Cor. 13: 14; Rom. 5: 11; Luke 2: 52; John 2: 19 which correspond to the Greek. Luke 2: 52 and John 2: 19 are also quoted in this form in other parts of C.

IIIa–d: MICHAEL MALPANA OR BADOQA,[1] PP. 105–113 (TEXT), 'A TREATISE'

Baumstark[2] calls III, according to Scher's description of S, 'a treatise against the Jacobites'.[3] These opponents do not appear in the lemma of III in C, but perhaps S had a fuller lemma. Michael was a pupil of Ḥenana and a teacher of Nisibis; he left the school with his fellow-teachers because of his orthodox opposition to the master. Since Ḥenana was head of the school from 572 to 610, Michael's activities can be dated about the turn of the sixth century to the seventh century.

Lemma and colophon designate III as 'a treatise'. From this one would expect that the text was not an excerpt but a short complete tract. However, the subheadings begin in each case with 'By the same', which suggests that they do not subdivide a continuous text, but introduce new excerpts.

III*b*, *c* and *d* are expressly directed against different schools of the opposing christology and their main tenets: against the hypostatic and confused union of Cyril, against the Severians and their comparison of body and soul and the two natures in Christ, and finally against the Julianists and their own particular interpretation of Christ's human nature.

III*a* has no special heading of this kind; it attacks the expression 'theotokos' common to all three schools, which accounts for the placing of its refutation at the beginning.

Michael's style is characterized by the extreme brevity of his sentences which distinguishes it fundamentally from II. It is stated three times (at the end of *a*, at the last but one section of *b*, and at

---

[1] A. Vööbus, 'History of the School of Nisibis' (*CSCO* **266**, Subs. 26), Louvain 1965, p. 278 and nn. 16–19, lists these and other titles of Michael which designate him as 'teacher'.

[2] *Geschichte*, p. 129 with n. 7.

[3] So does Vööbus, p. 279 and n. 28. Vööbus takes no notice of Goodman, 'Jenks Collection', and therefore does not know of the actual existence of this text in C. The only reference to Cambr. Univ. Libr. Or. 1319 in V.'s book is to the edition of the new Theodore fragment from it in *Muséon* **17** (1958).

the end of *d*): 'This little will suffice', or words to that effect. The author is not only fond of short sentences, but also likes to condense as far as possible the matter about which he writes. Like the anonymous author of IV, Michael proceeds by syllogisms, though the chains of conclusions are much shorter in III. Each short group of conclusions is introduced by 'And again'. The record in brevity is reached in *a*, where every sentence begins with 'And again'. We have not bothered to reproduce these minute divisions in print. Michael likes to end the argument in the form of a dilemma, especially so in *d*.

IV*a*, *b*: ANONYMOUS, PP. 113–16 (TEXT), 'CHAPTERS OF A TREATISE AGAINST THOSE WHO CONFESS CHRIST AS ONE NATURE AND ONE HYPOSTASIS', EXCERPTS FROM THE DOCUMENT OF 612

The 'chapters' consist in fact of two excerpts (*a*, *b*) from the document of 612, and therefore are to be found again in VII*b*, where they occur in the order *b*, *a*. The Syriac text contains indications of agreement with *Synodicon Orientale* over against VII*b*, though not so clearly as in the excerpt from the document of 612 in I. In spite of this, the text of IV, like that of VII, is better than the text of *Synodicon Orientale*.

A marginal note in C ('This chapter is written in its place below') shows that at one stage of the history of our collection, a scribe has noticed that IV reappears as part of VII.

V: ANONYMOUS, PP. 117–30 (TEXT), EXCERPT FROM AN APOLOGY FOR NARSAI

The lemma announces a collection of biblical sayings about the distinction of the properties of the two natures 'before and after the taking' (*sc.* of the human nature by the Logos). The author of the lemma has formed his impression of the content by looking at the beginning of V and the first sections. P. 67, 36–68, 5 (transl.) consists of a passage commencing: 'Now, before the taking: for instance...', and this is followed by p. 68, 6 ff.: 'Those which [belong to the category] "after the taking" are as follows...' How inadequate the lemma is can be already gathered from the fact that a third category of biblical sayings is listed, p. 68, 16 ff.:

'Now these things which were spoken concerning the prosopon of the manhood are as follows...' Whereas the first two categories only occupy two short sections, several pages are devoted to the third. On p. 72, 10 ff. it is stated that three categories of scriptural sayings about the economy in Christ have been listed (cp. also p. 73, 10 f.). The categories are, however, described in a manner not quite consistent with the preceding groups of quotations: 'the first kind – [of] the divine nature only; the second kind – from the prosopon of the union,[1] that is, the name of Christ; now that is the third kind – also after the taking and the union: in word only have the divine scriptures distinguished the two natures, while they have not confused the properties of the natures.'[2] One possible explanation of the inconsistency is of course that, V being an excerpt, there was more biblical material preceding its actual beginning.

But a second difficulty could point in another direction. After the sentence just quoted there follows without introduction (p. 72, 19 ff.: 'For Christ, it is said, is consubstantial with us and our Lord...') a passage which speaks about the distinction of the natures in Christ; it is only at the end that the contents are designated as quotations from the sermons of Nestorius. We suppose that between the last Bible quotation and the first excerpt from Nestorius, the author's original text must have been heavily abbreviated either by the compiler or at some earlier stage (perhaps the compiler found V already in its present anonymous and incomplete form). The description of the three categories of biblical christological sayings may have survived from the original or may have been composed by somebody to bridge something which to the attentive reader seems unconnected.

The small Nestorius florilegium consists of four quotations. Some lines similar to, but not identical with the first are to be found in Loofs and Severus, therefore the authenticity may safely be assumed; the second is identical with some lines in Loofs; the third is new for the greater part, the fourth in half. Slight as this new material may seem, it is particularly welcome since the three last fragments belong to the sermons 12 and 23 of which very little has survived. Also our knowledge of the development of Nestorius'

---

[1] This qualification of prosopon is taken from Nestorius; see below.

[2] 'In word only – properties of the natures' shows the author to be acquainted with the Syriac translation of the letter of Andrew of Samosata to Rabbula; see L. Abramowski, 'Peripatetisches bei späten Antiochenern', *Zeitschrift für Kirchengeschichte* **79** (1968), p. 359 with n. 4.

christological terminology is increased in a small way. The term 'prosopon of the union' was previously only contained in the Second Apology (i.e. the genuine parts of the *Liber Heraclidis*).[1] The new fragments here show that Nestorius already used it in his sermons.

On p. 73, 6 ff. it becomes clear what the author intended with the biblical material and what the real object of his treatise is. He is referring back to something which he had already said about it, but that passage is not contained in the excerpt (V):

> Now *what I have said,* that *there are those who rend sections of the treatise of Mar Narsai and calumniate us by them,* as though he was saying that '*lordly manhood' is simple and divested of the godhead.* . .But the blessed Mar Narsai, *in these three ways in which the holy scriptures have been set down* by the Holy Spirit through the tongues of the blessed apostles, *like them he speaks,* and with them he agrees, and in their footsteps he walks.

So we are in the presence of an apology for Narsai; opponents are to be refuted who isolate statements of Narsai in his treatise (which?), where he speaks about the manhood of Christ, that he, *and* people who think like him, may be accused as making of Christ a *psilos anthropos.* To show that Narsai's christology agrees with scripture, biblical sayings and excerpts from Narsai are now put side by side in pairs. We get 8 fragments from Narsai in this way, the last of which is rather long and apparently ends with V itself. We have not been able, so far, to find the fragments in the published texts; it is to be hoped that research on Narsai will procure one day the whole treatise from which these fragments are taken.

Since Narsai is called 'blessed', he must have been already dead when the apology was written, therefore the *terminus a quo* is the year 502. The Nestorius fragments exceed Cyril's collection of excerpts which was known from the conciliar acts; since the complete sermons of Nestorius seem to have come to Persia only with the great writings of Nestorius after 530 and were then translated into Syriac, the *terminus a quo* should be 530.

The biblical florilegia reproduce the Syr. vg. text, sometimes abbreviated, sometimes with words added; once only is found a deviation in favour of the Greek text.

[1] Abramowski, 'Untersuchungen zum Lib. Her.', pp. 221 ff.

VI: ANONYMOUS, PP. 130–47 (TEXT), REFUTATION OF CYRIL'S ANATHEMATA

The lemmata at the beginning of VI are not quite to the point. First there are simply announced 'The chapters of Cyril' (p. 75, 15 transl.), with the first anathema following. After that again a lemma appears: 'Refutation and interpretation from the famous fathers in the church' (p. 75, 20 f.), and indeed until the second anathema the reader has before him patristic quotations only. But later occur refutations of single anathemata which are not taken from the fathers but written by someone who calls himself 'the orthodox' (that is the usual practice in the polemical literature about the anathemata, found also in Cyril's defence against his Antiochene opponents). The term 'orthodox' appears the first time after anathema 4; it has to be supplied after the second and third anathema, where the rubrication was forgotten. The refutation as a whole is finished with a creed: 'Our faith' (p. 88).

In VI not every anathema is followed by a refutation from the pen of the 'orthodox' and the existing refutations differ considerably in length. The following is a schematic survey of the contents of VI:

anath. 1, no refutation, 5 quotations
anath. 2, short refutation, 1 quotation
anath. 3, long refutation, 1 quotation
anath. 4, refutation, 2 quotations
anath. 5, no refutation, 3 quotations
anath. 6, refutation, 3 quotations
anath. 7, no refutation, 3 quotations
anath. 8, no refutation, 2 quotations
anath. 9, rest of a refutation, 2 quotations
anath. 10, lemma to a quotation, but without the latter, refutation, 1 quotation
anath. 11, short refutation (without 'the orthodox'), 2 quotations
anath. 12, refutation (on the distinction between the biblical sayings about Christ, 15 (or 16) quotations
'Our Faith'

Some of the refutations (of anath. 2, 3, 4, 6) contain formulas of rejection, 'who says this and that, rejects the truth', analogous to Cyril's 'anathema sit'. The particularly long refutation of anath. 12 shows no such formula. Sometimes there is an explicit transition from refutation to quotations (anath. 3, 6?, 9, 10?, 12);

in the case of 9, the transitional part alone does duty for the whole refutation, that is to say, it is all that is left over from the original refutation. This case and the case of anath. 10, where a lemma appears which has lost its quotation,[1] point to the possibility of abbreviations. The abbreviator is then responsible for the loss of some of the refutations and the cutting back of others.

Clear evidence of the abbreviation of the original text is afforded, when we turn to the quotations. The refutation of anath. 3 mentions Athanasius and Gregory of Nyssa, but then only Gregory is quoted, while the Athanasius fragment is missing. The procedure of abbreviating executed without the necessary attention, explains the cases where the lemmata to the patristic excerpts are wrong or not quite correct.

13 'Of Athanasius': here two numbers of the Ps. Athanasian *Sermo maior de fide* are coupled together, nos. 40 and 45 of Schwartz's edition; between them should be a 'By the same'. We have distinguished them as **13** and **13a**.

19 'Athanasius, from "Concerning the soul"': a rather complicated case; the title of the writing excerpted is in any case not Athanasian. Indeed, in the Nestorian florilegium in *Vat. Borg. syr.* **82**, which is called by its editors 'Florileg mit den Gregor-Scholien' (Flor. Greg. Schol.), the same fragment is to be found (in another Syriac translation) under the name of Eustathius of Antioch. Now Eustathius is the author of a *De anima* – but the lemma of Flor. Greg. Schol. **30** attributes the excerpts to his treatise on Prov. 8: 22. Thus the authorship of Eustathius is a certainty, but in which of the two works written by him it originates is not so certain. Since the fragment is unknown, it is not possible to decide the latter question beyond doubt, though it is permissible to guess that the error is on the side of our abbreviator who took the author's name from a first excerpt, the title from a second and the text from a third, misled probably by recurring 'Again's or 'By the same's.

27 'Clement of Rome': only the first third is an excerpt from 1 Clement. The origin of **27a** is still to be found, the lemma belonging to it having been lost by the abbreviation.

29 'Of the same' – i.e. Eustathius, the author of **28**, but in fact it is a quotation from the *Sermo maior de fide*, therefore an Athanasian

---

[1] This particular quotation could also have been omitted by homoioteleuton if the cited text had ended with 'high-priest', as the lemma does.

quotation now lost must have preceded **29** in the original. For other similar cases see the apparatus.

Finally, we think that the extreme brevity of some of the quotations (**10, 11, 18, 32, 35, 36, 38, 39**) is due to the abbreviator. So the original writing of refutation has suffered contractions and abbreviations in all his elements except the anathemata. Presumably the compiler found it already in its maimed state and without the author's name, perhaps included in another writing. He may have had a special interest in the excerpts from the fathers.

The florilegium of patristic quotations (=Flor. Cambr.) in VI is related to some other florilegia (for the details see the apparatus): to the Flor. Greg. Schol., to the florilegium attached to the document of 612 (Flor. 612),[1] and to the great collections of Theodoret. The relation of Flor. Cambr. to the two Nestorian florilegia in Syriac is particularly interesting: the identical excerpts appear in entirely different Syriac translations. Some of the excerpts which are common to two of the Nestorian Syriac florilegia are also contained in Theodoret. Many more of the fragments in Flor. Cambr. are to be found in Theodoret without Syriac Nestorian parallels. Sixteen excerpts are unaccounted for in this way, among them several we have failed so far to identify, though the one or the other may be really unknown. The latter is the case with the new fragments from Eustathius, two of which have a second witness in the Flor. Greg. Schol.

Can anything be said about the author of VI? We get some glimpses of his christology in spite of the contractions his work has suffered. The author shows the greatest reserve in the use of technical christological terms, except 'two natures'. He more than once stresses the incomprehensibility and ineffability of the union of the two natures in Christ: see the refutations of anathemata 2, 3, 4 and 'our faith'. The word *synapheia* is not used in the preserved text; once the 'union of sonship' is mentioned (refutation of anath. 4). The union of the two 'complete natures' (refutation of anath. 2 and 6), of God the Word and the complete man ('our faith') results in the 'one Son'. But no mention is made of the one prosopon; the division of the one Son into two prosopa is rejected (refutation of anath. 3 and 4).

'Hypostasis' is used only of relationship within the Trinity ('our faith'). Quite revealing is the way in which the 'orthodox' reacts against Cyril's assertion that his opponent (Nestorius) teaches two

---

[1] Only one fragment has a parallel in Flor. 612; the common ancestor is Theodoret.

hypostases in Christ (refutation of anath. 3): Cyril's reproach would be justified if he had attacked two prosopa; in place of that, Cyril is attacking two hypostases, which procedure is nothing else than the masking of his own opposition to the doctrine of two *natures*; and in this the Alexandrine is of course wrong. The author therefore does not hold up two christological hypostases, he belongs to the large group of theologians who took a long time to become accustomed to the use of the word hypostasis in christology at all, no matter if it were one or two hypostases. We know of Greek-writing Antiochene theologians of this kind in the fifth century, and the Syriac diophysite church maintained its reserve officially until 612 as the conciliar creeds in the *Synodicon Orientale* testify.

In the final sentence of 'our faith', the author quotes Heb. 12: 14, commending peace to his readers. Can we see here a hint as to the date of VI? A peace between Cyril and his Antiochene opponents was concluded in 433. The formula of mutual consent was a creed drawn up by Theodoret, and this 'creed of union' was as devoid of technical christological terms as the text of our author, neither prosopon nor hypostasis figuring there. The Antiochene concession to Cyril in the creed was the term 'theotokos'; this our author does not use, he calls Mary 'forever virgin'. The anathemata of Cyril, however, nobody on the Antiochene side was prepared to swallow; it is therefore by no means improbable that the author of VI sought to combine refutation of the chapters with an inclination towards peace, when the latter was in preparation, if not already concluded. So VI would have been composed originally in Greek somewhere in 433; the translation into Syriac took place early enough to use the unrevised older version of the anathemata in Syriac. This would make VI the oldest of the parts of C (except the Ephrem texts, if they are genuine). The reason for the many abbreviations and contractions it suffered may perhaps be found in that very mild form of Antiochene christology which the author teaches: it did not contain enough ammunition for Nestorian orthodox polemic.

If the date attributed to VI should be correct, the patristic material gains further in interest. The quotations which have parallels only in the *Eranistes* of Theodoret (written in 448) could not have been gathered from this famous work, but from some earlier florilegium of the bishop of Cyrus. The lost *Pentalogos adv. Cyrillum* (432) suggests itself; it is generally considered as certain that the florilegium of lib. IV of the *Pentalogos* has survived in Latin in Pope Gelasius' *De duabus naturis* either in whole or in part. There are quotations in Flor. Cambr. which occur in Gelasius with and without parallels in the *Eranistes*. If the *Eranistes* parallels to Flor. Cambr. which do not occur in Gelasius should originate in the *Pentalogos*, this would be a proof against the completeness of the *Pentalogos* material handed down by Gelasius. But is Theodoret the only source for the Flor. Cambr.? Neither in Gelasius nor in the *Eranistes* do there appear quotations from Clement of Rome, Arius and Epiphanius, as they do here.

The Bible text in VI is on the whole that of Syr. vg.; agreement with the Greek is very rare.

VII*a, b*: PP. 150–69 (TEXT), 'CREED', 'CHAPTERS' AND 'RESPONSES' DELIVERED BY THE PERSIAN BISHOPS TO KOSROES (IN THE YEAR 612)

These texts are already known from one of the appendices of Chabot's *Synodicon Orientale* (= *Syn. Or.*). The frame of protocol which surrounds the creed in the *Synodicon* is omitted here (the compiler did not transcribe: 'Remerciements et apologie au Roi', pp. 580 f. of the French translation, the epilogue, pp. 584 f., and the 'Supplique que les pères présentèrent au roi pour qu'il leur accorde un chef en Orient', pp. 585 f.). The creed detached from its framework is treated by us as excerpt *a*.

What in the *Syn. Or.* is called 'Objections des orthodoxes contre les séveriens θεοπασχίται' (p. 586), is headed in C as 'Controversial chapters which the fathers drew up and affixed to the creed' (p. 93 transl.). The Severians and theopaschites are mentioned in C, in the little historical introduction to the creed (p. 88), which is not a copy of the historical introduction preserved in *Syn. Or.* C takes for granted that the cause for the bishops' writing to the Persian Great-King was Severian doctrine ('to show the truth of their faith in a reply to the Severians'),[1] whereas *Syn. Or.*

---

[1] The epilogue to the creed in *Syn. Or.* shows the tactical motive for denouncing the group round Gabriel as 'Severians' (pp. 584 f.): in this way they can be called a heresy whose origin lies in the Roman empire, and the old Persian distrust of Christians as sympathizers with the enemy is turned here against dissenting Christians. A hundred years earlier Barsauma had used the same tactics against Philoxenian monophysite propaganda. The *Vita Georgii martyris* by Babai, which is not destined for the eyes of the political authorities, is more honest about the relations between the dissenters and monophysite doctrine; see *Syn. Or.* pp. 627 and 629. From the *Vita* it is quite clear that the dissensions which resulted in the document of 612 arose not with the monophysites but with disciples of Ḥenana.

says that 'Gabriel the *drostbed*'[1] caused the dispute 'with the heretics, his partisans'.

The above mentioned 'Controversial chapters' are numbered consecutively within their groups in *Syn. Or.*, but not in C. Both witnesses differ also in the arrangement of the groups of chapters. They both begin with the chapters against the doctrine of one nature and one hypostasis. The remaining groups are produced by *Syn. Or.*, in this order: (*b*) against the suffering and death of God in the flesh, (*c*) against the alternative 'theotokos' or 'anthropotokos', (*d*) against the accusation of quaternity, (*e*) against the accusation of the doctrine of two sons; C on the other hand arranged them as follows: *d, e, c, b*. The order in C is more systematic in that the series about the trinitarian implications does not separate the proper christological questions. We are not sure which arrangement is the original one.

The first group of chapters in *Syn. Or.* shows a confusion which can easily be corrected with the help of C. In *Syn. Or.* the number 1 is written against the *title* of the group. Accordingly, the following chapter there has the number 2 (p. 586). The chapter, however, to which no. 1 really refers is not lost. C has it, showing it to be identical with chapters 8 and 9 in *Syn. Or.* (p. 587). Chabot recognized (n. 2 to this page) that the division into two chapters is erroneous; from C it can be seen that in the process of displacement and chopping into two the original ch. 1 has lost also a sentence.

The Persian king asked the bishops three questions in C (p. 100); *Syn. Or.* has only two of them (p. 591); 'Did Mary bear man or God?' is omitted. That C has preserved the correct number is shown by the account of the prehistory and circumstances of the events of 612 contained in Babai's *Vita Georgii martyris* of which the relevant passages are conveniently printed in French translation in *Syn. Or.* pp. 625 ff. There Babai tells us that the king put the questions in writing; the questions are the same as in C, only in different order, the third appears in the middle between the two others (p. 632). In the formulation of one of the three questions there is a difference between C on the one hand and *Syn. Or.* and *Vita Georgii martyris* on the other. The first question reads in C: 'Have the Nestorians or the *Severians* deviated from the foundation of the faith which the first doctors made?', whereas *Syn. Or.* has: 'Sont-ce les Nestoriens ou les *moines* qui se sont écartés des fondements de la foi enseignée par les anciens docteurs?'; Babai in *Vita*

---

[1] '*Drostbed*' corresponds to Greek *archiatros* (*Syn. Or.* p. 580 n. 2).

Georgii martyris supports this opposition between Nestorians and monks.

It is quite certain that the Persian king in this question did not call the group of disciples and sympathizers of Ḥenana (whose spokesman was the physician Gabriel), Severians. It is the intention of their opponents, the authors of the document of 612, to classify them as Severians. C has followed the impression thus created[1] and lets the king speak of Severians as opponents of the strict diophysites. In fact these opponents had the favour of the king, therefore the strict diophysites get the term of abuse, 'Nestorians'; we may see in this the influence of Gabriel. The dissenting group around Gabriel undoubtedly designated themselves with a name which was also used by the king in his question. This name must lie behind 'monks', the Syriac word 'monks' we now have seems to be the result of some misunderstanding or some erroneous translation of the term from the Persian into Syriac, perhaps both.[2]

Unfortunately the text of C breaks off, due to the loss of one quire, at *Syn. Or.* p. 591, 22 with the words 'une seule majesté, une seule'.

VIII: ḤENANISHO' THE MONK, PP. 170-9 (TEXT), 'CHAPTERS FROM DISPUTATIONS'

Baumstark mentions this piece according to the description of S by Scher and puts it beside a writing described by Sachau, ms. Petermann I 9, f. 180u – 182r (=B).[3] Baumstark refrains from suggesting any relationship between the two; Ortiz de Urbina goes further and identifies them,[4] asserting that the piece in S is part of B. He is right in the identification, but the text of Ḥenanisho' at least in C is longer than the parallel in B, because of 'an addition which we found in another copy' (see above, pp. xvi f. and xx). That the addition is of the same author is borne out by the contents and the style. Vööbus draws quite another conclusion from Baum-

---

[1] Chabot is influenced in the same way; see his explanatory notes in *Syn. Or.*

[2] In the historical introduction to the document of 612 in *Syn. Or.*, 'monks' are mentioned as partisans of the bishops and fathers who stood up for the doctrine of two hypostases.

[3] Baumstark, *Geschichte*, p. 134 n. 5. E. Sachau, *Verzeichniss der syrischen Handschriften* (*Die Handschriften-Verzeichnisse der Kgl. Bibliothek zu Berlin* 23, 1. 2), Bd. 1, Handschrift 88 = Petermann I 9.

[4] *Patrologia Syriaca*, p. 128.

stark's references: he thinks that B and S contain two different texts of Ḥenanisho'[1] – in which he is wrong.

The lemmata of the two witnesses B and C are complementary to each other. C calls the text 'chapters of disputations', B 'a treatise in the disputative manner'. C is probably right in presenting the short piece as an excerpt. Both mss. introduce the author as nephew of Mar Elijah; C, however, adds: 'who founded the monastery in Assyria'. According to C, the writing is directed against heretics who teach the 'unity of composition in Christ'. B gives the name of the opponent: Isaiah of Tahal; B explains also that the treatise is aimed against the Chalcedonians. From this we can conclude that Isaiah of Tahal taught the doctrine of the one composite hypostasis. Isaiah was a disciple of Ḥenana of Adiabene. Even if we still do not know whether Ḥenana himself propounded the one composite hypostasis, the fact seems certain that Isaiah did. Since the orthodox Nestorians knew that the one composite hypostasis was also neo-Chalcedonian doctrine,[2] it is understandable that they called the dissenters Chalcedonians. To denounce them as Severians (as VII does, see above) was a tactical measure of defence over against the political authorities in favour of the dissenters.

There are some interesting textual differences between C and B and it is at first glance difficult to say which form is the original one. The solution of the problem is complicated by the irreparably bad state of B, which is for the greater part corroded by the ink: only beginning and end and a very small piece in between are legible. But even so, some conclusions are possible. C makes the peculiarity of the author's style more evident than B. The author inclines to a brevity even more extreme than that of Michael Malpana; pairs of two membered syllogisms follow each other in quick succession. The brevity is accentuated by the omission of the copulae 'is' (ܐܝܬܘܗܝ) and 'he (is)' (ܗܘ), whenever the sentence is complete without it. Now B shows a clearly recognizable tendency to soften the precision and brevity of the author. A good example is the sentence p. 170, 8 f. (Syr. text). In B the subject of this sentence is twice expanded by a relative clause with a copula; in addition to this the fuller forms of words are preferred by B (ܕܡܢ for ܕܡ, ܡܛܠ for ܥܠ);[3] two short sentences are linked by

---

[1] *History of the School of Nisibis*, p. 276 with nn. 6 and 7.

[2] See Babai in *Vita Georgii martyris*, *Syn. Or.* p. 627: 'Et si une portion de nature et une portion de nature constituent *une hypostase composée, comme le prétend Justinien, l'empereur impie*: il y a alors *composition*, division et deux parties.'

[3] On p. 177, 22 (Syr. text) B has ܐܝܬܝܗ, C ܐܝܬܝ.

'and'. Other cases are: Syr. text pp. 170, 10 and 177, 9, where B adds ܘܢ; p. 170, 12 B adds ܗܠ as a dativus ethicus; p. 177, 5 B adds ܗܝ; p. 176, 24 B adds ܝܗܠ – all of which is superfluous. In two places B tries to enforce the argument by adding words (transl. p. 101, 17. 20). At one point B draws attention to the fact that one of the most frequently cited lines from Phil. 2 is an apostolic saying. On the other hand there are two omissions, a small one (transl. p. 105, 10) by haplography and a whole sentence by homoioarkton (transl. p. 105, 23–5).

Finally there are the differences in christological terminology. Where C has (p. 105, 17 f. transl.) 'his constitution' (ܩܘܢܡܗ) B reads: 'the ousia', meaning the human nature of Christ. ܐܘܣܝܐ is certainly the more difficult word; in this case the rule of lectio difficilior has to be applied. 'Ousia' is intended to simplify the text and to make it unambiguous. In fact the result in B is almost a tautology, that is to say a deterioration of the sense, while the reading in C gives an excellent meaning.

Other examples are: p. 105, 7 f. transl. – C: 'the man who is spoken of in Christ', B: 'Jesus from our race'; p. 105, 15 – C: 'from whence is our Lord perfect man?', B: 'then Jesus in his hypostasis is not complete', the transformation of the question into a conclusion makes the text easier, and is therefore secondary.

The curious thing is that these kinds of alteration (of which we would certainly have more, if B were complete), in spite of their concern with theological terms, do not cause doctrinal differences between C and B; B is as strictly diophysite in the orthodox Nestorian sense as C. The intention of B seems to be to conform Ḥenanisho's expressions to a standard terminology (Babai's?). Taken together, all these differences allow only one conclusion: C has preserved the author's original text.

IX: (PS.) NESTORIUS, PP. 179–206 (TEXT), 'VARIOUS CHAPTERS AND DIVERSE QUESTIONS'

For IX we have, fortunately, a parallel witness in R which corrects a considerable textual error (see above, p. xiii). For three chapters there is a further parallel in Vatic. syr. 179 (= V); they follow in this ms. after the so-called Syriac counter-anathemata (which form the second half of XI in C). The order of the three chapters in V is: 28, 17, 18. There are some minor variants, and one difference shows V with the inferior text on its side. We have already said (above, p. xx) that both Ps. Nestorius pieces in V are perhaps taken from a collection of the type of C. V is in any case a later ms. than U or S.

Loofs has printed and translated the three chapters from V in his *Nestoriana* (p. 371 text, with a misreading in the last line, pp. 218, 13 – 219, 17, German translation).

According to Scher the number of chapters was 38 in S and not 36 as in C. If this difference is not simply an error it could have been caused by the dividing up of one or two of the longer chapters.

A study of the chapters has been given earlier by A. E. Goodman.[1] The new quotation from Theodore of Mopsuestia in ch. 1 has been published after C in 1958 (see apparatus). But in spite of the fact that the interest of the editors in C began with IX, and that IX has been read carefully again and again, this part of C remains the most difficult text of the whole compilation. The peculiar style has been described already by Goodman, and his explanation was that the chapters must have been written originally in Greek. However, VI is a translation from the Greek and did not offer the kind of difficulties that IX does. The man who translated the Greek chapters into Syriac did his work very badly and we are not sure whether it was his Greek or his Syriac that was not quite up to the task.

But are all 36 chapters really translated from the Greek? Here the problem of the literary unity or of the unity of authorship arises. And what of the literary form? Was the text composed in chapters, or has a continuous text been divided by titles, or have excerpts from different sources been strung together by numbers and headings? In the last case a gradual growth of the collected chapters in IX can be imagined. Apparent differences in style between the chapters may point to more than one author. But efforts to divide them up in this way have not produced any results.

The Bible text used offers no help. There are two great deviations from Syr. vg. in Jer. 5: 8 and Heb. 12: 16 and some other slight variants. Elsewhere Syr. vg. is followed, although it differs from the Greek. And at the end of ch. 34 there is a discussion about a Syriac verb in Luke 23: 46 which presupposes acquaintance with Ephrem's commentary on the *Diatessaron* and is therefore possible only on a Syriac basis. However, this sentence goes so badly with

---

[1] 'An Examination of Some Nestorian Kephalaia (Or. 1319, University Library, Cambridge) ', in: *Essays and Studies presented to S. A. Cook*, London 1950, pp. 73 ff. See also Abramowski, 'Untersuchungen zum Lib. Her.', pp. 143 ff.

the preceding text that one would be tempted to see in it an addition.

The christological doctrine of IX is marked by the notion of the prosopon of revelation: the Logos took on the human nature to reveal himself in the prosopon of Christ. Ch. 8 attacks the christology of 'becoming', that is to say the christology of Philoxenus of Mabbug. The composite hypostasis is, as in many other texts of C, more than once opposed in IX.

Attempts to fix a date of origin for IX are easier to make if we begin to consider the reason why the 36 chapters are attributed to Nestorius: these considerations also apply to the second half of XI. Syriac speaking diophysites had to wait for the translation into their language of the complete writings of Nestorius until 539/40 (translation of the *Liber Heraclidis*) or thereabouts. Until then they had to take refuge in pseudonymous attribution of which we have two examples in C. So we come to the first part of the sixth century as the period of origin at least for the Syriac form of IX, the (possibly) Greek elements preceding it of course, but not too far back. The composite hypostasis attacked is, then, the neo-Chalcedonian notion, as has already been said in the discussion of the new Theodore fragment.

X: 'FROM BABAI THE GREAT', PP. 207–9 (TEXT)

The lemma gives only the name of the author, but no indication of the title of his work. It is difficult to say whether X is an excerpt from a greater writing or a short independent tract. The latter is by no means impossible, for X is a brief, self-contained presentation of Babai's christology. It begins with definitions of nature, hypostasis and prosopon (there is some similarity with ch. 1 in IX). The treatise ends with the condemnation as 'outcasts from the church and deniers of the truth' of those who do not confess two natures, two hypostases and one prosopon.

Since Babai the Great (d. *ca.* 628) was according to tradition the author of 83 works, it is surprising how every possible reference to his dogmatic writings is applied to the one *De unione*. Thus even the cautious Baumstark attributes our text to this work,[1] in spite of the fact that the description of S by Scher gives no reason for this. In consequence, X receives no mention in the short notice by Ortiz de Urbina on *De unione*.[2]

Baumstark also reproduces Assemani's erroneous assumption

[1] *Geschichte*, p. 138 n. 1.   [2] *Patrologia Syriaca*, pp. 130 f.

that *De unione* is identical with the treatise 'Against those who introduce the one hypostasis of body and soul as analogous to the one hypostasis of Logos and man'.[1] The latter is in fact a separate writing and has been available since 1915 as an appendix to Vaschalde's edition of *De unione*. The notices of Baumstark and Ortiz de Urbina were therefore already incomplete at the date of their publication. With the text preserved by C we now have three dogmatic works of Babai: *De unione*, the tract published in the appendix to *De unione* and our piece.

XI: CYRIL AND (PS.) NESTORIUS, PP. 211–18 (TEXT), 'KEPHALAIA' AND 'THESES'

Cyril's anathemata appear here for the third time in C (in the Syriac version used also by I). They are followed by 'theses of Mar Nestorius', of which there are also twelve. The theses without Cyril's anathemata are found in Vatic. syr. 179 f. 101u–104r (= V). The combination of the two series as we have it in C is likely to be the original form. The theses are also formulated as condemnations, only in a milder way: 'Whoever says...denies the truth.' The Ps. Nestorius text from V has been edited by J. S. Assemani, *Bibliotheca Orientalis* III, 2 with a Latin translation; the latter is reprinted in Loofs, *Nestoriana*, pp. 220–3. Loofs recognized the inauthenticity.

In spite of the similarity of the external form between the two series of condemnations, we do not find that every one of the theses refutes the corresponding anathema. Rather, over against a christology for which Cyril's anathemata were canonical, the theses insist on a firm diophysite doctrine, while at the same time defending themselves against accusations of teaching two sons, etc. Unlike Cyril, the author begins with the Trinity, on which there are seven theses. Only five theses are left for the *oikonomia*, but they are so long that in fact the christological part is the larger. The lemma in V indicates the contents as follows: 'On God and the *oikonomia* in the body.' The Trinity and the homoousia of the persons of the Trinity as a starting point for the argument is reminiscent of II*b* (Ps. Isaac), where this procedure is recommended for discussions with the Severians. Are the Severians the opponents here as well? It seems more likely to be Philoxenus of Mabbug with his christology of 'becoming', as theses 4 and 8 are opposed to it. For the author of XI the right way to speak of the incarnation is

---

[1] *Geschichte, loc. cit.*

to speak of the 'taking on' of the man for the 'purpose of revelation' (theses 8, 9, 11). It is evident that the theological background
of XI is the same as that of IX, though the authors need not be
identical (in fact the style tells against identity). The author avoids
as far as possible the christological use of the terms prosopon and
hypostasis; he does not say '*prosopon* of the revelation' (though
prosopon is used in a trinitarian passage). He prefers the traditional
biblical pictures for the description of the relationship of the two
natures in Christ (IX, too, is fond of these pictures). None the less,
it appears at the end of thesis 10 that the author teaches two
christological hypostases.

XII*a–d*: EPHREM, PP. 219–23 (TEXT), SERMONS AND HYMNS

So far we have not found any of the four pieces in the great
editions of Ephrem. XII*a*, however, is identical with the first part
of a *memra* published in 1904 by A. S. Duncan Jones from a ms. of
the India Office, London, Ethiop. and Syr. Nr. 9 (=I), and
with the first part of the same *memra* published, also in 1904, by
I. E. Rahmani from a ms. in the possession of D. Elia Mellus of
Mardin (= M), see apparatus. I and M tend to agree against C.

1

NOTE ON TRANSLATION AND APPARATUS

The translation does not make easy reading, for not only is the style of some authors extremely difficult, but also the subject matter of all of them. It often took a long time to understand the syntactical construction of a sentence, as well as the meaning of the author. The aim has been to give a translation as exact as possible, avoiding unnecessary paraphrase. The reader will perhaps bear this in his mind if the translation at times appears stilted.

We have tried to be consistent in translating the christological technical terms. ܐܘܣܝܐ is rendered by 'ousia' (plur. 'ousias'), ܐܝܬܘܬܐ and ܟܝܢܐ by 'substance' (except in the case of Ephrem, where the latter terms have the wider sense of 'divine being'), ܩܢܘܡܐ – 'hypostasis' (plur. 'hypostases'), ܦܪܨܘܦܐ – 'prosopon' (plur. 'prosopa'). However, 'consubstantial' stands for both ܒܪ ܟܝܢܐ and ܒܪ ܐܝܬܘܬܐ (ܒܪ ܟܝܢܐ is the older translation of ὁμοούσιος, ܒܪ ܐܝܬܘܬܐ is the more literal one). An important role is played by the notion of ܪܘܟܒܐ (σύνθεσις) – 'composition' and ܩܢܘܡܐ ܡܪܟܒܐ (ὑπόστασις σύνθετος) – 'composite' or 'compounded hypostasis'; these terms are violently rejected by nearly all the authors.

The page numbers of the Syriac text appear in the translation in square brackets. The English translation has a double apparatus, and the biblical references, which are very numerous, are printed in the margin. The first apparatus contains text-critical matters, and differences of Bible text over against Syr. vg. The second apparatus contains explanatory notes, and locates quotations. There are, however, several of the latter which we have not been able to identify.

li

ABBREVIATIONS AND SIGNS USED IN TRANSLATION AND APPARATUS

Mss. containing the whole text:
C = Cambridge University Library Oriental 1319
U = *Vorlage* of C
S = Séert 87 (only known from Scher's description)

Ms. or published testimonies for parts of C:
for VII (and IV where it does not agree with VII): *Syn. Or.*, see below
for VIII: B = Petermann I 9 (Sachau 88)
for IX: R = photostats formerly in the possession of Chabot, now in that of van Roey
for 3 chapters in IX: V = Vatic. syr. 179
for XI, second half: V = Vatic. syr. 179
for XII*a*: I = India Office, London, Ethiop. and Syr. 9, as published by Duncan Jones; M = ms. in the possession of D. Elia Mellus, as published by I. E. Rahmani, see apparatus

ACO = Acta Conciliorum Oecumenicorum, ed. E. Schwartz, Strassburg/Berlin 1914 ff.
Braun = O. Braun, *Das Buch des Synhados nach einer Handschrift des Museo Borgiano*, Stuttgart und Wien 1900
CSCO = Corpus Scriptorum Christianorum Orientalium
Eran., *Eranistes* = Theodoret, *Eranistes*, PG 83, cols. 28–317; the Roman numerals designate the dialogues, the quotations are numbered for each dialogue
Flor. Greg. Schol. = *Florileg mit den Gregor-Scholien*, ed. L. Abramowski and A. van Roey, *Orientalia Lovaniensia Periodica* 1, 1970, pp. 131–80
Gelasius = florilegium attached to Gelasius, *De duabus naturis*, ed. E. Schwartz, *Publizistische Sammlungen zum acacianischen Schisma* (Abh. d. Bayr. Akad. d. Wiss., Phil. hist. Abt. NF 10), Muenchen 1934, pp. 96–106
GCS = Die Griechischen christlichen Schriftsteller der ersten drei Jahrhunderte
Lietzmann = H. Lietzmann, *Apollinarius von Laodicea und seine Schule*, Tuebingen 1904
Loofs = F. Loofs, *Nestoriana. Die Fragmente des Nestorius*, Halle 1905

Philox. = Philoxeniana

Sermo maior de fide = E. Schwartz, *Der s.g. Sermo maior de fide des Athanasius* (Sitz. ber. d. Bayr. Akad. d. Wiss., Phil. hist. Kl. 1924, 6), Muenchen 1925

Spanneut = M. Spanneut, *Recherches sur les écrits d'Eustathe d'Antioche*, Lille 1948

Syn. Or. = J.-B. Chabot, *Synodicon Orientale ou recueil des synodes nestoriens (Notices et extraits...de la Bibl. Nat.*, vol. **37**), Paris 1902

Syr. vg. = Syriac vulgate, Peshitta

Syr. vt. = Syra vetus, Old Syriac version of the gospels

cf., cp. = confer, compare

conj. = coniecit (-erunt), conjecture(d)

del. = delevit (-erunt), delendum, delete(d)

edd. = editores, editors

exemplar = U

gr. = graece

ms., mss. = manuscript(s)

om. = omisit, omits

plur. = pluralis, plural

script. = scriptor, scribe (Daniel)

seqq. = sequentes

suppl. = suppletum, supplied

⟨ ⟩ addendum, to be added

[ ] delendum, to be deleted

( ) explanatory additions by edd. in the translation

TRANSLATION

[1] By the power of the Trinity I am collecting a little from the confession of the heretics from the writings of the fathers, and questions and responses against them.

5 First from the book which the holy of memory, Mar Shahdost, bishop of Tarihan composed, why we Easterns have separated ourselves from the Westerns, and why we are called Nestorians.
    From the second synod of Ephesus whose heads were Dioscorus, who was after Cyril in Alexandria, and Eutyches the monk... the
10 synod... the wickedness of Cyril... that everybody who (...) not (say) one nature and one hypostasis... unity, should be accursed. Whoever... twelve chapters of the blessed... ⟨bish⟩op Cyril, which the ⟨synod⟩ which was in Ephesus defined and approved ...he who speaks against them shall be accursed. ⟨He who
15 does not⟩ approve the anathema which the synod which was in Ephesus has drawn up against Nestorius such a one shall be ⟨accursed⟩. Whoever does not say that the blood of Christ is of (divine) substance shall be accursed. Because if the blood of Christ is consubstantial with us, how is it distinguished from the blood of
20 bulls and of goats? Again: Dioscorus [2] says: I confess that Christ our Lord is from two natures before the union. But after the union we confess one nature.

12] 'bishop': completed by the edd.
13] 'synod' supplied by S. Brock.
14/15] 'he who does not': supplied by the edd.
17] 'accursed': supplied by the edd.

5] 'Shahdost' here; pp. 22, 29 and 36, 20 the author is called 'Eustathius'.
7] 'we are called Nestorians'; below, p. 31, 8 the author speaks of 'Nestorian Christians' – the name given them by their enemies they have taken on their own by this time.
12–20] not in the preserved parts of the acts of the Robber synod (449) neither in the Greek acts for the first session (read at Chalcedon) nor in the Syriac ones of the last session.
17–20] cp. the closely similar expressions in Dioscorus' letter from exile at Gangra to Alexandria, quoted by Justinian, Ctr. Monophysitas, ed. Schwartz, Drei dogmatische Schriften Justinians (Abh. Bayer. Akad. Wiss., Phil. hist. Kl., NF **18**, 1939), p. 24, 11–14.
20–22] not said by Dioscorus in the first and last sessions in 449, so perhaps in the session (or sessions) between them the acts of which are lost. But considering the way Shahdost makes use of quotations, another explanation seems most probable. In the first session in 449 the minutes of Eutyches' case at Constantinople were read. There Eutyches said: ὁμολογῶ ἐκ δύο φύσεων γεγενῆσθαι τὸν κύριον ἡμῶν πρὸ τῆς ἑνώσεως, μετὰ δὲ τὴν ἕνωσιν μίαν φύσιν ὁμολογῶ (ACO

Things similar to these Cyril also says in his letter to Acacius of Melitene: We say Christ consisted of two natures, but after the union of the Son there ceased (to be) that which divided the two. We confess one nature of our Lord who is one, as one. And again, the same: For this reason they are considered to agree 5 with the blasphemies of Arius, because they are unwilling to distinguish between the variety of utterances – those, he says, which befit God, those which belong to the manhood and refer to the dispensation in the flesh. But to what extent I am removed from these things your perfection bears witness also to others. And 10 again, the same in Eustathius: It is not right to understand two natures, but one nature of the Word made flesh. Now the view of Apollinarius is: A new creation, a glorious mixture, flesh and God have perfected one nature. The same: The nature of the godhead (together) with the body is one, and is not divided into two. From 15 Cyril: The Word suffered in the flesh. – Wherefore, according to

3] 'of the Son' not in the Greek.
4] 'we confess': gr. πιστεύομεν.
4] 'our Lord': gr. τοῦ υἱοῦ.
7] 'he says' does belong to Cyril's text.
8] 'refer': gr. +μᾶλλον.
10] 'bears witness': gr. μαρτυρήσειεν.

11 1, p. 143, 10 f.). This sentence is in 449 at once commented on by Dioscorus as expressing his own opinion (and consequently that of his synod): συντιθέμεθα τούτοις καὶ ἡμεῖς πάντες (*ibid.* p. 143, 12). As Eutyches' deposition in the acts and Dioscorus' quotation in our text are exactly identical, it looks as if Shahdost did not scruple to put the words of one into the mouth of the other.

2–4] *ep. 40, ACO* 1 1, 4 p. 26, 7–9. PG 77 col. 192 D–193 A.
5–10] *ep. 40, ACO* 1 1, 4 p. 29, 24–7. PG 77 col. 200 AB.
11/12] bishop Eustathius of Berytos gives this as a quotation from Cyril twice, at Ephesus 449 (*ACO* 11 1, p. 112, 62 f.) and at Chalcedon 451 (*ibid.* p. 113, 13 f.). On the latter occasion it is made clear that he is quoting from memory. The first half of the alleged quotation must be an inference drawn by Eustathius. In one of the mss. used by Schwartz for the edition of the Chalcedonian acts (M = Venetus 555) it is accordingly glossed at in both places: ποῦ λέγει εὐστάθιος μὴ νοεῖν κύριλλον (the name is lacking in the second gloss) δύο φύσεις (see Schwartz's first apparatus). This way of 'quoting' Cyril justifies our explanation of the Dioscorus quotations above.
13/14] =Lietzmann, fragm. 10 (p. 207); a quotation given by the *Doctrina Patrum*, Justinian, Photius.
14/15] from *ep. ad Dionysium* 1, Lietzmann p. 258, 2–4; a quotation in Leontius Hier. (see Lietzmann p. 257 app.) ends with the words given here.
16] from the 12th anathema.

your saying, O impious one, [3] his incarnation earned death for
him, and it would have been better for him if he had not become
incarnate. And who would not suffer were he to see an immortal
who had come to rescue mortals from death, who (however) was
5 unable to free mortals from death, but was held and enclosed
within the cage of mortality? And what is deserving of sorrow is
that (bad) custom has firmly implanted presumption throughout
the whole of the western regions of the world.

10 The same.   1*b*

That Cyril formerly agreed with orthodoxy is known moreover
from that book called Thesaurus, written by him. For he says in it
thus: The ark signifies the coming of the manhood. For the gold
which is overlaid within and without is a type of the godhead,
15 whereby the manhood was anointed and it became as though one
might say 'He who ⟨was⟩ anointed'. Gold remains gold, but...of
the wood, the same. The ark, which contemptuously is called...,
and nothing which restrains, so also Christ, when two ousias are of
necessity to be understood, as the likeness of God and of a servant,
20 one Son and Lord is confessed and worshipped by us. And again,
in his treatise to the emperor Theodosius, he has written: [4] For
thus it is right, that we should not treat God the Word as foreign
to those things of the manhood after he had clothed himself with
the body, nor, moreover, that we should deprive the manhood of
25 the glory of the godhead when anything concerning Christ is said.
For the nature of God the Word, because it took the manhood, was
not by itself, for it was glorifying it with the divine glory, and it

16] 'was': edd. suppl., copyist's note at the lacuna: 'The leaf is torn.'
25] 'when anything concerning Christ is said': the Syriac text of this is
evidently corrupt, gr. εἰ ἐν Χριστῷ νοοῖτο καὶ λέγοιτο.

11] Theodoret in his *Apology for Diodorus and Theodore* made a point of Cyril's
former diophysite pronouncements, if we may judge from Barḥadbeshabba and
Facundus of Hermiane, who are both dependent on Theodoret on this point.
Our page in Shahdost certainly shows acquaintance with the same work; thus
the following quotations from Cyril perhaps go back to Theodoret.
13–20] not found in the *Thesaurus*. Another comparison of the two natures in
Christ with the wood and gold of the ark is made in the *Scholia de incarnatione
unigeniti*, c. 1, PG 75 col. 1381 AB. Facundus (via Theodoret) quotes the latter
passage.
21–5] *ACO* 1 1, 1 p. 60, 9–12. PG 76 col. 1173 B.
26–p. 6, l. 2] is that still Cyril speaking? The continuation of the preceding
quotation in the Greek reads differently.

was staying in it for ever, being unchanged, and not turned aside
from that natural greatness. Moreover, he distinguishes the natures
also in those three treatises which were composed by him against
those who would confound the natures. But his envy of Nestorius,
who became patriarch of the royal city, blinded his power of dis- 5
cernment, and drove him away from the truth though it was not
hidden from him...

[5] The sect of the followers of Peter, those who deny the taking
(of the human nature), are they who have done most evilly and
wickedly of all, in order that they might corrupt the utterances of 10
holy scripture. For they have supposed that they would be making
powerful the sickness of their mind if they were to turn away from
and forget the words which were preached to them openly concerning the manhood of our Lord; and they have cut off and cast
out and led them by force in accordance with the weakness of 15
their bitter mind. And while they were making use of their customary wiles, and found the wickedness of the emperor Anastasius to
be nourishment for their error, they were confident (in themselves).
And in the likeness of the swine of the forest they dared to corrupt
the vineyards of the divine scriptures. For they have warred with- 20
out shame against the words which are spoken about the manhood
of our Lord, and which manifestly declare the duality of his
natures. And they changed and drew them after their opinions
which they had learned from the ancient Jews. For they are like
the enemies of the life of all. They corrupted all the words which 25
they found written about God the Word, born of the Father – like

Mt. 22: 44   that passage, 'The Lord said unto my lord, Sit on my right hand'.
(Ps. 110: 1)   [6] That was when in the temple the saviour asked the gathering
Mt. 22: 42   of the quarrelsome, their fathers: 'What do you say of Christ,
ff. (Ps. 110:   whose son is he?' and they answered him: 'The son of David'. He 30
1)   refuted them: 'And how does David in spirit call him Lord?
(namely), "The Lord said unto my Lord, Sit on my right hand"'.

7] copyist's note at the lacuna: 'This part was left out; the latter part of (this
page) is blank in the exemplar.'
31] 'in spirit': ܒܪܘܚܐ: Syr. vg. ܒܪܘܚ.

3/4] 'three treatises...' = *Ctr. Synousiastas.* That this book was in *three* volumes
we learn here for the first time.
8] 'Peter': Petrus Fullo, monophysite patriarch of Antioch, the first time
before 475, then 475–6 and 484–7/8, in which last year he died. Cp. below,
pp. 19, 6 ff.; 23, 1–3.
17] emperor Anastasius, 491–518.
32 – p. 7, l. 6] see Introduction pp. xxviii ff.

They knew not, neither did they understand, and in place of the four letters (*sc.* of the Tetragrammaton) which were preserved in the Hebrew, and by which, so they say, one signifies the name of God which is above all, (and) which is used in the same way in
5 both expressions, namely 'the Lord' and 'to my Lord' (respectively) – having erased these four dominical letters, they have written (in their place) this (rendering) 'to my lord' in ordinary writing.

Moreover, in the account of the birth of the manhood of the
10 Son, when they saw that the evangelist records and says that that was fulfilled which was spoken of by the prophet when he said: 'Behold, a virgin shall conceive, and shall bear a son, and they   Mt. 1: 23 shall call his name Emmanuel, which is, being interpreted "God   (Is. 7: 14) with us"', they have written: We have 'a young woman' not 'a
15 virgin', and she bore after marriage, and not without marriage according to your prating, O Christians.

Those of the party of Paul of Samosata also have done things which resemble these. For wherever there have been words [7] in the scriptures concerning the eternity and the godhead of the Son,
20 they have removed them, and introduced others, human (words) in their place. For it is right for us to set down these words which they have disregarded and corrupted, which they are, and how they have changed and (what) written in their place. For example: 'Apart from God, on behalf of all men, he tasted death', they have   Heb. 2: 9
25 changed and written in its place: 'He, God, in his goodness, tasted death for all men.' And for example, what is said in Acts: 'Take care of the flock over which the Holy Spirit has appointed   Ac. 20: 28 you as bishops so as to feed the church of Christ which he purchased with his blood', they have written 'to feed the church of God which

14] 'young woman': νεᾶνις in the Greek versions of Aquila, Symmachus, Theodotion; Hebrew עַלְמָה.

24] 'Apart from God': the author follows the reading attested *i.a.* by Theodore of Mopsuestia.

25] 'He, God, in his goodness' ܣܠܐܘܒܣܘܬܗ ܐܠܗܐ ܗܘ ܗܘ: Syr. vg. changes the order of the two last words.

27] 'Take care of the flock': Syr. vg. 'Take care therefore of yourselves and of the whole flock.'

28] 'the church of Christ': so some Syr. vg. mass., see Lee's edition *ad locum*, app., following the Greek.

29] 'the church of God': some Syr. vg. ms. and editions S. Lee 1821 and British Foreign Bible Society 1905–21.

17] The name of Paul of Samosata belongs to the apologetic-dogmatic argument about biblical translations.

Heb. 2: 16   he purchased with his blood', and that (saying): 'He did not receive from angels but received from the seed of Abraham', they changed and wrote thus: 'For it was not over angels that death had authority, but over the seed of Abraham death had authority.'

Joh. 2: 19, 21   And that: 'Destroy this temple, and in three days I will raise it 5 up – but he spoke concerning the temple of his body', they have changed it to: 'but he spoke concerning the temple of his

1 Tim. 2: 5   church'. And that: 'One is the mediator [8] between God

Ac. 2: 36   and men, the man, Jesus Christ'; and that: 'This Jesus whom you crucified, God has made Lord and Christ'; these, and many 10 other (words) like them, they have extracted and made as they desired.

See then, O hearer, of what kind is the love of truth of the heretics who, like diligent labourers in the destruction of their lives, with great care take pains to corrupt the utterances which are 15 spoken in the Spirit by the apostles. And when the writers were not persuaded to do this, they brought forth against them an edict (σάκρα) so as to cause them to cease from their work, and left only a few – those who were obedient to them – and the rest they drove away from their houses and compelled them to depart to other 20 cities. And together with these (matters) they were zealous in cursing the renowned teachers of the church, Diodore and Theodore, so that there was not found with any one a trace of the sane and true teaching of the apostles. And they established their own error through worldly authority, persecuting the true ones 25 with the power of money and obscuring the truth by the statement of their words.

1/2] 'He did not...Abraham' = gr.

3/4] 'For it was not...had authority' = Syr. vg., only 'death'² has been added (by the author? or did he read it in his Syr. vg.?).

5] 'Destroy' ܐܘܦ: gr. λύσατε Philox. ܐܘܦ, Syr. vg., Syr. vet. ܣܘܬܪ; cp. II p. 44, 31, VI p. 84, 18, VII p. 92, 18.

5/6] 'I will raise it up' ܘܣܩܝܡܝܘܗܝ ܐܢܐ: Syr. vg. ܠܗ ܐܢܐ ܡܩܝܡ ܐܢܐ; cp. II p. 44, 32, VII p. 92, 19.

7] 'spoke' ܐܡܪ: Syr. vg. ܐܡܪ ܗܘܐ.

7/8] 'of his church': see Introduction, p. xxxi.

13–27] here the time of Peter the Fuller and of Philoxenus of Mabbug is still treated. Philoxenus attacked Diodorus and Theodore, see A. de Halleux, *Philoxène de Mabbog*, Louvain 1963, pp. 31 ff. Is the 'sacra' (line 18) the *Henotikon* (mentioned below, p. 19, 19)?

[9] Against those who confess one hypostasis.   Ic

Let us see whether this 'one hypostasis in two natures' stands, or whether it has a leg to stand on alongside the examination of the truth. And from the divine books let us learn whether the Father
5 has ungiven life in his hypostasis. And everything the Father has, so also has the Son. There is then to the Son ungiven life in his hypostasis. If therefore the Father has given to the Son to have life in his hypostasis as the divine book says, there is then in the Son an hypostasis endowed with ungiven life, and an hypostasis (which is)
10 a recipient of given life. And if this is so, as it is the truth, what is the hypostasis which is admitted, and what is that which is omitted, that of the godhead or that of the manhood? If that of the manhood is omitted then there is no taking, and he was born in an ordinary manner. And if that of God the Word was omitted then
15 there would be no union. Tell me: you profess the union absolutely? And if you do profess (so) – if then the nature is one and the hypostasis one – tell me, is there a nature which is not in the hypostasis under which it is known; or (is there) an hypostasis not indicative of the common nature? Therefore, in this [10] one
20 hypostasis which you speak about, are there known in it two natures preserving their properties, or one? And if there is one nature – then which is it? If (it is) that of God the Word, then there is no nature of his manhood, and if (it is) that of manhood, there is no nature of godhead, and if half nature and half hyposta-
25 sis, they have established a compounded hypostasis, as the impious emperor Justinian says: Here is a composition and a division and parts, and this one hypostasis is singular in its species and separate from the eternal substance and from the nature of men. Then God is not perfect God in hypostasis, nor is man perfect man in hypo-
30 stasis and ceases to be confessed consubstantial with the Father. For neither the Father nor the Holy Spirit have a compounded hypostasis like this; nor is there throughout all creation an hypostasis which is compounded of godhead and flesh according to the blasphemy of Justinian. But perhaps you will say: Hypostasis has

26–7] 'Here is...one hypostasis' cf. Justinian, *Edictum de recta fide*, ed. Schwartz, *Drei dogmatische Schriften*, p. 74, 14–21. There are to be found the catchwords σύνθεσις, μέρη, μία ὑπόστασις and between them διαίρεσις, but the latter is *negated* by the emperor. The 'quotation' belongs in fact to a long passage borrowed from Babai's *Vita Georgii martyris*: p. 9, 15 f. = *Syn. Or.* p. 627, 10 f. (French transl.); 9, 16 f. cf. 627, 11 f.; 9, 17–32 = 627, 15–25; 10, 4–24 (with alterations) = 628, 5–21; 10, 25–27 = 627 (sic), 11–13. See index of quotations. 34 – p. 10, l. 3] is best explained by p. 20, 28 ff. below.

been set down here in place of prosopon and it is possible that your error is that you have read hypostasis as *hypostasis*, that you call prosopon *prosopon*. And look, this reading and change of terms refutes you. Say to me now: [11] This prosopon of the unity of the whole Trinity, is it conjunctive or that of God the Word – about 5 whom it is said: 'The Word became flesh', and: 'The form of God, took the form of a servant'. And in this prosopon, moreover, was united the human nature also; all nature of men is perceived in him, of men and of women in common. Or (is it) that one hypostasis, man, he sends forth, who is the form of a servant; and from the 10 seed of Abraham was he taken – as it is said: 'He did not receive from angels but from the seed of Abraham', 'and he did not say to him to your seeds as to many but to your seed as to one, namely Christ', and he was man, and from the virgin Mary was he born. Therefore in this one prosopon of Christ not only natures are per- 15 ceived in one conjunction, but also hypostases preserving their properties, namely that of God the Word, complete hypostasis, like Father, Son and Holy Spirit, and that of the man Jesus, a complete hypostasis like Abraham and David from whose seed he was taken. And he was united in one unity and conjunction, the 20 temple and its inhabitant, the taker and the taken, the perfecter and the perfected; [12] man and God in the one inseparable union, of one prosopon, of one Lord Jesus Christ, the Son of God – yesterday, today and for ever.

If then before the union one is the nature and one is the hypo- 25 stasis, and after the union likewise, one nature and one hypostasis, there is no union and the name of union is vain. Or do you not know that the denial of the hypostases is a denial of the nature? But you have confused the manhood with the godhead, and the godhead with the manhood and you have destroyed the properties 30 of the hypostases, like water and wine when they are mixed.

But what will you do with that (passage): 'For it befits him through whom is everything and because of whom is everything', who is God the Word, as it is said, that 'everything came about through him', 'that he should make perfect through sufferings the 35 captain of their salvation', his unified temple, 'Jesus of Nazareth, whom God anointed with the Holy Spirit and with power'? For God the Word was not perfected in sufferings, O Egyptian. For

Marginal references:
Joh. 1: 14
cf. Phil. 2: 6, 7

Heb. 2: 16
Gal. 3: 16

cf. Heb. 13: 8

Heb. 2: 10

Joh. 1: 3
Heb. 2: 10
Ac. 10: 38

11/12] 'He did not...Abraham': see above, p. 8, 1 f.

2/3] 'hypostasis'² and 'prosopon'² are trans*literated* here from the Greek.
38] 'O Egyptian' is addressed to Cyril of Alexandria.

one is the perfecter by nature and another the perfected by nature, just as one is the anointer and the other the anointed. And just as also Paul says when he throws light upon that (passage) from the blessed David: 'For this reason God, your God, has anointed you   Heb. 1:9
5 with the oil [13] of gladness more than your fellows.' Well then, who is the God of God the Word, who anointed him? for look, he says: 'I and my Father are one', and they are his fellows, above   Joh. 10:30, whom he is exalted by anointing. Well then, in respect of what   cf. Heb. 'gods', his 'fellows', does he say concerning his manhood which   1:9
10 was anointed, 'the spirit of the Lord is upon me, therefore he has   Lk. 4:18, anointed me'? This therefore is so, in accordance with what the   cf. Is. 61:1 scriptures have said. Who is he who will confirm all this, who supposes that Christ is neither perfect in the nature and in the hypostasis of his godhead, nor perfect in the nature and in the
15 hypostasis of his manhood? Because true God from true God, consubstantial with the Father joined himself to the true man consubstantial with us which was complete in body and soul, that is: God the Word, made one (with himself) the true hypostasis from our race, willingly, and prosopically. Wherefore the two natures
20 are preserved in conjunction and in union, without confusion and without change. In this one is one united prosopon, one Lord Jesus Christ, Son of God and for ever in one lordship and authority and worship with Father and Holy Spirit. And for this reason the fathers say: God who was made man, and man who was made
25 God, in order that they may make clear the property of the natures.

[14] How is it possible that God the Word should be formed from the Holy Spirit? If without his godhead, Christ is not God, yet in his godhead was not born of the virgin, how could the virgin be
30 God-bearer? If, because Christ is God and for this reason the virgin is God-bearer, how much more because Christ is man, should the virgin be called man-bearer. But if he who calls the

7] 'my Father'= Syr. vg., gr. ὁ πατήρ.
27] 'How is it': p. 98, 4 f. 'But if it is not'.

15–17] 'true God...Father' and 'true man...us' from the Nicene creed.
19] 'prosopically' (ܐ ܒ ܘ ܦ ܪ ܨ) shows that the Greek προσωπικῶς had been introduced into Syriac theological language; again p. 35, 18.
24/5] 'God who...made God': Gregory Nazianzen, *ep. ad Cledonium* (*ep.* 101). PG 37 col. 180A.
27 – p. 12, 15] is a quotation from the documents of 612; below (VIIb), p. 98, 4–27. We have to thank Dr Sebastian Brock for the observation that this passage occurs twice in our collection.

virgin 'man-bearer', calls Christ an ordinary ⟨man⟩, also he who names the virgin 'God-bearer' speaks of Christ as God divested of manhood. Because he who is confessed as born of the virgin, of necessity is the same who was circumcised and has grown in stature, in wisdom, and in grace, and was crucified and suffered 5 and died according to the witness of the scripture. Wherefore it is clear that it is not for the honour of Christ or of his bearer that the heretics name the virgin God-bearer, but in order that they might find occasion to attribute all these weaknesses and sufferings to God. If there is no God who has a God, also there is no God who is 10 more than God; but it is said of Christ by the prophet, [15] and the apostle expounds it: 'For this reason God your God has anointed you with the oil of gladness more than your fellows' – who now, is the God of God the Word who with the oil anointed him, or those his fellows above whom he is anointed? And if you 15 are willing, hear from the illustrious Eustathius, bishop of Antioch. For he says: If he was God the Word and consubstantial with the Father and, we say, everything through him came about, then he who was the cause of the origin of all was not from a woman, but he was in the divine nature powerful, and without limitation and 20 incomprehensible. From a woman there became man, he who was fashioned in the womb of the virgin by the Holy Spirit. For this one did Mary bear.

If the virgin, being the daughter of a man, precisely and really bore God, it follows perforce that the Father also precisely and 25 really bore a man, for they speak of our Lord as God and man. And if we ascribe the birth of his godhead in a precise manner to the virgin, of necessity we must ascribe the birth of his manhood exactly to the Father. Now what (was the reply of) that one persecuted by you, the illustrious herald of orthodoxy, the blessed 30

Marginal references:

cf. Lk. 2: 52

Heb. 1: 9
(Ps. 45: 8)

Joh. 1: 3

1] 'man'²: edd. suppl., cf. *Syn. Or.*
6/7] 'Wherefore it is clear that it is': p. 98, 18 om.
8] 'virgin' (=*Syn. Or.*): p. 98, 20 'holy virgin'.
9] 'and sufferings' (=*Syn. Or.*): p. 98, 21 om.
14] 'with the oil': p. 98, 26 om.
17] 'God the Word': Spanneut Λόγος καὶ Θεός.
17] 'consubstantial with': Spanneut ἀνέκαθεν παρά.
20] 'in the divine nature powerful': Spanneut τὴν φύσιν Θεός αὐτάρκης.

17–23] from the *Commentary on Prov. 8: 22*; the quotation here overlaps with Spanneut Nr. 18: 17 begins with Spanneut p. 101, 9 Εἰ δὲ Λόγος. The last sentence: 'For this one did Mary bear', is unknown, but may be an inauthentic addition.

Nestorius, when much persuasion was presented to him by those [16] who for love of leadership and love of the (episcopal) throne, inclined to the left side, that he might call the virgin 'God-bearer'? He answered them at the commencement of his speech: It is clear
5 that this is an heretical utterance. And again, against the impious Cyril, who sometimes confessed the taking (of the human nature), and spoke impiously of the hypostasis of the manhood of our Lord, and at other times spoke impiously of the natures and rent the taking, he spoke as follows: If, then, he who is born of the virgin is
10 Christ, why do you go about seeking another name for her who gave birth, as though it was something else apart from Christ who was born of her, and do not name the virgin with that which befits her, namely, 'Christ-bearer', as Christ is God and man? Now if anyone should say that Mary is (either) 'God-bearer' or 'man-
15 bearer', he ought to say, in addition to 'God-bearer', 'man-bearer'. For when one of these utterances is made alone, it is not without danger – when both are made, they achieve safety – in that this (expression) 'man-bearer' signifies that his birth was from a mother who gave birth to a [17] body consubstantial with herself,
20 but that (expression) 'God-bearer' (signifies) that Mary is divine.

I desire...you Chalcedonians, in what way do you differ from the Jacobites? For they say to everyone who becomes a disciple of theirs...only: 'Say: Mary is God-bearer, and: God suffered in the flesh, and curse Nestorius, and see, you are a son of the king-
25 dom, and not a son of Gehenna.' And you are saying that God the Word became flesh hypostatically, and that Mary bore God. Well then, according to your statement, he who became flesh and man, him did Mary bear. Therefore it was a man whom she bore, a man, you say, who became God. And if he became man, and you
30 reply that she bore God, therefore she bore not him who became. But this blasphemy will turn upon you. Again, to put it in another way, if Mary is God-bearer, then it is fitting that she be called goddess, and it is right that we should reckon her mother and her

21] a short word illegible.
23] one long or two short words illegible.

4/5] In this form not be to found in the texts of Nestorius.
9–20] not found; for similar passages see the index in Loofs, *Nestoriana*, *s.v.* Maria.
15/16] 'man-bearer': one would expect an analogous clause to follow: 'and in addition to "man-bearer", "God-bearer"'.
17–20] 'in that this...': these lines explain the 'danger' of line 17.

mother's mother, and her father and her father's father and the absolute entirety of her family and her kin to be gods and goddesses. This is to stop the mouths of the heretics.

However, because to ridicule heretics is not in itself sufficient for a demonstration of the truth, we will take up against them the hope which is in the venerable scriptures, where the hope [18] of our lives is defined. And first I will speak of those (words) of prophecy in Genesis, of David, Isaiah and the twelve, of Jeremiah, Ezekiel and Daniel. Then we will set down also the stories of Exodus and Numbers, and Deuteronomy and Joshua and Job, and Judges and Ruth and Samuel and the book of Kings and Acts. We will set down also the depositing of the laws, the book of Leviticus and the Wisdom of Solomon, Ben Sirach, Koheleth and Song of Songs. We will set down also those things which concern apostleship which are also an establishing of laws, the proclamation of the gospel, the letters of Paul, and we shall seek and see whether there is in them at all the term 'God-bearer'.

cf. Lk. 1: 26–56   Now we will begin with the gospel. In the sixth month of the conception of John, 'the angel Gabriel was sent from God to Galilee to the town of which the name was Nazareth, to a virgin espoused to a man whose name was Joseph'. 'And the name of the virgin was Mary. And the angel entered in unto her and said to her: Peace be to you, full of grace. Our Lord is with you, blessed are you among women.' 'For you have found favour with God, for behold you will receive conception and bear a son, and call his name Jesus.' 'Mary says to the angel: How shall this be, because no man is known [19] to me?' 'Mary says: Behold I am the Lord's handmaid.' 'Now Mary arose in those days and went.' 'And it came to pass, when Elizabeth heard the salutation' of the virgin, she said to Mary: 'Blessed are you among women, and blessed is the fruit which is in your womb.' 'Mary said: My soul magnifies the Lord.' 'Mary stayed with Elizabeth for about three months.' –

cf. Mt. 1: 16–23   'Jacob begat Joseph the husband of Mary from whom was born Jesus who is called Christ.' – 'The birth of Jesus Christ was in this manner.' – 'While Mary his mother was espoused to Joseph.' – 'Joseph son of David, do not fear to take Mary your wife.' 'All this that took place was in order that that which was spoken by the

Is. 7: 14   mouth of the prophet might be fulfilled: Behold a virgin shall conceive and bear a son and they shall call his name Emmanuel,

Lk. 2: 5   which is, being interpreted, our God is with us.' – 'With Mary his espoused, being with child, that he might be registered there.'

Lk. 2: 16   'And they found Mary, and Joseph, and the infant laid in the

manger.' 'Now Mary was keeping all these words and meditating   Lk. 2: 19
upon (them) in her heart.' – 'And Simeon blessed them and said   Lk. 2: 34
to Mary, his mother.' – 'And the mother of Jesus was there.' –   Joh 2: 1
'And with Mary the mother of Jesus, and with his brethren.'   Ac. 1: 14

5   Like the shame of a thief when he is discovered so is Cyril put to
shame [20] through the writings of the apostles. But like a drunkard
falling this way and that, he chatters that the name of Mary
(occurs) also in the prophets. And it happens that this saying is
written there: produce it (and) let us see: 'And Amram took as a   Ex. 6: 20
10 wife Jocabad, his uncle's daughter, and she bore him Aaron,
Moses and Miriam.' – 'And Miriam the prophetess, Aaron's   Ex. 15: 20f.
sister, took a tambourine in her hand', 'and Miriam was answering
them'. – 'And Miriam and Aaron spoke against Moses.' 'And the   Nu. 12: 1ff.
Lord said suddenly to Moses and Aaron and Miriam.' 'And he
15 called to Aaron and to Miriam.' 'And behold Miriam was leprous
like snow. And Aaron turned to Miriam and saw that she was
leprous.' 'And Miriam dwelt outside of the camp for seven days.
And the people did not journey until Miriam entered.' – 'And   Nu. 20: 1
Miriam died and was buried there.' – 'And I sent before you   Mic. 6: 4
20 Moses and Aaron and Miriam.' And look, from the books also of
the prophets is the Egyptian put to shame.

But to where does he stumble? For he says that the name of
Mary is to be found also in the writings of Josephus, the Hebrew.
And in order that there should not remain to him one single
25 excuse, let us investigate this also.... But, he says, there was a
woman and her name was Miriam and who was in the direct
succession of the house [21] of David...now she, without marriage,
bore many, a foolish thing to be said. But lest he should be
crowned, the Egyptian (was) opposed...and Miriam, the daughter

25] copyist's note at lacuna: 'In the exemplar this place is empty.'

6–8] is this an allusion to *Glaphyra in Exodum* III 2 (PG 69 col. 493)? Most of the
following biblical quotations are used or alluded to in this passage. Aaron's
sister, however, is for Cyril ordinarily an image of the church.
22/3] Aubert's indexes in PG show that Josephus (*Bellum judaicum*) is
mentioned once in Cyril's *Comment. in Joh. Evang.*, but the passage does not
help to explain our text.
25 – p. 16,3] 'But he says...they know': since the text has suffered damage, it is
difficult to say where Shahdost reports Cyril's (alleged) meaning and where he
refers to Josephus.
26] 'Miriam': which of this name?
29 – p. 16, 1] 'Miriam the daughter of Hyrcanus': if she is Mariamne I, 'the
wife of Herod the Great', then Hyrcanus was her mother's father.

of Hyrcanus...she was the wife of Herod the Great. Antipater...
and was covered with ...but the shamed one did not stand in awe
of...they know. But again he dares to say...

In the holy writings there is no mention of this expression, but
whoever does not use it is not orthodox. Well then, Simon Peter 5
Mt. 16: 16f. who confessed in the midst of the apostles: 'You are the Christ,
son of the living God', and our Lord to him: 'Flesh and blood
have not revealed (it) to you', – he is not orthodox because he
doesn't say, as you do, 'You are God the Word, born of Mary,
God-bearer, according to the flesh'. And all the apostles and 10
teachers after them, and to put it briefly: the Christian people
from the time of the apostles until Cyril, who have not called Mary
'God-bearer', are not orthodox. The Orientals in any case, who
never mixed this expression with their confession of faith, even
after Cyril, are not orthodox. And behold, the east until... [22] 15
scorned by you. The common guardian has not left it...profitable,
and of rejoicing and of knowledge of praise...but once by means
of Jonah and Daniel and Ananias, Azarias and Misael and
Ezekiel and Zechariah. Now what is greater than all...in flesh
was revealed to the Easterns before all peoples. They blessed... 20
and they offered his worship. And if...this he asks Jerusalem...
Once again, by means of Nathaniel and Thaddeus and Thomas,
and Addai and Aggai and Mar Haddi, its sons (were brought) to the
knowledge of this faith which the Easterns have kept, not without
the variety of their sufferings and the diverse kinds of their deaths. 25

But you, because there dwelt in you an abundance of envy and
cf. Lk. 18: 11 the pride of your heart caused you to err, you are proud: I praise
you, O God, that I am not like the Easterns, or even like this
Nestorius. Where then can be put all the holy blood of all those
martyrs, thousands without number, which has been shed in the 30
East for the name of Christ? Cease therefore from your quarrelling
with us, you (who are) instructed in error. It is enough to make
accusation before her of many blessings, (even) the holy one, full of
joys – (saying that) the Easterns do not [23] desire to call her
'God-bearer'. And if they ask us, saying: Christ – is he not God? 35
we answer: Yes, God, and everlasting and (divine) substance. But
the writers of the gospel, have refused to use these expressions in the
account of the birth of our Lord, who from high...you are not

1] 'Antipater': which of this name?
4] 'this expression' = God-bearer.
13] 'Orientals': the diophysites of Persia.
23] Who is Mar Haddi?

enslaving. And in short, they have supposed...writers of the incarnation, Christ...and saviour, and Lord, who together... they will confine within finity the maker of times and finities, and that they may make a complete confession of the likeness on behalf
5 of our salvation: so far that he receives that, God has humbled   cf. Phil. 2:7 himself. If then, since Christ is God, they command us to confess that God was born, let them concede the same of the everlasting one, and (divine) substance. Let them say then of the virgin, in accordance with their foolish judgement: 'bearer of the everlasting
10 one and (divine) substance', for Christ is both – however they do not say (so). For they do not accept that those expressions 'everlasting one' and '(divine) substance' should be submitted to a beginning (in time). If then, because Christ is God, they name the virgin 'God-bearer', then moreover because Christ is created and
15 a man, they should name her 'bearer [24] of the created and of man'. But it is absurd, for she is neither 'man-bearer' nor 'God-bearer', but 'Christ-bearer'. Now, in accordance with the mind of those who have written by the Spirit of God, listen, O contentious one, and be persuaded, O heretic, more than you do I
20 honour the honoured one, but I do not call her 'God-bearer' – unless you are going to show me that it is written: 'The book of   cf. Mt. 1:1 the nativity of God. Now the birth of God was thus. And when   cf. Mt. 1:18 God was born in Bethlehem of Judah. And when they had ful-   cf. Mt. 2:1 / cf. Lk. 2:21 filled eight days that God should be circumcised. And rise up and   cf. Mt. 2:13
25 take God and his mother, and flee to Egypt. And Herod was ready   cf. Mt. 2:16 to seek out God in order that he might destroy him. And God grew   cf. Lk. 2:40 in stature and in wisdom and in grace. Now when God was   cf. Mt. 4:1 baptized, and then God was led by the Holy Spirit into the desert to be tempted by the devil. And Pilate scourged God. And the   cf. Mt. 27:
30 soldiers, having crucified God. Now God cried with a loud voice   26, 35, 50 and delivered up his Spirit. And when they came to God, they saw   cf. Joh. 19: that he was dead already and they did not break his legs, but one   33 f. of the soldiers smote him in his side with a spear, and immediately there came forth blood and water. And: I know that you seek God   cf. Mk. 16:
35 who was crucified, [25] and you seek God the Nazarene who was   6 crucified.' But the shameless one persisted with his customary impudence and was saying in addition that it is written so in the Greek copy.

He neither knew nor understood that Ptolemy, king of the West,
40 puts him to shame even from there, and this...who in a precise inquiry learned that not...of writings, and concerning this I call

39–41] see below, p. 35, 19 ff.

heaven and earth (to witness)...this expression is without a writer. And who, were he more obstinate in his mind than a beast, would forsake that which is written in the gospel and go out into the error after the Egyptian, who, though it is not written that God was born, says that he was born? And not only does he make 5 this statement, but also he curses everyone who does not say as he does. Well then, how have you made a book which is a refutation throughout the length of (its) lines of that opponent of the gospels, Julian the heathen? And now you overthrow these things which once you built up. 10

But the effective cause of your malady is known and manifestly clear. Because Nestorius the righteous martyr and christophorous, who was patriarch of the royal city, (strives to) convince you, saying: If you had cursed me alone, a crown of cedar [26] would I be placing for you and (a crown) of laurel, but since you have 15 cursed both us and the gospel at the same time, am I considered... and with its preachers. But the Egyptian has despised and rejected the counsel of the evangelists, and by blinding the sight of his discernment by the desire of his will, has carried the shield against the pilot who did not become weak. Nestorius...'God-bearer'. 20 That...the holy Nestorius was not persuaded by him; he (sc. Cyril) out of his envy for and his contest with the athlete was raving, as he also wrote to the clergy of Constantinople: I will not give sleep to my eyes, nor rest to the temples of my head until I have avenged myself on the son of the Antiochene. 25

But how long am I to remain with the Egyptian? Let us proceed first a little, and show the things which took place afterwards. Now Yazdegerd reigned seventeen years and died, and Peroz, his son, reigned after him. Marcian reigned seven years. Now he died in the first year of Peroz, and there reigned after him Leo the illus- 30

Ps. 131: 4

7–9] Shahdost refers to Cyril, *Adversus libros athei Juliani*; another allusion below, p. 33, 18 f.

14–16] where does Nestorius say this? In the first *Apology* (= *Tragoedia*)? Or has the author himself made up the quotation?

23–5] Cyril to his apocrisarii at Constantinople (*ep.* 10), *ACO* 1 1, 1 p. 12, 15–17. PG 77 col. 68 D – 69 A. The second half (lines 24 f.): 'I have avenged myself on the son of the Antiochene', is a malicious substitution for οὗ ἀγωνίσωμαι τὸν ὑπὲρ τῆς ἁπάντων σωτηρίας ἀγῶνα.

28 ff.] cp. the synchronism for an earlier time p. 23, 6–21.

28] Yazdegerd II 438–57.

30] Peroz 457(9)–84, Marcian 450–7.

30] Leo I 457–74.

trious and fearer of God, and his life and that of Anthemius continued for nineteen years, while the two of them strengthened the
synod of Chalcedon.

Now this Zenon [27] was the son-in-law of Leo, and his up-
5 bringing had been in one of the monasteries of the heretics, and
the name of the head of this monastery was Peter who, as they say,
was a fuller, and he was hated by the followers of Cyril, and he
was made a bishop. Now in the time of this (man) there took place
amongst the Romans a controversy concerning the faith in the two
10 natures clamorously. And he confirmed the faith of Eutyches...
and one...and there was a great war amongst the Romans which
was worse than that which took place in the days of Cyril. And the
bishops assembled together, and anathematized the synod of
Chalcedon and the tome of Leo, the bishop of Rome, which he had
15 written to Flavian, the bishop of the royal city, in which he had
anathematized Eutyches, and all who had imputed suffering to
God in a natural and hypostatic union...(affirming) that I do not
recognize any synod except that of Nicaea. And the heretics read
the uniting document of the churches, and thenceforward were
20 bold to proclaim openly 'one nature'. The dexterity of Zenon
effected these things.

Let us recollect here moreover the ignominy of the Westerns as
to where they found this expression 'one nature'. Now I say
assuredly and clearly [28] that the Apollinarians, when they per-
25 ceived their own malady, and the glory of the catholic church, all
began in some small degree to partake in saluting him as mortal
without relinquishing their former malady. But they instilled their
bitterness into many who previously were healthy and made them
sickly. And from this root there sprang up in the church that (ex-

3] after 'Chalcedon' there is room for one word.
14] after 'Chalcedon' there is room for one word; copyist's note: 'In the
exemplar this place was empty.' But nothing seems to be lacking.
17] after 'union' a small blank.

1] Anthemius 467–72.
4] 'Now this Zenon' presupposes that Zenon was already mentioned
before; one sentence seems to be missing.
4] Zenon 474–5, 476–91.
6] 'Peter': cp. above p. 6, 8 ff. and below, p. 23, 1–3.
17/18] '(affirming) that...of Nicaea': who and what is quoted here?
19] 'uniting document': the *Henotikon* of 482.
26] 'him': Jesus Christ. The sense of the sentence seems to be: 'They considered Christ not only as divine but also as human.'

pression) that one is the nature of the godhead together with the manhood, and the (fact) that they introduced suffering into the godhead of the only begotten. For this was the father and begetter of this expression, and not a man of foolish talking. Wherefore, how can anyone who calls Christ one nature, anathematize 5 Apollinarius?

Now the athletes of the fear of God – I refer to Mar Acacius, pillar of the land of the Persians, and Mar Barsauma, light of the East – when they heard of the evils which had taken place amongst the Romans, diligently assembled the bishops of their dioceses, and 10 made a synod, and confirmed in it the true faith of the two natures and the two hypostases. And although they did not accept the synod of Chalcedon for the reasons I have mentioned above, nevertheless they did not entirely reject it. They did not accept it because of the (expression) 'God-bearer' apart from that of 'man- 15 [29] bearer', and that of 'one hypostasis', and again because of the impiety which was wrought in (the expression) 'prosopon', which (expressions) were partially set down in the definition of that synod. And for all these (reasons), the Easterns were unwilling to accept it, but neither would they anathematize it 20 because of the (expression) 'two natures' for 'their properties were preserved', which was set down in the definition of that synod.

It will not mislead us that the heretics and also the followers of the synod dare to say that 'the synod of Chalcedon anathematized Nestorius'. But we say to them: 'You lie, for it has called him 25 lacking in understanding but has placed no anathema upon him. This is much more tolerable than those things which it has presumed against God.' And for this reason, although they exercised

7] Acacius, catholicos 485–95/6.

8] Barsauma, metropolitan of Nisibis 449 (so de Halleux, *Philoxène*, p. 14 n. 18)–92/5.

10/11] Of Barsauma's otherwise schismatic synod at Bet-Lapat in 484, a protestation of adherence to Theodore of Mopsuestia is quoted with approval in 605, *Synodicon Orientale*, pp. 475 f. (transl.). The synod of the catholicos Acacius in 486 has a theological statement in its first canon, *loc. cit.* pp. 301 f. (transl.).

11/12] 'the two natures and the two hypostases': the formula of 486 speaks of two natures and one prosopon only, and it is improbable that in 484 two hypostases were spoken of in an official document. Shahdost is reading the view of Nestorian orthodoxy since 612 into the earlier history of his church.

12/14] Chalcedon is not spoken of at all in 486 (and the same was probably the case in 484): the matter in hand was *monophysite* propaganda, not Chalcedonian doctrine.

20/1] note the author's kind attitude towards Chalcedon.

great pressure on the Easterns to accept the synod of Chalcedon,
and made a considerable defence on behalf of the 'one hypostasis'
that was set down in it, saying, 'qnoma is here set down instead of
prosopon', the Easterns did not accept their persuasion. But when
5 the Easterns saw here that the lives of the Christians of the West
were standing in affliction amounting to despair, because they
found them heretics...

[32] ...if it effected a blessing upon the nations in the seed of cf. Rom. 4:
10 Abraham, according to the saying of the apostle, the hypostasis of 13
Christ in the flesh is not now in its sense, according to the scripture.
In vain then is the blessing of Abraham and the promise spoken to
him. If when we worship God in spirit and in truth, we worship cf. Joh. 4: 24
one nature of the godhead, which is known in three hypostases of
15 Father, Son and Holy Spirit, are we not (to be) called worshippers
of many gods? Also when we worship Christ who is perfect God,
is it not right that we be called worshippers of two sons? If when
the evangelist says: He gave his only begotten Son for us, are we cf. Joh. 3: 16
to understand of the godhead of Christ that it suffered? Also when
20 he says: Why do you seek to kill me, a man who has spoken truth cf. Joh. 7:20,
with you, are they to understand it (to be) about an ordinary man? 8: 40
This is shocking. If when the apostle says: 'He in his hypostasis Heb. 1: 3
effected a cleansing of our sins', they understand of the hypostasis
of God the Word that it suffered, then are they to understand that
25 (text): 'He made him inheritor of everything', as referring to the Heb. 1: 2
same hypostasis? This is shocking. If when our Lord says: 'Destroy Joh. 2: 19
this temple, and in three days I will raise it up', do they not make
a distinction between the inhabitant and his temple, and between
him who is destroyed and him [33] who raises up, nor again will
30 there be a distinction between the creator and creation? If, when
the blessed John says: 'The Word became flesh', do they say of Joh. 1: 14
the mystery of the incarnation that with mixture and confusion he
was changed and became flesh, also, when the apostle says: 'He Gal. 3: 13
became a curse and sin for us', do they understand (it) in a similar

7] pp. 30 and 31 of the text are empty; lacuna of what extent?
18] 'we': S. Brock prefers to read 'they'.
20/1] 'Why do you...with you' while here John 7: 20 (Syr. vg.) and 8: 40a
are conflated, the *Diatessaron* (see Ephrem's *Commentary* XVI 26) combines 7: 20
with 8: 40b.
26] 'Destroy': see above p. 8, 5. 'I will raise it up' (line 27) follows Syr. vg.:
ܐܢܐ ܡܩܝܡ ܐܢܐ ܠܗ, another reading p. 8, 5 f.

3/4] cp. above, p. 9, 34 f.

way? But if it is neither one thing nor the other – if when our Lord says: 'No man ascended into heaven save he who came down from heaven', with reference to the manhood of our Lord do they say that it 'came down from heaven' – that which is particularly 'son of man'? If the word concerning the ascending and the exaltation 5 (has) its established meaning, then also the descending and the ascending may be understood, and which each one of them fits. If the vision which Stephen saw was true: 'I see the heavens opened, and the Son of man sitting on the right hand' – and the revelation to Paul – 'Who are you Lord?', and the voice of our Lord to him: 10 'I am Jesus of Nazareth whom you are persecuting', there is established the distinction of the properties of the hypostases and the definition of the natures from which Christ is called God and man in names and in the understanding of the names. And one name of the Son (belongs) to both of them because of 15 the union of the prosopon. These things did he write to [34] Nestorius.

But the apostles, impelled by the Spirit of God, though the heretics were scandalized by them because they made a distinction between the godhead and the manhood of Christ, we the Easterns 20 warmly espouse as homilies and words of God. The divine teaching away from which the heretics turn their faces, the holy apostles teach us with a few words. But if these erring ones do not believe, Paul then shall say to them: 'Because they have not believed, have they brought to naught the faith of God?' For the 25 faithlessness of these does not bring to naught the true faith. Let the faith enter and prosper in your own heart, O king.

Id Again, another extract, also from the book of Mar Eustathius of Tarihan. 30

Now it is time for us to turn also to our neighbours, and to that which they prate: Look, the synod of the 318 anathematized Nestorius. Let us examine them because perhaps you may have

16/17] 'These things...Nestorius' ('he' is evidently Cyril): should this remark take up p. 18, 23 ff., in spite of p. 18, 26 ff.? Or was Cyril mentioned again in the lacuna between p. 21, 7 and 9? Or has some reader made a gloss, after loosing the thread?

27] Who is the king addressed? And is he addressed by the author, or by some later hand?

29] 'Eustathius' here and p. 36, 20, 'Shahdost' p. 3, 5.

32] 'The synod of the 318': Nicaea 325.

33 – p. 23, 3] The patriarch is Petrus Fullo, already mentioned p. 6, 8 ff. and p. 19, 6 ff.

Marginal references:
Joh. 3: 13
Ac. 7: 56
Ac. 9: 5
cf. Rom. 3: 3

learnt from your patriarch, who when he dwelt like a beggar in the monasteries was not ashamed to write himself down as patriarch of Antioch. Otherwise from where has this any sense, or from where is there [35] any occasion (for this)? The prophet shall say to you
5 through me: 'By day has stumbled the chosen one who (is) with   cf. Hos. 4: 5
you, and he has stumbled by night.' For, look, from the time of the synod of Nicaea until the synod of the 350, there have mounted up 105 years... ⟨years of the reign⟩ of Shapur, king of Persia, son of Hormizd, he who prolonged his days, as it is written, for 71 years,
10 and of Constantine the victorious and of Constantine and of Constantius and Constans and Julian and Jovinian (sic) and Valentinian and Valens and Gratian and Theodosius the Great, Greek kings. And from the synod of the 150 until the time of the synod of Ephesus in which Nestorius was (present), there mounted
15 up 50 years, ⟨years of the reign⟩ of the other Shapur who was after Shapur and of Ardashir and Bahram and Yazdegerd, Persian kings, and of Theodosius the Great and Honorius and Arcadius and Theodosius the Less, Greek kings. See, the kings who were in the midst of the three assemblies which took place in Roman
20 territory, and their years without addition and omission, I set down for you.

5/6] 'By day has stumbled the chosen one who (is) with you, and he has': Syr. vg. 'By day you have stumbled and the prophet who (is) with you has'. 'stumbled'¹: Sept. ἀσθενήσεις, Rahlfs conj., mss. ἀσθενήσει.

8] blank space in the exemplar, copyist's note: 'Even though this place is blank, nothing is lacking in these places' – in which he errs. 'years of the reign' edd. suppl.

15] 'years of the reign': edd. suppl. for blank space.

7] 'synod of the 350': considering the distance of years this is Ephesus 431; but 350 is nearly the exact number of participants in 451. Possibly the words 'and twenty' after 'hundred and five' have been lost in the lacuna (see the arrangement of words in the Syriac).

6 ff.] cp. the synchronism for the second half of the fifth century p. 18, 27 ff.

8] Shapur II 309–79.

9] Hormizd II 302–9.

10] Constantine I 324–37. Constantine II 337–40.

11] Constantius 337–61. Constans 333–50. Julian 361–3. Jovian 363–4.

12] Valentinian I 364–75. Valens 364–78. Gratian 367–83. Theodosius I 379–95.

13] 'synod of the 150': Constantinople 381.

15] Shapur III 383–8.

16] Ardashir II 379–83. Bahram IV 388–99. Yazdegerd I 399–420.

17] Honorius 395–423. Arcadius 395–408. 18] Theodosius II 408–50.

...that in the first place: [36] Mar Nestorius was not born. In the second place: He did not reach primacy. In the third place: His teachers departed from amongst the living. And henceforward, the Egyptian, Cyril, in his vain envy and unlawful revilings, commenced a calumny of the blessed one, and of those who shared 5 his views after him. And Nestorius lived after the council of Ephesus for 22 years. These are for the termination of your dream-like chattering.

But if you are willing, be persuaded and rest from wrath and rest from anger. Because, just as there is an abundance of reason in 10 the holy angels, so also is there an abundance of wrath in the wicked demons. And whosoever is gnawed by wrath is no different to the demons. And for this reason, one of the holy ones says: If you have seen a man continuously wrathful, know that an evil demon ministers to him; and he says again: Do not trust a wrathful 15 man, even if he raises the dead. Because from wrath, hatred is born, and he who hates his brother is a man-slayer. And the prophet in the name of God warns: 'Call those who hate you and spurn you, your brethren, for my name's sake.' To you also we say: You fellows, we are brethren. May there be no [37] quarrel be- 20 tween us and you. Therefore Christ is for us, who is against us? 'On behalf of Christ, therefore, I beseech you, be reconciled to God.' Relinquish warfare with God. For it is a shameful thing that peoples should be against us, and we against ourselves so that we should never accomplish our warfare. And this, although we hold 25 one scripture which is established from (one) prophecy and apostleship, and one is the baptism which Christ has demanded.

cf. 1 Joh. 3: 15

Is. 66: 5

cf. Rom. 8: 31

cf. 2 Cor. 5: 20

1] lacuna.
22] 'I beseech': Syr. vg. (=gr.) 'we beseech'.

6/7] If we count 431 for the first year, that brings us to 452; but the author's ciphers are not always quite exact. In any case this is a new affirmation for the fact that Nestorius died about the time of Chalcedon.

13–15] cf. apophthegma by Pithyrion in the *Alphabetikon*, PG 65 col. 376A: ἕπεται, φησὶ, δαίμων τῇ ὀργῇ. ἐὰν τῆς ὀργῆς κρατήσῃς, ἀπελήλαται ταύτης ὁ δαίμων. This saying is not included in Ananjesus' Syriac translation of the apophthegmata.

16/17] 'man...slayer': cp. apophth. 19 by Agathon, *loc. cit.* col. 113C: ἐὰν ὀργίλος νεκρὸν ἐγείρῃ, οὐκ ἔστι δεκτὸς παρὰ τῷ θεῷ (Ananjesus: τῷ ἀνθρώπῳ). Syriac translation of Agathon 19 by Ananjesus ed. P. Bedjan, *Acta Martyrum* VII, Paris/Leipzig 1897, p. 632 No. 479; Engl. translation E. A. W. Budge, *The Wit and Wisdom of the Christian Fathers of Egypt*, London 1934, No. 484.

'Go forth, teach all peoples, and baptize them in the name of the   Mt. 28: 19
Father, the Son and the Holy Spirit.' And shall our building not   cf. Mt. 7: 27
be upon the rock but upon the sand, which is blown upon by every   cf. Eph. 4:
wind and overwhelmed by the waters and increases joy for our   14
5 enemies? But come, let us proceed to our Father's house, and let us   cf. Mt. 25:
divide there the inheritance which is prepared for us.   34

If therefore you adhere to the divine books, for them I call
fathers, the word against you causes us no difficulty. For it would
have been easy for the evangelists that from here they should
10 commence to write that God the Word after that he was eternally
begotten of his Father before times and seasons, in the last times   cf. Heb. 1: 2
was conceived and born in a confusion with flesh, and that he
partook of his suffering and his death, according to nature and
will. For if they had done this, there would have been occasion for
15 your error. [38] But because the Holy Spirit knew beforehand of
the deceit of Satan and his angels, he curbed your error beforehand through the prophets together with the apostles, through
whose mouths he said: 'Now the birth of Jesus Christ was like   Mt. 1: 18
this' – and relating all those things which came one after the other,
20 setting down about the name of Jesus, the birth, growth, progress,
exaltation, and the rest of the whole divine dispensation, whilst
they set apart expressions befitting the godhead and confession of it.
And when they were speaking about the dispensation which is in
the cross, and the mystery which is in the resurrection, they
25 removed their word from the godhead and put it upon the manhood. For this reason, the blessed evangelists make mention of the
name of Jesus and of Christ – who was born, circumcised, and on
whose behalf the offer was presented, fled to Egypt, was subject to
Joseph and to his mother, was a reader, was baptized, fasted,   cf Joh
30 prayed, was agitated in the spirit, was arrested, bound, was mocked,   11: 33
despised, led, escorted, was judged, did not turn away his face   cf. Is. 50: 6
from shame and spitting, carried his cross, was delivered up, was
crucified, drank vinegar, was pierced with a lance, was embalmed,
was wrapped [39] in linen, was buried, and rose from the dead,
35 appeared to his apostles, was touched, and ascended into heaven.
But if, in demonstration of their blindness they throw a covering
over their wickedness, they resort to expressions pertaining to the

1] 'Go forth' ܩܘܦܘ: Syr. vg. ܐܙܠܘ ܗܟܝܠ gr. πορευθέντες οὖν. ܩܘܦܘ is 'a
familiar Old Syriac reading which enjoyed a wide circulation', A. Vööbus,
Studies in the History of the Gospel in Syriac (*CSCO* **128**, Subs. 3), Louvain 1951,
p. 161, with examples.
30] 'was agitated' ܐܬܥܝܩ: Syr. vg. ܐܙܕܥ.

Joh. 1: 14
Joh. 3: 16
Joh. 3: 13

Lord – like that one: 'The Word became flesh', which the evanglist has said, and like the one: 'God so loved the world, as to give his only begotten Son', and: 'No man has ascended into heaven', and those things which were spoken of the saviour concerning the greatness of the familiarity. And lest we should doubt 5 the greatness of the blessing which happened to us at his hands, we have demonstrations greater than these to bring against them, those which are spoken concerning the death alone of Christ. And we are not because of this (reason) speaking of Christ as an ordinary man.

And I will begin with that which is from scripture and from 10 liturgy. Listen: If scripture has said: 'A star shall shine from Jacob and a chief one shall arise from Israel', where is God the Word? If the aged Jacob has said: 'The sceptre shall not depart from Judah, nor the law-giver from between his thighs, until there come that which is his', and after that: 'he shall bind his colt to 15 the vine, and his young ass to the shoot of the branch. He will cleanse his garment with wine, and with the blood of grapes his clothing. His eyes are redder than wine, and his teeth [40] whiter than milk' – where and in what part shall I call to mind the only begotten? If David has said: 'The Lord said to me, you are my 20 son, and I today have begotten you. Ask me and I will give you.' And: 'What is man that you have remembered him and the son of man that you have visited him? You have made him lower? etc.' – where is he 'who is in the bosom of his Father?' If that same prophet shall say: 'Because of this, God your God has anointed 25 you with the oil of gladness above your fellows', and: 'The Lord shall send the rod of power from Zion', and: 'From the brook in the way shall he drink. For this reason his head shall be lifted up'– where is the everlasting Son? If Isaiah said: 'There shall come forth a rod from the stem of Jesse and a shoot shall spring up from 30 its root, and the Spirit of God shall rest and stay upon it', and another: 'The sun of righteousness shall rise upon those who fear my name, with healing upon its wings', and another: 'Behold the man whose name is "shining" and from beneath him shall we shine' – where is the Lord? If Isaiah points out in advance con- 35 cerning the suffering of the saviour and says: 'He was despised and

Nu. 24: 17
Gen. 49: 10ff.
Ps. 2: 7f. (Heb. 1: 5)
Ps. 8: 5f. (Heb. 2: 6)
Joh. 1: 18
Ps. 45: 8
Ps. 110: 2
Ps. 110: 7
Is. 11: 1f.
Mal. 4: 2
Zec. 6: 12
Is. 53: 3

14] 'his thighs' ܘܐܠܨܘܗܝ: Syr. vg. ܘܪܓܠܘ Sept. τῶν μηρῶν αὐτοῦ.
16] 'of the branch' deest in Syr. vg. and Sept.
17] 'his garment' ܠܒܘܫܗ: Syr. vg. ܠܒܘܫܐ, Sept. τὴν στολὴν αὐτοῦ.
32] 'shall rise' ܢܕܢܚ: Syr. vg. ܢܕܢܚ.
33] 'upon its wings' = Sept., Syr. vg. 'upon his tongue'.
34] 'and from beneath him' = Sept., Syr. vg. om. 'him'.

humiliated by men, and we saw him that he had no appearance   Is. 53: 2
and we acted deceitfully towards him', and: 'A man of pains and   Is. 53: 3
acquainted with sufferings. Truly, he has carried and endured our   cf. Is. 53: 4
pains. And he was delivered up because of our sins, by whose   cf. Rom. 4:
5 stripes we are healed' – where is God? If Jeremiah has said: 25 + Is. 53:
'I will cause [41] to spring forth for David a branch of righteous-   5
ness, and he shall reign over his kingdom and be wise; and this is   cf. Jer. 23:
the name which they shall call him, "The Lord, our righteous-   5
ness"' – where is he who holds all by the power of his word? If   Jer. 23: 6
10 Daniel has said that 'King Messiah shall be slain and there shall   cf. Heb. 1: 3
be nothing any more, and the holy city shall be destroyed, together   cf. Dan. 9:
with the king who is coming' – where is God the Word? But if   26
against these things you should say that the prophets, as those who
foretell things to come, are prophesying about his manhood only,
15 who of you shall believe the truth, that concerning his godhead
also have they proclaimed in a way that corresponds to the divine
nature. 'Your throne, O God, is for ever and ever', and: 'From of   Ps. 45: 7
old I bore you as a child', and: 'His going forth is from the   cf. Pr. 8:
beginning, from the days of eternity', and: 'O Lord, our Lord,   22 ff.
  cf. Ps. 19: 7
20 how glorious is your name in all the earth', and: 'This is our God   Ps. 8: 2
for whom we have waited. This is our God, and there is none   Is. 25: 9
other who can be reckoned with him'. And afterwards he appeared   cf. Is. 40: 18
on earth. But if the erring ones, in opposition to all these things,
obstinately persist in asking moreover: Is Christ (a member) of the
25 Trinity or (does) he (stand) apart from the Trinity? – If we say to
them that he is of the Trinity, they immediately reply: Christ,
then, is one hypostasis. And if we say that he is apart from the
Trinity, they quarrel with us and say: You are confessing four
hypostases. And this [42] would be (the case) were we to proclaim
30 the Son of man who was taken, with an appellation foreign to the
Son of God. But if we confess with the one appellation of the Son
of God at the same time the Son of man, they will strive with
St Paul who proclaims concerning his Son, that he was born in the   cf. Rom.
flesh of the seed of the house of David. And the Son of God was   1: 3
35 known in the resurrection from the dead as Jesus Christ, our Lord.
We then shall ask them: Was God the Word known to be Son of

7] 'over his kingdom': Syr. vg. 'over the kingdom'.
10] 'King' deest in Syr. vg., Sept.
11] 'any more' deest in Syr. vg., Sept.
17] 'Your throne' ܟܘܪܣܝܟ ܕܝܠܟ: Syr. vg. ܟܘܪܣܝܟ.
20] 'our God' = Sept., Syr. vg. 'the Lord our God'.
21] 'our God': Syr. vg. 'the Lord our God', Sept. 'the Lord'.

God by the resurrection, or was the Son everlastingly, from before the ages, the Son of the everlastingness of the Father? And if Christ, through all the lordly expressions, (and) through the two-fold sense of the expressions concerning him, has proceeded to bring us near to an understanding of his godhead and of his man- 5 hood, he has also collected together those (things) which relate to the one prosopon and that he lived among men, and those things which resemble them, saying: 'I go to my Father and to your Father, and to my God and to your God', and: 'I am the living bread who came down from heaven', and: 'No man has ascended 10 into heaven except he who came down from heaven the Son of man who is in heaven.'

What do we answer them? For they do not know what they are saying or what they are contending about. Again, (we) say: 'He who was begotten of the Father essentially was not born of Mary 15 in the nature. And he who was born [43] in the nature of Mary was not begotten of the Father in the nature. And the properties of the nature before and after the incarnation are distinguished.' But perhaps you will say: The Nestorians wrote that, and not the apostles. Do you ask them: Is Christ simple or compounded? Is he 20 man or God? Is he finite or infinite? Is he the taker or the taken? Is he of the form of a servant or of the form ⟨of God⟩? Is he the sanctifier or the sanctified? Is he the offering and the sacrifice or is he the receiver of these things? High priest or God? Judge or judged? Passible or impassible? When they are refuted by these 25 matters, a sign of their folly and ignorance is revealed in the fact that they will not obey the scripture, nor the confession of the holy teachers. They lack only that they should abolish and steal the holy words of the prophets and apostles which contain an investigation into the incarnation of our Lord. For the true faith is a rock 30 of offence to those who are doubtful in their faith. But for Peter, and for all those who confess rightly, God has made Lord and Christ this Jesus whom you have crucified. [44] Now when Stephen was filled with the Holy Spirit, he was crying out to you, O impudent ones: 'Behold, I see the heavens opening, and the Son of man 35 sitting at the right hand of God.' But if you flee from the name of Jesus, you are foreign to the covenant of promise. For us there is 'no other name given to man whereby it is right to live'. And

Joh. 20: 17
Joh. 6: 51
Joh. 3: 13

cf. Ac. 2: 36

Ac. 7: 55

Ac. 4: 12

8] 'I go' ܐܙܠ (πορεύομαι) Syr. vg. ܣܠܩ (ἀναβαίνω).
22] 'of God': edd. for ms. 'of man'.
38] after 'name', 'under heaven' is omitted with part of the textual tradition, and against Syr. vg.

together with the blessed concourse of the apostles, we say with
loud voice: 'You are God who has made heaven and earth and the   Ac. 4: 24–7
seas, and all that is in them, and you are he who spoke through the
Holy Spirit by the mouth of David your servant, "Why have the
5 nations raged together etc." For truly they have gathered together
in this city against your holy Son, Jesus, whom you have anointed.'
And again, the blessed David, in the prophecy which the apostle
Paul expounds, says thus: 'Your throne O God is for ever and   Heb. 1: 8
ever', and again: 'You at the beginning have laid the foundation   Heb. 1: 10
10 of the earth, and the heavens are the works of your hands.' And
John the evangelist says: 'In the beginning was the Word, and the   Joh. 1: 1
Word was with God, and the Word was God.' And the blessed
Paul says: 'He is the brightness of the glory of the Father, and the   Heb. 1: 3
image of his being. And through him, he made the worlds, and he   Heb. 1: 2
15 holds everything by the power of his word.' And those things which   Heb. 1: 3
are said concerning the manhood of Christ are [45] as follows:
Isaiah said: 'Behold my servant with whom I am well pleased, my   Is. 61: 1
beloved for whom my soul longs. I will put my spirit upon him.'   Mt. 12: 18
And this our Lord in the gospel expounds (as referring) to himself.
20 The blessed Paul says: 'He has appointed the day on which he is   Ac. 17: 31
prepared to judge the whole earth with justice, through the man
whom he has designated', and again: 'Who was faithful to him who   Heb. 3: 2
made him, like Moses in all his house.' And many others like these.
Now if the apostles were not ashamed to speak distinctly about
25 the godhead and the manhood of Christ, why are you cunning to
bring to us utterances of impudence, foreign to the scriptures, and
new to the hearers, in that you cast the godhead of the Son under
sufferings, and prate of one nature and one compounded hypostasis? But if you say that it is (only) in appearance (schema) that
30 the words of the scriptures are spoken, then the whole dispensation
is (only) appearance (schema). And give us another gospel which
will instruct the whole world that Christ is not in his godhead one
of the hypostases of the Trinity or in his manhood of the seed of
David and of Abraham. And those things which are said con-
35 cerning his godhead cannot be in the nature of his manhood. And
clearly is it known that Christ is perfect God [46] and perfect man.
He is then spoken of as perfect God, being perfect in the nature and
the hypostasis of the godhead. And he is then spoken of as perfect
man, being perfect in the nature and the hypostasis of the man-
40 hood. And just as from the contradiction of words spoken about
Christ, it is known that Christ is two natures and two hypostases,
so also (from) those things which are spoken concerning the one

Christ, Son of God, it is known that Christ is one, not in singularity of nature as hypostasis, but in one prosopon of sonship. Now the prosopon is the recipient of the distinct actions of the distinct natures, which take place by the imposition of one of the names which is conferred upon its fellow (-nature by the other fellow- 5

Heb. 1: 2 nature), like that which Paul said: 'In these last days, he has spoken with us by his Son.' For he has set down the name of the Son by itself and concerning him he expresses human and divine things.

Heb. 1: 2 For this reason he says: 'He made him heir of everything', that is to say – in his manhood, because it is that which received uni- 10 versal lordship. Now God the Word, together with the Father and the Spirit, is the creator of all, and not an inheritor of the

Heb. 1: 2 Father. And again, he adds: 'And through him he made the worlds' – this is (said) of the godhead, which made and established [47] everything. For the manhood is after many ages and was not 15 the creator of the ages. Because then the name(s) of Son and Christ are in common with those of his manhood and of his godhead, as (resulting) from the union, they speak sometimes of the prosopon of God, and sometimes of the prosopon of his manhood,

Joh. 16: 28 as for example: 'I came forth from the Father and have come into 20 the world' – (here) the manhood makes use of the prosopon of his godhead. It was not from there that it (*sc.* the manhood) came forth, because the godhead is spoken of as having gone forth from

Joh. 16: 28 the Father. And again: 'I leave the world and go to the Father' – (here) the godhead makes use of the manhood, for it (*sc.* the god- 25 head) did not depart as at the end. Because the manhood is common (by the union to both natures), it is: 'I go', for the man-

cf. Joh. 6: hood departed in the end. And again: 'I am the living bread,
41, 48 which came down from heaven.' For because of the Word which came down, the descent is said (to be) in common with his man- 30

cf. Joh. 3: 13 hood also. Now whenever we say concerning the Son of man that he ascended to the place where he was before, he showed the ascent to be in common and that the godhead was revealed because of the manhood, for it (*sc.* the manhood) was not there before. While he is adhering to these same things, even he who is 35 illustrious among the saints, the great Mar Nestorius, says: Because

19–25] (two) 'prosopa of godhead and manhood' and the 'use the manhood makes of the prosopon of his godhead' (and *vice versa*) are expressions characteristic of Nestorius in the *Liber Heraclidis*. It is noteworthy that the two Ps. Nestorii in C do not use them.

36 – p. 31, 2] there are similar utterances of Nestorius, but we have not found this one.

then Christ calls himself by them both, [48] the apostles also and
the evangelists refer to him by them both.

From these (considerations) therefore it is evident that it was
not ourselves (who) have turned aside from the foundation of the
5 faith, we who, in the orthodox way, believe that in Christ are two
natures and two hypostases. But Severus and his disciples have
turned aside, they who confess Christ to be one nature and one
hypostasis. But we, the Nestorian Christians, cry with John the
evangelist: 'The Word became flesh and dwelt among us.' Joh. 1: 14
10 Therefore, God the Word 'dwelt' according to the preaching of
the son of thunder 'among us'. How? In the holy womb of the
virgin. He wove for himself a human robe, and clothed himself
with it, and he went forth into the world. The eyes of those who
are created were not able to observe the glorious brightness of his
15 godhead without the veil of his body or the curtain which was his
flesh. And he would not have been able to suffer on behalf of our
sickness, had he not taken to himself from our nature a passible
body, 'who was tempted in all points like us, except (that he was Heb. 4: 15
without) sin'. This being so, how can the Adamite body be con-
20 substantial with the Trinity, and quaternity be confessed in the
nature of the Trinity? For God the Word gave him all that
belonged to him – lordship and power and authority, in a uniting
way and not in his nature (*sc.* as man). And his manhood took [49]
all those things which could be taken, for the manhood did not
25 take the infinity of his nature or the eternity, or the invisibility,
but, as he said from the prosopon of his manhood: 'There has been Mt. 28: 18
given to me all authority in heaven and on earth', and he did not
say: 'There has been given to me to be the nature of God'. But
because of the union and the exact conjunction, the one is named
30 by the other, and the other is called by the one, the two natures
being preserved in their hypostases in one everlasting union.

Now those who are lacking in this perfect faith fall into a pit.
Now moreover it is time for us to set down the burning arrows of
the Egyptian, in order that all who pass along the way may see
35 how he pierces and rends the body of the gospel. 'Incline your ear, Is. 37: 17
O Lord, and hear: open O Lord your eyes and see'; and hearken
to the words of the Egyptian who has dared to blaspheme the
living God. His Chapters: 1. Whoever does not confess that
Emmanuel is in truth God, and for this reason the holy virgin is

8] 'Nestorian Christians': cp. above, p. 3, 7.
38] Cyril's anathemata appear here for the first time in our ms. to be refuted.
For the same reason they are quoted again in VI and XI.

God-bearer, for she bare after the flesh the Word which is from God the Father when he became flesh – let him be anathema. 2. Whoever does not confess that the Word which is from God the Father is united hypostatically to the flesh, and that Christ is one with his flesh, that is to say, [50] the same one at the same time 5 God and man – let him be anathema. 3. Whoever makes distinctions concerning the one Christ into hypostases after the union, whilst mingling them in the conjunction alone, which is with authority and command and power, and not rather by a collecting together of the natural union – let him be anathema. 4. Whoever 10 divides into two prosopa or into two hypostases the utterances made about Christ in the scripture of the gospel or of the apostle, or those things spoken about him by the saints, or by him about himself, and applies some of them to the man who is deemed to be alone, apart from God the Word, and others of them, as though 15 they were utterances befitting the godhead, to the Word which is from God the Father – let him be anathema. 5. Whoever says of Christ that he is God-bearing man, and not rather that he is God

Joh. 1: 14 in truth, as an only son in nature, in that 'the Word became flesh' and shared like us blood and flesh – let him be anathema. 6. Who- 20 ever says that the Word of God the Father is the God or Lord of Christ, and does not rather confess that he is God and man simultaneously, in that 'the Word became flesh', as it is written – let him be anathema. 7. Whoever says [51] that Jesus was energized as a man by God the Word, and says that he took the glory of the 25 only begotten on himself, as though he was another, apart from him – let him be anathema. 8. Whoever dares to say that it is right that the man who was taken should be worshipped and glorified with God the Word, and together with him should be considered as God, as if he was one with another – for when there is added 30 this 'together with', it always gives us to understand this – and does not rather in one worship honour Emmanuel and cause to ascend to him one glory, because 'the Word became flesh' – let him be anathema. 9. Whoever says concerning our one Lord Jesus Christ that he has been glorified by the Spirit, as though he had 35 made use of a strange power in the power of the Spirit, and that from him received power against the unclean spirits, and so as to do signs among men, and does not rather say that the Spirit is his in a singular manner, through whom he wrought the divine

cf. Heb. 3: 1 miracles – let him be anathema. 10. The high priest and apostle 40
cf. Eph. 5: 2 of our faith, Jesus Christ, says divine scripture, and he who offered

40] 'The high priest and apostle': Syr. vg. (= gr.) *vice versa.*

32

himself for us, a sweet-smelling savour to God the Father. And
whoever says therefore that the high priest and our apostle was
not the Word of God [52] at the time when he became flesh and
man in our likeness, but another man who was of a woman,
5 manifestly apart from him; or whoever says that he made an
offering on behalf of himself, and not rather on behalf of us, ⟨for⟩
he who knew no sin ⟨was⟩ not ⟨in need⟩ of an offering – let him be
anathema. 11. Whoever does not confess that the body of our Lord
Jesus Christ is life-giving and belongs singly to the Word which is
10 from God the Father, but as though it was another man who
cleaves to him in honour, or that only the indwelling of God was
in him, and not rather that it was life-giving, as we have said, in
that it belongs singly to the Word who is able to give life to all –
let him be anathema. 12. Whoever does not confess that God the
15 Word suffered in the flesh and was crucified in the flesh, and
tasted death in the flesh, and became the first-begotten of the dead
because he is alive and gives life – let him be anathema.

Ah! Cyril, more heathen than Julian, like him you have destroyed the gospel. But to what degree do you darken the vision of
20 your judgement? Lift up your eyes, and see whom you have
anathematized. Is it not the whole apostolate of the house of
Simon? 'The mighty Lord tries the righteous.' I will look upon
retribution from Egypt, because I have revealed to you my judge-
ments, [53] you snake, listen: Who accepts that the holy virgin
25 bore after the flesh? Who speaks of the natural union, and by this
something enforced upon nature and reason? Who confesses one
nature of the form of God and of the form of a servant? Who dares
to anathematize those who justly write exalted things of the godhead and inferior things of the manhood, whilst in no place the
30 union is rent asunder? Because the apostles and evangelists have
said that, have they been anathematized by this teaching? Who
assents to the fearful judgement against the holy and glorious
bishop, Basil, who says: The flesh of our Lord is clothed with God,

cf. Heb.
3: 1

Jer. 20: 12

cf. Phil. 2: 7

1] 'the Father' deest in Syr. vg. (=gr.).
6/7] lacuna (only *one* in the Syriac) edd. suppl.

18 f.] An allusion to Cyril's refutation of the emperor Julian; cp. above p. 18,
7–9.
33] 'clothed with God' ܒ݁ܠܺܝܫ ܐܰܠܳܗܳܐ is the ordinary Syriac translation for θεοφόρος. Basil the Great uses indeed the expression ἡ θεοφόρος
σάρξ, for instance *Hom. in Ps. 45*, PG 29 col. 424 B; *ep.* 261, PG 32 col. 969 B, and
again C. In all these passages the expression 'of our Lord' (see above the text)
does not occur.

who has been anathematized together with those who consent to say, is clothed with God? Who let our Lord lie, who said: 'I ascend to my God and to your God', and Paul, who said: 'The God of our Lord Jesus Christ', and (who) will receive whomsoever anathematizes him who says this? Who will be a partaker with 5 him who has anathematized the chosen vessel, Paul, through these (words) which he has said: 'If any man shall say: Jesus as a man was energized by God the Word, let him be anathema'? While the holy Paul manifestly says: 'According to the working of the strength of his power which he wrought in Christ, he also raised 10 him from the [54] dead.' Who severs the flesh from the Word and then offers the due worship as he commands who says: 'Whoever dares to say the man who was taken deserves to be worshipped and glorified with God – let him be anathema'? Who now, when he hears that our Lord through the Spirit of God casts out demons, 15 and (when he) learns from Paul that he who was revealed in the flesh was justified in Spirit, refuses (to accept) that our Lord Jesus Christ was glorified by the Spirit, or anathematizes that which is confessed? Who dares to say, according to the unspeakable prating of this (man), that God the Word became apostle and high 20 priest, who shows furthermore that he was made, since the blessed Paul proclaims: 'See this apostle and high priest of our faith, Jesus Christ who was faithful to him who made him'? Who will accept concerning him to say or to hear that the body of our Lord was not taken from our nature, but was God the Word's own, so that it 25 might be established next (to him)? Who would place all the saints together under the sentence of anathema – such as have not said that God the Word suffered in the flesh and was crucified in the flesh, and became the first-begotten [55] of the dead, he who at all times is alive and immortal? 30

Now it is easy to refute this spiritually. If the soul which by (its) creation even is immortal, cannot die in the body, how can God the Word, who is immortal, essentially die in the body? If our Lord Christ has immortal life eternally, and immortal life temporarily, how can Christ not be two natures, one of everlasting life, 35 and the other which has assumed immortal life temporarily? And

Side notes (left margin):

cf. Joh. 20: 17
cf. 2 Cor. 1: 3
Eph. 1: 3

Eph. 1: 19, 20

cf. 1 Tim. 3: 16

Heb. 3: 1

7] cp. Cyril, anath. 7.
12] cp. Cyril, anath. 8.
18] cp. Cyril, anath. 9.
20] cp. Cyril, anath. 10.
23] cp. Cyril, anath. 11.
27] cp. Cyril, anath. 12.

31]'If the soul'–p. 35, 16] a quotation from the documents of 612; below (VIIb), pp. 99, 14–100, 2. See index of quotations.

if in the natural and hypostatic union the godhead of our Lord was united to his manhood, just as his soul was united to his body, how, while the godhead was with his body, did he not live and arise, though when his soul returned into the midst of his body, he did
5 live and arise? One of the two (only can be right), either the godhead is weaker than the soul, or the godhead was not naturally united for the resurrection of the nature, but willingly and prosopically for the provision of the dispensation. If, because the soul is united to the body naturally, it is impossible for the man to
10 die as long as his union is preserved, how, if the union of the godhead and the manhood of Christ is natural, did Christ die whilst the union of Christ was undivided? If (there is) one hypostasis when he dies, he has need of another to raise him up. [56] But if the hypostasis of Christ is one, how could Christ say of his body:
15 'I will raise it up'? Death is the taking away of life. How is it Joh. 2: 19 possible that the life of God should be taken away?

But because Egypt cast God from it like chaff on the face of the waters, the abortive child whom she had begotten thrust out his tongue saying that God suffered in the flesh. And he was not
20 abashed not even by the seventy elders whom Ptolemy, the king of Egypt sent for, summoning them from Jerusalem, in order that they might translate for him the books of the prophets from Hebrew into Greek. In order that these might be free from all disturbance, and translate rapidly, he commanded that there
25 should be built for them small lodgings corresponding to the number of them, not in Alexandria, but at (a distance of) seventy stadia, so that each one of them should complete his translation by himself alone. And it was commanded the attendants who were stationed with them that they should meet every need. They
30 should prevent them from talking with one another – so that it

24 ff.] A marginal note in the ms.: 'And this took took place 300 years before the epiphany of our Lord and 7 years after the return (conducted) by Zerubbabel.'

8] 'prosopically', cp. above p. 11, 19.
19 ff.] An allusion to king Ptolemy already above p. 17, 39–41. The story given here does not paraphrase the relevant passage from the *Letter of Aristeas*, but Ps. Justin, *Cohortatio ad Graecos* c. 13, PG 6 cols. 265–8. It is the merit of A. Pelletier's edition of Aristeas in *Sources Chrétiennes* **89** to give in its introduction the history of the developing legend (pp. 78 ff.), making our form of the legend recognizable from its characteristics ('les petits maisons' p. 81, 'les petits appartements' p. 82, cp. above in our text l. 25 'small lodgings'). Pelletier quotes the chapter from Ps. Justin's work (which he calls 'Exhortatio') in French translation, pp. 82 f.

should be possible that the accuracy of their translations would be manifestly known, through the conformity of their words. Now because he knew that these seventy men employed not only the (same) sense but also the (very same) words, and had not deviated among themselves in a single word from [57] the conformity of 5 words, but had written there the same (words) and about the same matters, then he believed that the translation had been made by the power of God. And he knew that they were worthy of all honours, as men who love God. He gave instructions that they should return to their own land with many gifts. 10

Those who until ⟨then⟩ excluded the name of abuse from God, and put in its place: 'Bless God and die', and in another place: 'Naboth blessed God and the king', and they were not any more ashamed ⟨...⟩. And not from Moses, who counted it equivalent to presumption if he should reveal the name which the son of the 15 Israelite woman had pronounced. ⟨...⟩ And in that he had found for himself the kingdom in which he might play in accordance with his desire, he supposed that the gift of God might be acquired with worldly possessions.

Ended is the selection of the book of the holy Mar Eustathius, 20 bishop of Tarihan. May his prayer be with us all. Amen.

IIa [58] And now, of the holy of memory, Mar Isaac, bishop of Nineveh, true recluse, and orthodox in truth. May his prayer assist us. Amen. 25

For the confirmation of the orthodox faith which the holy church of the East has held, in accordance with the apostolic teaching, against the confession 'God-bearer', and that of the one hypostasis, and the natural union, and the rest.

Those who by verbal attacks think to denounce the truth in the 30 guise of love of the truth, by the demonstrative word, their lies are refuted without disguise before all. And when, by the power of the distinctness of demonstrative inquiry, they are compelled to confess the revelation of the truth in the orthodox faith, by praise of truth which is in their mouths, falsehood turns upon their skull to 35

cf. Jb. 2: 9
cf. 1 Kg. 21: 13
cf. Lev. 24: 10f.

12] 'Bless God': Syr. vg. 'curse your God', cp. *Biblia Hebraica*, ed. Kittel *ad Job* 1: 5.
13] 'blessed': Syr. vg. 'cursed', cp. *Biblia Hebraica*, ed. Kittel *ad Job* 1: 5.
14] lacuna edd. conj.
16] lacuna edd. conj.
21] rest of p. 57 (text) blank. Gloss transcribed by Jenks: 'A star has risen from Tarihan', cp. Num. 24: 17.

denounce their word, as contrary to the truth. The sane conscience
of reason is demonstrating between the two parties, and making a
distinction, even for those who wish to assist the fraudulent party.

  Now Cyril, who was permitted by God to introduce impiety
5 into the faith of the church, which was cleansed by the blood of the
orthodox fathers, for the manifest [59] ultimate condemnation of
him who was (so) permitted, when compelled by the truth,
because of the revealing of his wickedness, to confess the faith of the
two unmixed natures, passible and impassible, in Christ – contrary
10 to his kephalaia which impute passibility to God – has again, in
another form, introduced his impiety into the pure faith. With
cunning he compelled the orthodox by (recourse to) imperial
authority, to agree to that confession of the two natures, not united
according to nature, (and) moreover to agree to the collection (of
15 the two natures) that (results in) the union of the hypostasis, so
that while one hypostasis is confessed, by all means the common
suffering and death should be considered to be of the two natures.
Even after his death, his adherents confirmed this in the bad
synod of Chalcedon, while by the magnitude of the strength of
20 their adherents, and (by means of) the imperial edict, they compelled even the firm ones to (do) this. And some of the orthodox,
being armed with burning zeal, scorning worldly authority, and
despising honour, took upon themselves affliction and exile and
expulsion from their (episcopal) thrones. Nor would they accept
25 persuasion at all. But some, disregarding fear of the heavenly king,
so as not to estrange themselves from the honour of their position
of leadership, to the dishonour of the faith, expressed their agreement, and in the guise of their not being said [60] to be confessing
with the heretics duality of sons, they received and assented to the
30 (doctrine) of the one hypostasis.

  About those of the orthodox who had agreed to the confession,
mixed with impiety, of the synod of Chalcedon.

  Some, though recognizing God the Word, perfect in his hypostasis, and the nature of the manhood, perfect in its hypostasis, and
35 confessing Christ, passible and impassible, distinct and not confused, in order that they might avoid being accused of the confession of the duality of sons, and the duality of worship in their
confession, shun in a wicked manner the confession of the duality
of the hypostases. And in place of one prosopon of Christ in his two
40 natures, they postulate one hypostasis in Christ from the two
natures. And though properly confessing the distinction of the
properties of the natures, and their continuous preservation, they

37

are wronging the rectitude of the confession, by taking part in the impiety of the union of the hypostasis with which they are in the end joined, assenting in this to all the heresies of old.

The hypostasis of the sonship, then, of God the Word, is not a half hypostasis in Christ, in that it also is not perfected with the 5 human hypostasis to the one hypostasis of sonship, God the Word. And if before the taking (of the human nature), the hypostasis of the only begotten, of the one son, is confessed by you as not perfect [61] (that makes) an heretical distinction.

Now, from (the time) when corruption began to enter the 10 church of God against the orthodox confession of the dispensation of Christ to the present, there has not been any one of the heresies and its adherents, which has confessed Christ to be two hypostases, save the orthodox only, those who (were) wise in God, to whose footsteps we in this are keeping. But all the heretics keep atten- 15 tively to 'one hypostasis'. Since then, of those who gradually sprang up, some said: 'One hypostasis of phantasia, from the god-head alone, without the nature and the true hypostasis of the man', phantastically, like Mani and Marcion and Bar Daisan, and those like them. And some said: 'Without phantasia, and in truth, from 20 God the Word and a half of the manhood, (that is the manhood) deprived of the soul, while God the Word filled the place of the soul', like Arius and Eunomius, and those like them. And some said: 'One hypostasis from the godhead and the manhood, without the intellect, whilst the godhead filled the place of the intellect', 25 like the Apollinarians, devoid of intellect, and the rest of their com-panions. And some of them said: 'One hypostasis of an ordinary man, without the godhead', like the senseless Paul of Samosata, [62] and the whole company, barren of understanding. And some said: 'One hypostasis of God alone who was changed into flesh 30 whilst he had not taken flesh. The Word became flesh, etc.', like Eutyches, with Severus, and Jacob of Sarug and Aksenaya of Garmek, and the rest of the whole band, foreign to God. And some said: 'One hypostasis from two perfect natures which were com-pounded into an hypostatic union, and together endured suffering 35 and death, etc.', like the foolish Cyril, together with the whole crowd who make God to suffer. And in brief, there is not one of the heretics who has not said of Christ 'one hypostasis'. Last of all are those who have rightly confessed and have distinguished the nature

Joh. 1: 14

32] 'Jacob of Sarug': should it not be Jacob Baradaeus? 'Aksenaya of Gar-mek' is Philoxenus of Mabbug, called by his Syriac name, and after his birth-place.

of the godhead from the manhood in humility and ⟨weakness⟩, and from suffering, and from all those things that befit the created nature – even they have turned to speak of one hypostasis in Christ, and have corrupted their confession by the agreement to
5 this word with all the heresies.

Again, under the guise of their not being considered to be confessing Christ as an ordinary man, they say of his mother 'God-bearer'. They are cunning with an evil cunning. But let us examine whether it be possible, on the basis of the true faith, for
10 Christ to be spoken of [63] as one hypostasis. Where truly can we speak of the hypostasis of the manhood and the hypostasis of the godhead, complete and unmixed and free from the confession of the union of nature in Christ, finite and infinite, as one hypostasis? What cannot be (at once) a definition of the finite and infinite,
15 must also not be said by an inquiring mind. First we will demonstrate that 'God-bearer' is the first door leading to impiety, because it effaces the appellation 'Christ' from the church which indicates the natures and their properties, and how this confession is contrary to the teaching of the holy scriptures.
20 Against those who say that it is right for blessed Mary to be called 'God-bearer', and not 'Christ-bearer'.

'Now has Christ arisen from the dead', says the blessed Paul, 1 Cor. 15: 'and became the first fruits of them that sleep.' Who is he who rose 20 from the dead in the birth of the resurrection for the confirmation
25 of our resurrection? This is Christ, according to the preaching of Paul. But he who was born of the virgin is God and not Christ, according to what the heretic says. Wherefore, he whose resurrection Paul preaches is one, while he who was born of the virgin is another, according to the confession of the heretics. [64] From a
30 mother, this one says, God was born, but from the resurrection, Paul preaches Christ (was born). Wherefore the apostle says: 'If cf. Gal. 1: 8 an angel from heaven should preach to you anything other than we have preached to you, let him be anathema.' When, again, the heretic is presumptuous against the word, saying that even Paul
35 has called Christ God in another place: 'Christ who is God over Rom. 9: 5 all', the heretic speaks against himself and does not realize it, in that he himself confesses that the apostle first of all wrote down the name of Christ, and then called him 'God of all'. You, O heretic, do not loathe the appellation 'Christ' but confess it, like the
40 apostle, who everywhere preaches this honoured name in all his epistles, and do you be naming his mother thus, namely: 'bearer

1] 'weakness': edd. pro ms. 'quality'.

of Christ who is God of all'. And do not forget his name in your confession which in all the scriptures is written down gladly, and this name of Christ is preached by his saints, which is sweeter in the mouths of those who preach it than honey and the honeycomb.

And the members of his household are known by this appellation, for they are called 'Christians' – that is to say 'Meshiḥayē', for it is 'Christos' in the Greek tongue, and (that) is not translated 'God', but 'Christ'. Many saints were inebriated with the memory of this name [65] and received death in all manner of forms. Why therefore do you abhor this adorable appellation which was given to him by the angel at the commandment of God? 'Behold, I declare unto you great joy which shall be to the whole world, for to you is born today a saviour, the Lord Christ, in the city of David.' He did not say: 'There is born to you today the Lord God', but 'the Lord Christ'. Even if you will not accept it from those who preach it, as being from men, accept it from the angel, moreover, stand in awe of his nature. Do not desire to be even wiser than the angel, nor seek a teacher who is truer than a spiritual (leader). 'There is born to you today a saviour who is Lord Christ' – this which is also proclaimed by the evangelist, is handed down by the (whole) scripture, 'of God' being kept distinct from 'of Christ' in all the range of the scriptures. 'Christ purchased us from the curse of the law, and he, not God, became, on our behalf, a curse.' How can you listen to this saying, and apply the curse to God? But the apostle is not persuaded by you, nor is reason. And how, in the present case, are you to know him who 'received upon himself a curse on your behalf' to be Christ and not God? But the birth from the mother, you do not attribute to him, but to God. [66]

And again: 'God has made this Jesus, Lord and Christ', and: 'For God was in Christ who reconciled the world to his greatness.' 'Christ died and rose, and sat upon the right hand of God.' 'And Jesus Christ ministered circumcision on behalf of the truth of God.' Who is he who ministered circumcision? Paul knew that it was not God, but Christ. How can you attribute the birth from the mother, not to Christ, but to God? You are not afraid even of these weighty sayings which are irresistible. And, in brief, everywhere the scriptures, without confusion, exhibit a plain distinction between those things which pertain to God and those which pertain to Christ; like that saying: 'I have boasting in Jesus Christ toward God', setting down plainly Jesus Christ and God distinctly from

cf. Ps. 19: 11

Lk. 2: 10, 11

Lk. 2: 11

cf. Gal. 3: 13

Ac. 2: 36
cf. 2 Cor. 5: 19
cf. Rom. 8: 34
Rom. 15: 8

cf. 2 Cor. 3: 4

each other. And again, the saying: 'I confess God through our
Lord Jesus Christ', and: 'God has both raised up our Lord and
will raise us up through him', and: 'Grace and peace be with you
from God, our Father, and from our Lord Jesus Christ' – for
5 'God' and 'Christ' are not identical. For look, this name of God is
with all the nations: 'Great is my name amongst the nations', he
says in Malachi, 'and in every place shall they burn incense, and
offer to my name choice offerings, and my name [67] shall be
terrible amongst the nations.' But the name of Christ shall be
10 proclaimed in the church alone, while by him all Christians swear.
Why then are you at pains to root up the name of Christ from the
church, O heretic? For if you do not wish to do this, be persuaded
to call his mother by the designation indicative that her bringing
forth is Christ, together with the evangelist who begins in his
15 writing with the nativity of Christ: 'The birth of Jesus Christ was
as follows.'

Also in the great synod of the fathers, thus did they set down and
teach all the church beneath heaven to believe the fullness of the
faith: 'We believe in one God, the Father, and in one Lord Jesus
20 Christ, and in one Holy Spirit.' You alone, then, do not believe in
the name of Christ, and in the apostolic confession before the
altar by which are sanctified the mysteries of our salvation. In the
form of a blessing thus is it set down: 'The grace of our Lord Jesus
Christ, and the love of God the Father, and the communion of the
25 Holy Spirit.' And our Lord to his Father thus: 'This is [68] eternal
life, that they should know you that you are the God of truth alone,
and Jesus Christ whom you have sent.' Therefore, whoever does
not know Christ with God the Father through his being sent from
the Father, and through the begetting from the Father, and
30 through the rest of the dispensation and through him as mediator,
has no eternal life, according to our Lord's own word. And all the
apostles, when they were gathered together and were praying to
God privately, after other (things), said: 'Truly there were
gathered together in this city, against your holy son Jesus whom
35 you anointed, Herod and Pilate, etc.'

Now if everywhere, 'Christ' is handed down to us by our Lord

Marginal references:
cf. Rom. 5: 11
cf. 2 Cor. 4: 14
1 Cor. 1: 3
Rom. 1: 7
cf. Mal. 1: 11

Mt. 1: 18

2 Cor. 13: 14
Joh. 17: 3

cf. Ac. 4: 27

8] 'choice offerings': Syr. vg. and Sept. 'pure offerings'; 'and' 'terrible':
Syr. vg. and Sept. 'because great'.
23] 'grace': Syr. vg. 'peace'.
24] 'Father' deest in Syr. vg. et gr.

17] 'great synod': Nicaea 325.

and by his saints, for (us) to confess, why in the nativity from his mother do you call him 'God', you foolish heretic? While also they will not call you by that (name) of 'Christian', you consent to apostatize. Now you stand against yourself, and against the array of the whole dispensation which is set down concerning this 5 naming. Stand in awe of the revelation of the Father to Peter, who for the confession of messiahship, was counted worthy of blessing cf. Mt. 16: from our Lord, and was called Peter from [69] that time. 'Flesh 17 & 16 and blood has not revealed it to you', namely: 'You are Christ,' which you have confessed, 'but my Father who is in heaven.' Was 10 the revelation from the Father, which he spoke by the mouth of Peter, true or untrue? Did he receive a blessing from our Lord in return for the confession of his messiahship, rightly or falsely? Reply here Yes or No.

cf. Lk. 2: 26 Stand in awe also of the revelation of the Spirit to the aged 15 Simeon, to whom it was said by the Holy Ghost, that he should not Lk. 2: 27– taste death until he had seen the Christ of the Lord. 'And this man 30 came by the Spirit into the temple, and when his parents brought in the child Jesus, to do for him as is commanded in the law, he received him in his arms, and praised God and said: Now dismiss 20 your servant, O Lord, according to your word, in peace, for my eyes have seen mercy.' Do you confess also with Simeon that it was Christ whom he carried in his arms in accordance with the revelation of the Spirit, because his eyes saw mercy in that he had attained his hope, that Christ was born of the virgin, and he saw 25 him, and he asked henceforward release from life? For if he had not seen the Christ according to the promise of the Spirit to him, because it was not Christ who was born, in accordance with the confession of the heretic, who has falsified the whole order of the dispensation, then Simeon would have been confessing in vain, 30 according to the folly of the heretic.

II*b* Again, from the same holy Mar Isaac, [70] against those who confess that Christ is two natures (and) one hypostasis.

[This is the way of the heretic Cyril.] Tell us therefore, O 35 utterers of anathemata without sense, if now Christ is one hypostasis, is it right that he should be confessed (to be) of duality of his natures, in accordance with your word? How can you say of him, one hypostasis? Well then, (is) half of him God, and half of him cf. Joh. 12: man? And see, our Lord said at the time of his passion: 'Behold, 40 27

20] 'praised': Syr. vg. 'blessed', gr. εὐλόγησεν.
35] 'This...Cyril' edd. del. (gloss).

42

my soul is troubled.' Tell us therefore, whose was this utterance? Was it of the whole of that hypostasis that is compounded of God and man, or (was it) of half of the hypostasis? If (it was) of the whole of it, how do you not think to connect this utterance with
5 God (with the result that) he was troubled, and with that (other) part (of the hypostasis), his manhood, in accordance with your blasphemy? And if you are afraid of this, because it is a blasphemy, when you say of the manhood that it alone was troubled, then Christ was troubled in the passion (with) half of his hypostasis, and
10 (with) half of it (he was) not (troubled). And therefore not the whole Christ suffered in a complete hypostasis, but a half of him – a remark deserving of ridicule!

Again, our Lord said, 'El, El, [71] why have you forsaken me?' Mt. 27: 46 If the hypostasis from God and man is one, by whom do you
15 suppose this was spoken, the whole hypostasis of Christ, or a half of it? For if the hypostasis is one in Christ, and the whole of it was praying: 'My God, my God, why have you forsaken me?' then Mt. 27: 46 this utterance 'My God, my God' belongs equally to his godhead and his manhood; and that (saying) 'Why have you forsaken me?'
20 (means) that God was calling his God. If this saying belongs to his manhood alone, a half of the hypostasis of Christ was praying in the passion, and not the whole Christ; and also a half of the hypostasis of Christ suffered, and not the whole – which is a mad thing to say.

25 And again, that (saying): 'In the beginning was the Word', Joh. 1: 1 concerning whom does one interpret this? If you say that there is one hypostasis in Christ, (namely) of God and man, and of the whole of it you understand that it existed in the beginning, how do you not preach that his manhood was without beginning? But if it
30 is of his godhead alone, how do you not prate about the godhead of Christ as an incomplete hypostasis, when you do not confess that it is preserved completely in a true [72] hypostasis, unmixed, existing by itself alone, and without defect, throughout all time, and for ever?

35 But with another hypostasis which is from a foreign ousia, you know him (as) one. For if you confess him complete in the hypostasis of his godhead, and preserved in that which is his own continuously, and his manhood, subject to time, in complete hypostasis, though you are unwilling to do (so), you are compelled to
40 ascribe to Christ two complete hypostases. And (in the case of) that (saying) that Jesus was thirty years old, you will not perceive a half cf. Lk. 3: 23 hypostasis, nor will you perceive one hypostasis with the godhead,

43

thirty years old, but the complete hypostasis of the manhood. And if the hypostasis of Christ's manhood was thirty years old, it was always complete hypostatically, but the hypostasis of his godhead is not in any wise reckoned and shared with it (*sc.* the hypostasis of the manhood) in this enumeration of years.   5

How do you not confess two complete hypostases, each one of which is preserved distinctly with its properties in the one prosopon of Christ? And you have contended needlessly, who this one is. Tell us, now, O companion of ours, did now the whole of Christ suffer, or a half of him? If all of him, what was that all of him that   10 suffered – a half hypostasis or a whole hypostasis? And the part [73] of Christ which continued impassible, what was it? Expound to us. Did a half hypostasis remain without suffering, or a complete hypostasis? Because if it was a part of Christ that suffered it was a complete hypostasis, and not a half of it, and (if it was) a   15 part of Christ which remained impassible, it is a complete hypostasis, and not a half of it. How do you not confess two complete hypostases preserved, each in its own, unconfused, when from union they did not come to a hypostatic unity? You are turning against yourself, and destroying your true faith in the two hypo-   20 stases. Why therefore is the man who is of a hypostasis of soul and a hypostasis of body, the one hypostasis, man? (Is) Christ then from the hypostasis of soul and the hypostasis of body and the hypostasis of godhead? (Is) Christ (then) one hypostasis compounded from three hypostases? The godhead then of Christ is one of three parts   25 of the hypostasis in Christ? Judge then (and see) whether the man (composed) of soul and body is one complete hypostasis, while God the Word, apart from the body and the soul, is not a complete hypostasis, but one third of the hypostasis in Christ.

And do you confess [74] with John the evangelist the body of   30
Joh. 2: 19   Christ to be the temple of God the Word? 'Destroy this temple',
Joh. 2: 21   said our Lord, 'and in three days I will raise it up.' 'But he spoke
of the temple of his body', the evangelist expounded it. If therefore the body of our Lord is not confessed by you to be the temple, as the evangelist has expounded it, and from those things which were   35 said you rather separate his raising up and his being raised up (and if) instead of that (you claim) the destroyed body, which was named by our Lord and by the evangelist, the temple and the raised, to be a part of the own hypostasis of him who would raise it up, how do you not suppose you (can) speak against scripture in   40

31] 'Destroy': see above, I p. 8, 5; cp. VI p. 84, 18; VII p. 92, 18.
32] 'I will raise it up'. See above, I p. 8, 5 f.; cp. VII p. 92, 19 f.

this matter, by preaching in your confession God the Word in Christ (to be) a half hypostasis? Do you confess the body to be his temple, and not a part of the hypostasis of God the Word, i.e. (do you confess) the body in Christ as his own half hypostasis? How
5 can you say 'one hypostasis' of the temple, and his inhabitant at the same time? For not even of the human hypostasis of Christ do we say that it raised him, but the hypostasis of God the Word which was united to it in the taking of the prosopon (raised him).

And how can the hypostases which do not possess conjunction
10 according to nature, as you too confess, become one hypostatically? [75] You acknowledge the one everlasting Son, and the Son equal to the Father and the same complete in the nature and in the hypostasis before the union. Or do you confess before the union the incomplete sonship of God the Word and his hypostasis, but as a
15 result of the union (do you confess) his sonship was perfected with the man whom he took? But I know that there is none who says this last thing. And if, after this, one perfect Son in nature and hypostasis, is your confession, tell me, what do you call now the man who was taken? As an addition to the hypostasis of the Son
20 have you confessed him, or as the inhabitant of the sonship of him who is perfected at the same time? And if you call an addition the man who was taken to the everlasting Son, then you confess two sons, and you introduce quaternity into the Trinity, by the addition of another ousia foreign to it – that which you ignorantly
25 accuse others (of doing). And if, again, it is not thus, but the sonship of the Son was perfected from the godhead and the manhood, how can you not preach God the Word as assisted by the taking, and that the union was not for the benefit of man, but rather for its own profit, and (that) the perfecting of the sonship which
30 previously to this he did not possess is now completed?

If, however, you avoid this as [76] manifest wickedness, then you are confessing the lordly man, the mediator of the dispensation of the Son and the temple for his revelation and the demonstrative image of himself – a blameless confession with the apostle since
35 you will be compelled by the truth. And how then will you know the mediator of the dispensation, and the receiver of the mediator to be one in hypostasis, and the temple with its inhabitant to be one, and the image and the prototype to be one in hypostasis, (saying this) like a fool who has turned to the destruction of his
40 confession through lack of understanding? And again: Or how, when at one time you have confessed one Son, perfect and complete, according to nature, before the union, then after the taking

of the nature and another hypostasis, do you know two ousias at the same time as one Son in hypostasis?

But if it is impossible that this should be, then you must, compelled by the truth, confess this one who was taken, as has already been said, as the Son's own image, and the temple, and the 5 indicator and carrier of the prosopon of that one (*sc.* the Son's). And from the equality of honour and authority and worship which is with him, there should be confessed by you one Son in the equality of name and in singular glory; and not in equality of nature and in singleness of hypostasis. 10

Soul and body (are) indeed two natures, assisted by each other, and in need of each other, and this one comprehends that, and that is comprehended by this. [77] Therefore the one hypostasis of man is completed from the two of them, as also they are the perfectors of each other, and one without its fellow is of no use for 15 anything, or as a perfecter of any one matter, nor is set in motion towards anything without mutual motions and sensations. But God the Word is not spoken of with his man as one in hypostasis, like soul and body, for it is not comprehended in it like the soul in the midst of the body, nor indeed is there perfected with it the one 20 hypostasis of the Son, nor does it receive from it increase for itself like the soul in the increase of thoughts and knowledge and teaching from its body. The (fact) that 'Jesus grew in stature and in wisdom, and in favour with God and man', (does) not (mean) that God the Word also was growing with him in these divine and 25 human (attributes) like the soul with the body. For if at the same time, there is one hypostasis, it is necessary also to think of one growth of the growing infant.

For this reason the example (of body and soul) agrees in one way, while in another way, it does not. In the taking of exalted and 30 humble (things) which belong to the one prosopon, and the invisibility in the visibility, it agrees, while in the possession of a composition of the two for one commingling and conjunction which (leads) to the one hypostasis, and the rest of what has been said about them, it does not agree. [78] Just as we say: 'So and so 35 is a wise man' – we call him wise while saying this of the prosopon of his soul, knowing that the body does not possess it of its own nature; but in participation with the soul, it participates also in the calling of wisdom, not however naturally; yet neither for this cause do we call (him) 'two wise men' or 'two wisdoms' – in the 40

Lk. 2: 52

23/4] 'in stature and in wisdom': Syr. vg. 'in his...and in his', Philox. et gr. 'in wisdom and in stature'; cp. below p. 48, 40; V p. 68, 20.

same way also we call Christ (as being) in one prosopon with God the Word 'Son of God', together with that natural (son we call) the man, united to him, 'one Son', whilst we stress that he is not so by nature, but because of the union with the Son is he (thus)
5 called, and possesses this. Yet neither (do we speak of) two sons because of the duality of the natures and the duality of the hypostases, in that the human nature has served the revelation of the Son, and not because he has been completed with the hypostasis of the Son (so as) to (become) the one hypostasis of sonship.
10 'He was revealed in flesh', not that he was completed in flesh – 1 Tim. 3: 16 'and justified in Spirit', and that (refers) to God the Word while this (refers) to the man. But if (there are) two sons, then on all accounts (they are) two brethren. When (there is on the contrary) inequality of nature in this, and one is honoured in that of the
15 other, of necessity, one is Son in ousia; but of the other the apostle has said: 'He has given him a name which exceeds all names'; that Phil. 2: 9 he is worshipped and honoured more than all (means:) together with him who made him [79] a mediator of his revelation, not by himself, but together with him who possessed him as his prosopon.
20 Now when you hear how Jesus was about thirty years old, it is cf. Lk. 3: 23 not with God the Word that I know him to be one hypostasis thirty years old, nor as an ordinary man by himself do I know him, but as a complete hypostasis of the manhood, being glorified in a prosopon of union with God the Word. The prosopon of God the
25 Word is honour and greatness and authority and worship, in this he is one with God the Word, and not in hypostasis. He is the prosopon of God the Word, not his hypostasis, but the name of greatness is his own honour. This prosopon with which Christ was clothed in his manhood was the interpreter of hypostasis, its own
30 prosopon. 'He was revealed in flesh.' How was he revealed? In his 1 Tim. 3: 16 nature and in his hypostasis? Whoever saw God the Word in (his own) nature and hypostasis while he was revealed? But he was revealed in him, in glory and in great dignity which is in good pleasure, 'and he gave him a name which exceeds all names'. This Phil. 2: 9
35 name and honour and authority of the Son, we know as the prosopon of the Son, and not as the hypostasis of the Son; in that they are one, but in this (they are) two. See, here, 'Christ' is indicative of the prosopon of the union, [80] and shows him who was clothed in the prosopon of God the Word.
40 All his reflections and thoughts and will, were within him in a

13] 'two brethren': that is to say: 'two sons, equal in everything, even in nature'.

47

divine manner, while he has not reflection or thought or will in an
ordinary manner by itself at all, but all of them are moved through
the working of the Holy Spirit, for the use of the dispensation, and
everything is moved and moves in God. And these thoughts and
the will in him are those which are in the divine nature, and all of 5
them, which were his, were placed in him and were perfected in
cf. Col. 2:9   him in all the fullness of the godhead, save that the nature and the
hypostasis could not be one with him, created and creator, one,
after the nature and hypostasis.

    Questions: I asked the heretic on one occasion concerning his 10
saying 'God-bearer': 'You do not confess the name of Christ,
which is said over you.' He says to me: 'Yes, (but I do).' I say to
him: 'Do you confess Christ as born of a mother, or not born of a
mother?' He says to me: 'As born (of a mother): it is clear that
Christ was born also of a mother, and not without a mother.' I say 15
to him: 'And how, (seeing) that you confess Christ born of his
mother, and after he was born confess yourself as a Christian, do
you [81] not call her who bore him by the name of that one whom
she bore, but you call him by the name of another whom she did
not bear? For the blessed Mary did not bear God, but Christ – 20
and you have confesssd (it).' The heretic said to me: 'And you, do
you not call Christ God?' I say to him: 'In what way? God simply,
incorporeal and infinite? I do not call Christ thus, and not even
you will be persuaded to do so, but you call Christ God and man,
and at the same time he is not one hypostasis which is compounded 25
cf. Lk. 22:   from God and man. But when the scripture says: "An angel came
43   from heaven, strengthening him", was then the angel strengthening with him God also, who was compounded in the flesh?
Because it was not concerning a half hypostasis that the scripture
said that an angel strengthened him, but concerning the hypostasis 30
of the lordly man, he who was named Christ by the angel from the
day of his birth. But if the half of this one hypostasis is God, then
the angel was also strengthening God, according to what you say,
but if God, the angel strengthened neither a half hypostasis nor a
whole, complete hypostasis, nor the deficiency of Christ. And also 35
the whole dispensation of inferior and exalted (things), is transmitted as [82] to one hypostasis equally, without the distinction of
hypostases, according to the two natures of Christ, when you are
not excluding God from such measurings (as are mentioned in)
Lk. 2:52   that: "Jesus grew in stature, and in wisdom, and in favour." And 40
Joh. 1:1   (you do not attribute to his manhood) that: "In the beginning

40] 'in stature, and in wisdom': see above, p. 46, 23 f. app.; cp. V p. 68, 20.

was the Word", and that: "All came about through him", and that: "Before Abraham was, I am", and that: "By me the heavens and earth are filled", and that: "He is the pattern of the invisible God", and that: "Through him he made the world";

5 also you do not allow eternity to his manhood and (that it is) consubstantial with the substance (which is) without beginning. Otherwise do you appear by your word. And that he died and rose, and that he raised, your word refers to one hypostasis, the same one rising and being raised. And there is not (according to your

10 word) one and the other which do not partake in nature in these, except in the matter of the taking of the prosopon, but (you say) one hypostasis being created and creating, half of it subject to time, and half of it without beginning, which is not possible, nor can the reason accept it.'

15 He says to me: 'Let it be that this is so, as you say. But how do you say that he dwelt in him, and was united?' I say to him: 'First of all, I desire [83] to hear from you, how do you speak of God? Is he finite or infinite by nature? And when I shall have learned of you how you think of God, then I will know how to answer the

20 question.' He says to me: 'It is evident that he is infinite by his nature.' I say to him: 'At all times? Or was there a time when it was so, but it is not so now?' He says to me: 'God does not depart from the definition of infinity, nor can he (do so).' I say to him: 'He who is infinite, can it be in whole or in part, more or less than

25 the whole.' He says to me: 'It is known that the definition infinity is the same in all things.' I say to him: 'Then, because he should make a dwelling and a unity according to nature, you have released me from the dispute with you on this matter. For God is not to be comprehended by one of the natures of creation, whom

30 not even the whole of creation can comprehend; nor is it possible in any way for him who is without parts to dwell and be united in something with a part of his nature; for it is not said that a part of the godhead is in Christ, but the whole of it in (its) entirety.'

35 He says to me: 'But how?' I say [84] to him: 'You now tell me: He who in his nature is not comprehended by any boundary, and concerning whom there is no mention of a part, in what sense can it be right to suppose that he dwelt and was completely united, unless it be in good pleasure? It was not as in any one of the saints,

40 because no one of the saints has ever been seen who could be honoured with the name of godhead, or with worship together

Joh. 1: 3
Joh. 8: 58
cf. Jer. 23: 24
Col. 1: 15
cf. Heb. 1: 2

cf. Col. 2: 9

3] 'pattern' ‌‌: Syr. vg. , gr. εἰκών.

with him, but (it was) with exalted good pleasure, and that he should receive worship from all in one prosopon of sonship – as He
Mt. 3: 17   said: "This is my beloved Son, in whom I find pleasure".' He says to me: 'Because of this one saying, you claim that in good pleasure he dwelt and was united?' I say to him: 'And how can you regard 5 this one saying as not actually written – and we ourselves, have we fabricated it? Or do you not believe that which he witnessed concerning him? And is this saying little in your eyes? See also in Isaiah (how) he speaks of many generations before of the beloved
Is. 42: 1   servant in whom he found pleasure. "Behold, my servant in whom 10 I have found pleasure, my beloved, in whom my soul has found delight." And if you will not accept the prophets and apostles in the gospel concerning Christ, who will accept you among Christians? But even if you receive our word in that (matter) of infinity, yet expound [85] to us: though you secede in the matter of "ac- 15 cording to nature" from what you confess, because there is no word left for you about the infinity, yet you refuse to speak of "according to good pleasure". What else remains for you to say, save also that he did not dwell in the temple according to nature, nor according to good pleasure? And though you were seeking to 20 call Christ altogether God (born) of the virgin, also that God was in him in his entirety, you are renouncing your confession concerning him.'

The heretic said to me again: 'Like the sun which has entered through a window, and at the same time as it is in the house, is 25 also in heaven, and one does not speak of it as being cut off, but (that it is) whole, while it is whole also in the heavens, so do I say that God was dwelling in Christ.' I say to him: 'Even if this is so, the more do you confirm that there are two hypostases, in that the sun which shines in the house is not spoken of as of one hypostasis 30 with the house in which it shines. But again, even if it is thus, tell me: is the sun in the house as a finite thing within a finite thing, or as an infinite thing within a finite thing? Although even with its finity its power within the house is not equal to the (strength) in the heavens, so that the strength of its working is not equal in every 35 place where its rays are – how do you interpret that God dwells in his manhood [86] in this way? But in spite of yourself your demonstration resembles that of the two hypostases. You confirm (it) well!' He says to me: 'This demonstration, even if it cannot be adapted equally, in everything, it is a demonstration and figure 40 of the truth.'

I say to him: 'Let it be so, but that "like the sun in the house"

50

or that "like the soul in the body", as you are wont to say – how does he shine in it, and how does he dwell: according to nature, or according to something else?' He says to me: 'According to nature.' I say to him: 'And how is he there? Is the whole of him in
5 everything in every place, as it was previously to the union? Or a little more in his body, but in other places a little less? Or was it a half of him, or did he remove from everywhere (else) altogether, and was the whole of him contracted there (in the body)?' He says to me: 'No, but in everything in every place is the whole of him, as
10 before the union, so now too, just as he is not compounded from parts. But the union did not remove the infinity from the godhead.' I say to him: 'If then, in his body and in everything the whole of him was in nature, neither less nor more, as indeed it is true, and by this was one hypostasis with his body, i.e. with his manhood,
15 then God is compounded with everything, and is one hypostasis with everything, according to your foolishness, in that the whole of him is in everything [87] in nature as (it is) in his manhood.' And by this, the mouth of the heretic was muzzled.

Again the heretic said to me: 'But you are saying two sons and
20 your worship is divided into two.' I say to him: 'Do you not call the bread of the eucharist the body of Christ?' He says to me: 'Yes, without doubt.' I say to him: 'And do you worship him...or do you not?' He says to me: 'Yes, in common with the whole church.' I say to him: 'Do you know the body of the Son by itself (alone),
25 or as one body together with that natural one?' He says to me: 'One, lest Christ should be (considered as) many bodies.' I say to him: 'And since (the two of) them are one in hypostasis and in nature, do you acknowledge this one and that one who is in heaven, as one or two?' He says to me: 'How can the bread and
30 the natural body be one hypostasis?' I say to him: 'And since they are two, in the prosopon of that natural one do you worship and honour this bread as the mystery of his body, or by itself?' He says to me: 'How can I possibly honour the nature of things, like a worshipper of the creature? But I observe as it were one body in
35 them, because of the order of the dispensation. And though (they are) two in the hypostasis and in the nature, I do not think of two bodies; so that this one administers the mystery of the natural one.' [88] I say to him: 'Thus do we also think of the man of our Lord (as) one with the Son who took him, they being two in nature and
40 in hypostasis, like the bread and the body, in that this (the man) also administers the mystery of the Son. And though there are two

22] illegible in U.

hypostases, there are not two sons, but also two...there. But just as in that duality of hypostases and of the mysteries there is no distinction in the sight of the faithful, into one and the other, so (we know) also the man of our Lord with the hypostasis of the Son as two in nature and hypostasis, and as one Son in prosopon, whilst 5 we do not regard him by himself in distinction of appearance. And we call the nature of his manhood "Son" by the singleness of the prosopon. But as one Son we worship the image of the Son with his exemplar, as the bread with the natural body of Christ, as one body. But the natures and the hypostases are two.' And his mouth 10 was shut by this question and its demonstration, and by his own mouth he was convicted.

The heretic says again: 'You diminish the hypostasis of the manhood of Christ, in that you call him "son of grace", as though he were thought to be like all men, whilst not indeed attributing 15 to him that he is "true Son", in which you seem to agree with Paul of [89] Samosata.' I say to him: 'It is you who confess like Paul (of Samosata), if you examine (these matters), and not I. Now Paul did not confess two hypostases, as I do, but one hypostasis, like you. You therefore agree to his confession. Consider well this 20 matter. But do you also state in how many ways you know, in the divine order, sonship in scripture.' He says to me: 'In three ways I know (it): according to nature, according to grace, and according to supposition; according to nature, like (the saying) "God the Word, consubstantial with the Father", and like "the man of our 25

Joh. 1: 12   Lord, from the blessed Mary"; according to grace, like "He gave them power to become sons of God, (even) to those who received

cf. Lk. 3: 23   him"; according to supposition, like "Jesus was supposed to be the son of Joseph".' I say to him: 'And by which one of these kinds do you know the man of Christ to be Son of God – according 30 to nature, according to grace, or according to supposition?' He says to me: 'Not by one of these.' I say to him: 'Even if he was distinct and by himself exalted more than everything which is honoured through the grace of the adoption of sons, because of his unity with God the Word, by all means he has, by reason of being 35 taken, the name of sonship according to grace, or else Christ according to your confession is not Son of God, [90] either according to nature, or according to supposition, or according to grace.' Now when the heretic heard this, he was silenced, because he was cornered by the questions over matter in which he was unable to 40 make a defence by his devices.

1] lacuna of one word in U.

He says to me: 'Not in any one of these ways do I know him as Son...of Christ with God.' Now when I heard this from the heretic, I cried out with a loud voice and said: 'Come, listen to the heretic, who completely estranges Christ even from the name of 5 sonship in his manhood, and makes him an ordinary man!' I say to him: 'Since you have sought to recognize as one Son in hypostasis together with the everlasting Son, the nature of the manhood of Christ, which does not receive the ousia, you have slipped and fallen into wickedness worse than that of Paul of Samosata. For 10 you have completely alienated even him (sc. Christ) from the familiarity with God by your confession, because you have not ascribed to him a familiarity such as one of the saints (has) with God, which is the (kind of familiarity which) Paul (of Samosata gives to Christ). Listen, therefore, and I will show you: How, when 15 you know him in his manhood as Son through grace, can you foolishly be ashamed to confess (this), even though his own (familiarity with God) is distinct and exalted above that of all men? For the blessed Paul speaks concerning him thus: "He Phil. 2: humbled himself and became obedient even to death, the death of 8–11 20 the cross. [91] For this reason also God highly exalted him, and gave him a name which exceeds all names, that at the name of Jesus every knee shall bow, in heaven, on earth and underneath the earth, and that every tongue should confess that Jesus Christ is Lord, to the glory of God the Father." Again: "According to the Eph. 1: 25 working of the strength of his power which he wrought in Christ, 19–22 in that he raised him from the dead and caused him" to ascend and "to sit with him in heaven above all principalities and authorities and powers and dominions, and above every name which is named, not only in this world, but in the world to come, 30 and he placed everything in subjection under his feet, etc." Tell me now: all these exalted (things) and the greatness which Paul speaks about him, do they belong to the human nature naturally, or did he indeed receive (them) at the end, they being exalted above his nature? On this (point) answer me.' The heretic says to 35 me: 'It is evident that the reading of the words demonstrates that at the end he received what did not belong to his nature. For if they had belonged to him, how could they be given to him afresh?' I say to him: 'And who was the recipient of those (things) which were exalted above his nature? What do you call these things – 40 grace or, forsooth, debts?' He says [92] to me: 'It is obvious that a

2] lacuna of more than one word (illegible in U).
24] 'of God the Father': Syr. vg. 'of God his Father'.

matter, which is clearly known by all, does not need to be confirmed by an answer, (namely) that those things which do not belong to the nature are received by grace.'

I say to him: 'How do you know the sonship which is with God, to be of nature for the manhood of our Lord?' He says to me: 'This also is in no need of question, for if he is man, he cannot naturally be Son of God.' I say to him: 'Do you also then know another son of the Nature?' He says to me: 'Yes.' I say to him: 'Look then, you also are speaking of two sons, and to one of them you ascribe adoption to sonship by grace, by way of being taken, and not naturally. And how, when you are taking your stand in it (*sc.* this proposition), can you madly accuse others (of taking their stand) in it, as though you were removed (from it)?' And when he heard these things, he rose up like a man smitten with hallucinations, and went out, convicted out of his own mouth, because he had testified to the truth without realizing it, since in the questions he had been cornered and had been forced to speak, so that he said what he had never intended.

And now, against the Severians.

When you speak with the adherents of Severus and Jacob, who deny the taking (of the human nature), who speak of one nature and one hypostasis, and they ask you concerning Christ, ask them in return: 'First I wish to know whether you agree [93] with the 318 fathers of Nicaea, and whether you anathematize Arius, and those who confess like him that there is no consubstantiality in the Trinity, and whether you confess the equality of the hypostases in the Father, the Son, and the Holy Spirit, and the unity of the nature in which there is none less or more than the other, but that they are equal in honour and in power in everything, and that they are not distinct from one another, so that the Trinity should be rent asunder, but infinitely dwelling in another, and (that) Trinity is never also duality, and creation is not sufficient to contain them, and (that) there is no place which is unoccupied by each one of the hypostases, in the same way as the whole godhead (is there). For the Father does not dwell in one region, the Son in another, and the Spirit in another, as though they were dwelling in various regions; but the whole is filled by each one of the hypostases which are dwelling in each other. (This) is confessed as a definition of infinity. "My Father who dwells in me", and: "I am in my Father and my Father in me", and again: "The Spirit of truth which issues forth from the Father", and: "No man knows God except the Spirit of God which is in him." And the scriptures

Joh. 14: 10
Joh. 15: 26
cf. 1 Cor. 2: 11

54

say clearly that Father, Son and the Holy Spirit dwelt in another. –
This is the faith of those of Nicaea.' Demand this of them at the
beginning of your interrogation, and see, [94] they are already
convicted.

5 And if they profess that they agree with this, in that they too do
not refuse openly, turn to ask them: 'Who was it who was indued
with a body and sanctified in the womb, according to scripture,
by the Spirit, and was anointed by the Spirit, and received the
Spirit in Baptism, and went forth, filled with the Spirit, from
10 Jordan, and performed deeds of power by the Spirit, and was led
into the wilderness by the Spirit, and was known to be Son of God
by the resurrection through the power of the Spirit, and received
honour moreover in good pleasure which was in the sonship from
the Father, and received all authority over everything from the
15 Father, and prayed in suffering to the Father, and arose from the
grave by the power of the Father, and was exalted to the right
hand of the Father, and received the promise concerning the Holy
Spirit from the Father, and received by oaths the priesthood from
the Father, and entered heaven and appeared before the face of
20 God, and found everlasting salvation, as weak nature, from the
Father, and offered himself without spot to God the Father, and
entered once, by his own blood, into the perfect tabernacle, as one
who was finite, and received a seat on the right hand of the Father,
and was highly exalted, because he had been obedient, and
25 received at the same time a name more excellent than all names,
and it was commanded that the angels should worship him anew,
[95] by the commandment of the Father. For if the Son like the
Father and the Spirit, is equal in power and honour and authority,
and they are not in need that they should receive help or honour
30 from each other, for the reason that everything belonging to one
of them is (shared) in common, who (then) is this one for whom
all these things were done, and by whose power did he receive
strength and honour? "The Holy Spirit shall come, and the power
of the highest shall overshadow thee. Therefore he that is born of
35 thee is the holy one, and shall be called the Son of the highest."
And he did not say that he is the Son of God, but that this one

cf. Lk. 1: 35
Mt. 1: 18, 20

cf. Ac. 10: 38
cf. Mt. 3:
16, Joh. 1:
32, 33,
cf. Lk. 4: 1
cf. Mk. 6:
2, 5, cf.
Rom. 1: 4
cf. 2 Pet.
1: 17
cf. Mt. 28: 18
cf. Mt. 26:
36ff.
cf. Heb. 8: 1
cf. Heb. 6: 15
cf. Heb. 6:
17, 7: 28
cf. Heb. 9: 24
cf. Heb. 5: 9
cf. Heb. 9: 4
cf. Heb. 9: 12
cf. Eph. 1: 20
Col. 3: 1
cf. Phil. 2:
8, 9
cf. Heb. 1: 4
cf. Heb. 1: 6

cf. Lk. 1: 35

10] 'deeds of power' translates the one word ‏ܚܝܠܐ‎ which in the Syriac New
Testament is the translation of δυνάμεις. Within the chain of *biblical* quotations
and allusions about the Spirit and the human nature of Christ the clause 'and
performed deeds of power by the Spirit' is a *dogmatical* inference. That inference
is of old Antiochene tradition: it is already attacked by Cyril of Alexandria in
his ninth anathema.

"shall be called" the Son of God, so that he points to the other who is (Son from) the Father, by which name he is called. And because "grace has been poured upon your lips", for this reason "God has blessed you for ever"; and because "you have loved righteousness, and hated iniquity", for this reason "God, your 5 God, has anointed you with the oil of gladness more than your fellows." Concerning whom did David prophesy these (things) that he was blessed by God, and anointed with the oil of gladness? Was this prophesy then about God the Word? "But without any dispute", says the apostle, "the less is blessed of the better". And how 10 can you confess the equality of the hypostases, as (do) the fathers, when you say that God the Word was blessed by the Father and was anointed by the Father and the Spirit because of his righteousness [96] and when, as it is said, the prophets prophesied these things about him? "The Spirit of the Lord is upon me. For this 15 reason he has anointed me", and: "I will place my Spirit upon him", and: "God has anointed Jesus of Nazareth with the Holy Spirit and with power", and: "The Father has not given the Spirit to the Son by measure." To which Son did the Father give the Spirit – to that consubstantial with him, or to that one of 20 whom the angel said that he should indeed be called Son? And: "The Spirit descended upon him like a dove", and: "Jesus, filled with the Holy Spirit, returned from Jordan", and: Jesus was led by the Holy Spirit into the wilderness for temptation by the devil, and: "Jesus came forth by the power of the Spirit into Galilee", 25 and: "I, by the Spirit of God cast out demons", and: "The God of our fathers glorified Jesus, he whom ye have killed, hanging him on a tree; him has God established as head and saviour, and set him at his right hand." Whom? The Son who is everlasting like him – to him did he give the dominion and made him saviour. 30 And again: "And when they had fulfilled everything that was written concerning him, they took him down from the cross, and placed him in a tomb. But God raised him from the dead", and: "According to the working of the strength of his power which he had wrought through Christ whom he had raised from the dead, 35 and he caused him to ascend and sit with him in heaven." Whom did God raise, and in whom did he exhibit the working of the strength of his power, and whom did he cause to sit with him in heaven – him who was equal in power with him, and did not need to be [97] helped or honoured by him, or him who was less than 40 all these things in his nature and who was made by another

Margin references:
Ps. 45: 3
cf. Ps. 45: 8
(Heb. 1: 9)

Heb. 7: 7

Lk. 4: 18
cf. Isa. 61: 1
Mt. 12: 18
cf. Is. 42: 1
cf. Ac. 10: 38
cf. Joh. 3: 34
cf. Lk. 1: 32
cf. Mt. 3: 16
Lk. 4: 1, 2
Lk. 4: 14
Lk. 11: 20
cf. Ac. 5: 30–2
Ac. 13: 29, 30
cf. Eph. 1: 19, 20

25] 'came forth': Syr. vg. 'turned'.

56

power?' Speak with them (starting from) the equality of the hypostases, and demand of them that they show who these are.

And if they say: 'We do not confess these things with the fathers',
5 say: 'Then I have nothing to do with you, because I agree with the ecumenical faith. First of all confirm those (things) belonging to the ousia of the Godhead, and then we will approach the dispensation. For if you do not believe, like Christians, in the unity of the godhead, equal in hypostases, but like the heathen speak of a
10 multiplicity of gods, where one is stronger and more powerful than his fellow, and one is helped, even honoured more than the other, how can you ask us about the problem of Christ? Yet first, be Christians, and then make (your) investigation about Christ. Christ, by his unction, is the vicar of his godhead, he who
15 by unction received the appellation of the name of Christ, is not equal with his anointer with regard to the things of the nature. And let these things be judged justly, and do not be hasty to attack many things concerning the matter of "God-Bearer".'

20 Ask them (beginning) from the infinity and from the conjunction of the hypostases: 'Who was born of a mother, and who issued forth from the womb [98] – was it he who at one time was not there, and who, after he came forth, was no longer there, or (was it) one who, before the babe was formed, was there and everywhere, and
25 (who) when the babe came to the birth, did not depart, but is in the babe (and) also within his mother, and not restricted there, but was in everything equally in his ousia? How then was he born? (Thus), that when he was born, he was altogether without, and nothing of him remaining within his mother? Or was he born
30 in part only, and did something of him remain within the womb, so that his birth should be in part, and that within the womb there should be as it were a portion? Or was the whole of him changed into flesh, so that he became foreign to his ousia? Or while the whole of him stayed, infinite and simple, is he also finite and
35 compounded, both visible and invisible, and is it the case with him that he could not be seen, even by the cherubim, and (yet) that he should be seen by all men? And how can we speak of God as visible and invisible (at the same time)? All the scriptures alike have proclaimed only one thing, namely, that God is invisible.
40 Of him who, it is said, is invisible and incorruptible, Paul speaks as being the one God, and: "No man has seen him or can see him." 1 Tim. 6: And this, they (the scriptures) proclaimed after Christ's appear- 16

ance. Do they say: "Jesus Christ [99] my Lord, I have not seen, and God, no man has seen or can see"? And what is the distinction between "God" and "Christ"? Paul makes the distinction: "We have glory in God through our Lord Jesus Christ, through whom we have received now the reconciliation", and this (saying): 5 "We are ambassadors of Christ with God and as it were Christ is beseeching you through us. On behalf of Christ, therefore, we beseech you, be reconciled to God." While he has ascribed "reconciliation" to "God", to "Christ" "I would persuade that through you", but to themselves "ambassadors of Christ" in the 10 (things) of God. He has persuaded and taught in every way, that the visible one has proclaimed that he is another than God by nature; but he calls the nature of God invisible, because scripture has not taught you that he is subject to change, but that he took the form of a servant, not from the angels, but from the seed of 15 Abraham. And that: "He was revealed in the flesh", he taught for the sake of illuminating the (saying) "the Word became flesh", at which they stumble. The apostle has shown that it is revelation in the flesh and not coming into being. If he became flesh, how was he revealed in it? Well then, does all that happens to the 20 ousia, happen to the whole of it equally, or to a part of it, the rest of it being freed from that which happens? [100] Are the three of them in each other or not? If the Son is visible to all, then so are the Father and the Spirit. Such as they were (previously) they remained and none of them was a matter subject to sight; was only 25 the hypostasis of the Son separated from them both in this? Or how was the Word born alone, and the blessed one called "logos-bearer"? Because when the Father and the Spirit are in him, then he, the Word is in the Father and in the Spirit. Or, while the Trinity was rent asunder, did the Word remain by himself? And 30 if the virgin bare God, did she become the mother of all ousia, or of a part of the ousia, and how did she not bare the Father and the Spirit and you not call her their mother? Since they were not separated from the Word, and the three of them within the womb and in everything are equal, is she the mother of one of them only? 35 And if you say that the Word was changed into flesh, do these remain in their purity? Especially on this account, therefore, is she mother of flesh and not mother of God, because you have said that flesh was born, and not God without a body. If the ousia is com-

cf. Joh. 1: 18

Rom. 5: 11

cf. 2 Cor. 5: 20

cf. Phil. 2: 7 & Heb. 2: 16
cf. 1 Tim. 3: 16
Joh. 1: 14

4] 'We have glory' ܡܬܫܒܗܪܝܢ: gr. καυχώμενοι, Syr. vg. ܡܫܬܒܗܪ.
4/5] 'through whom' ܕܒܐܝܕܗ: Syr. vg. ܕܒܗ.
6] 'Christ'[2]: Syr. vg. (=gr.) ܠܡܫܝܚܐ.

mon to the godhead (and) you wish to call her "God-bearer", then you ought rather to be calling the holy virgin "Trinity-bearer". Because those (*sc.* the Father and the Spirit) also remain in ousia, the (expression) "God" is the more fitting [101] for them.

5 Or (would you rather say) "mother of the Father and the Spirit"? Because they have remained in that which is of ousia, in accordance with the simplicity of godhead. Equally with the Word were they within the womb too, and were never separated from each other. For if she bore the whole ousia in that the Word is in

10 the Father and the Spirit, and they are in the Word, without time or place, therefore she should be called mother in common of the (whole) ousia, according to the folly of your opinion. Again, on the other hand, if the Word was born of a mother, was it conceived and born finitely or in his infinity? If finitely, it changed therefore

15 from that which is in everything and all of it was withdrawn into the womb; and if he infinitely became an infant, and was conceived in the womb and was born, therefore he became this infant in the whole creation, both in heaven and on earth, and beyond them, and not only in the little land of Palestine, but everywhere

20 you might seek him, the infant would be found. So also with regard to his dimensions, no one has been overcome by his appearance in (the sense) that he became infinitely within the dimensions and like his nature which is in every place.'

And if they say that he remained in every place, simple and

25 infinite, but in one place did come into being and was seen (to be) compounded flesh – see (that is) the phantasia which Mani begat, (namely) that he (*sc.* Christ) showed himself (to be) flesh in one place, as a finite one, and (yet) in every [102] place remained as a simple one, and by that should be boundless. Whoever heard such

30 nonsense as this, or what intellect would not clearly and immediately grasp its foolishness: God the Word is in one locality a man, and simple spirit throughout the whole of creation, and outside of creation is he spiritual, and within it and throughout all of it found to be incorporeal, for he is more subtile according to his ousia than

35 the appearance of all beings, and invisible, and surpassing the sense, even of the ousia of the spiritual ones – and in a portion of the earth it is found that these are contrary? Well, when beyond the limits of creation where his corporeality is not found, all of him being subtile and simple beyond creation – does man know him

40 there, or (is he) spiritual and subtile (so that man cannot know him)? Then this will be a repulse to their senselessness as is fitting.

Concerning that 'He suffered and was crucified and died', they should be asked the same thing for they dare to speak presumptuously of his suffering and death. 'When he suffered, then, and died' – according to their word, but not according to mine – 'was he found to be dead in every place, or only where his corporeality was found? And was a part of him confined within death, or was 5 he absolutely mortal? And did he know himself [103] when he was outside of his life at the time when he was slain by death, or was he without knowledge, in accordance with the rule of mortality? Because, if everywhere he was found to be dead being an ousia without boundary, creation would have been full of his (ousia in 10 the) dead (state). Where forsooth would the infinite corpse have been laid? And how is the Trinity not dissolved through his death? And if he had been in possession of feeling and knowledge, then it was death in phantasia and not real death. Divine scripture knows of three kinds of death – first, that of the corruption of con- 15 stitution, like all bodies bereft of reasoning power; secondly, that of the departure of the soul from the body; the third kind is the

cf. Mt. 8: 22   death by sin, as our Lord has shown us by his living word: "Leave the dead" in sin "to bury those who are dead" in nature. Now the first kind is that of animals and beasts, and the second of human 20 nature, while that which is through sin is that of rational nature. By which of these three kinds of death did God die – by that of the corruption of constitution, like the animals, or by the departure of the soul, like a man, (or) by that (death) which is through sin? Because where these things are not happening, it is not called 25 death. Where have you found a fourth kind of death which divine scripture does not know? You are deserving of ridicule in the presence of wise inquiry in all [104] your speech.'

    Let the heretics be interrogated again whether they are the same who say that God the Word did not take a body, but was changed 30 into a state of being flesh; (to which) resembles (in their opinion)

Col. 2: 9   that which is said by the apostle: 'In him dwells all the fullness of the godhead bodily.' For they speak suddenly (and) unwisely, their folly being laid bare to all men by (their) reply, from the opposition of their sayings which (is manifest) in a changing of the 35

Joh. 1: 14   words of scripture; as e.g., 'The Word became flesh' is 'He was
cf. Col. 2: 9   dwelling in it bodily' i.e. (in their opinion) He was made a body and became flesh and dwelt in it (*sc.* in the flesh). See, they speak of two fleshes here. There they speak of one nature and one

Joh. 1: 14   hypostasis, (namely that) in the (saying) 'The Word became 40 flesh', the same one was flesh and God at the same time, and here they expound that flesh dwells in flesh. And without necessity they

confess here two natures – God made flesh, dwelling in flesh – and
they are made an open mockery and are convicted because of the
contradiction of their words. Now when, above, they take hold of
that (saying), 'The Word became flesh', (they take hold of) only   Joh. 1: 14
5 half of the saying, and that (saying) 'He dwelt among us' they
leave, fleeing from it, that it should not be shown that it is the one
(nature) in the other. Here, in this that the fullness [105] of God   cf. Col. 2: 9
dwelt in the flesh bodily, they say (there is) the other one. The
error which they reveal there, i.e. by means of error they struggle
10 against error, through exposure becomes clear. See then, O our
beloved one, (how) skillfully this question is answered by the
orthodox against the heretics, so that by it they are forced to an
exposure of their falsehood, not being able to leave it without reply.
But when they answer, they cannot for certain escape being burned.
15   Finished is the tract concerning the orthodox confession composed by the holy of memory Mar Isaac, bishop of Nineveh, the
faithful and orthodox recluse, in truth. May his prayer succour us!
2nd of Iyor, in the year 1545.

20 Again, a treatise of Mar Michael Malpana.   IIIa
If the holy virgin is alone God-bearer, like the Father she bore
the infinite God. And again, if she is alone God-bearer, she is
without time mother of God the Word. And again, if she is not the
(mother) of man, she cannot be mother of God, and if she is not
25 man-bearer [Christ], she cannot be, or be called God-bearer. And
again, if together with the seed from the virgin, the Word of the
Father received composition, growth, finity, creation and birth,
it received all [106] human attributes, that is things which (are)
subject to change. These few things will suffice for the discerning.
30

By the same, against the hypostatic and confused union which   IIIb
Cyril, the impious one, proclaims.
Let us now speak also against the confused union of the impious
Cyril. The Word in hypostasis is infinite, but man in hypostasis is
35 finite. He therefore who speaks of the hypostatic union of God and
man, either brings God down to the finity of man, or raises man to
the infinity of God. Since neither this nor that will be, it is impossible for God to be united hypostatically to man.
And again, the hypostasis of the Word is uncreate, while the
40 hypostasis of man is create, and man cannot be united to the Word

20] 'Malpana': in the margin: 'Badoqa'.
25] 'Christ' edd. del.

in an uncreated way, nor the Word, in a created way, be united to man. Therefore say, in what hypostasis did hypostatic union take place?

And again, on the other hand, if God the Word is man because of man, how much more the man is man because of his nature! 5

And again, if the hypostasis of the Son is one, how does it differ now after the birth from the virgin from that which it was previously, when he was not yet born of the virgin? If it is the same [107] one, then he did not take anything from the virgin. However, if (it is) one and the other, then he was not that former one. 10

And again, if one is the hypostasis of the Son, either the virgin bore him as all bearing women (do) finitely, or as the Father bore him, did the virgin bear him. If therefore the virgin bore him ⟨in⟩finitely, he came forth from the begetting of his Father. If (she bore him) like the Father, then infinite was Mary who bore him 15 who, being infinite, was born of the Father.

And again, if the hypostasis is one, (and) Paul calls him the 1 Tim. 2: 5 mediator between God and man – what do you say? Does this mediator stand between the Trinity and men, or between a 'duality' and men? If he stands between a duality and man, he 20 has left the Godhead, but if he (stands) between the Trinity and men, then he is not one hypostasis. What then will you do, O agitator? You are unable to establish the hypostatic and natural union, and you are unwilling to accept the voluntary (union). One of two things is required of you – either establish the natural union 25 or accept the voluntary one and that of order and honour, and show, if it is possible, which is the true and possible one. Therefore, concerning these (matters) of the union and of the God-bearer, the things which we have said suffice, which, though [108] said briefly, contain the power of many things. 30

Therefore in this manner and (with these) arguments, let us ask them also about the growth, the baptism, the contests, the sufferings, the resurrection and the ascension, joining to them words of the scriptures and thus demonstrating that it is impossible for God the Word to receive sufferings and stripes; but because of 35 cf. 1 Cor. the union are they spoken of concerning him, like that: 'They have 2: 8 crucified the Lord of glory', ⟨not⟩ naturally, and not from eternity.

14] 'infinitely' completed by edd.; S. Brock prefers to read the text as it stands. Both readings have something to recommend them.
37] 'not'¹ inserted by edd.

By the same, against the foul Severians, who say: 'As the man's IIIc
soul and body are called one nature and one hypostasis, so also the
Son, after the union in his two natures, is called one nature and
one hypostasis.'

5   Refutation. But here (in the case of man it is) the finite, and the
created with the created, all the parts being collected together into
one human hypostasis and into one nature. This is possible. But
above (*sc.* in the case of Christ) it is impossible that the uncreated
with the created, and the infinite with the finite should come to one
10 natural collection.

And again, on the other hand because here, the soul, confined
within the body, in being always with it, does not see it and does
not know how it is because of its union with the body – if therefore,
after this manner, God is united with man, neither is it possible
15 that he should see [109] him because of his union with the body.

Again, on the other hand, also in this union of soul with body,
it willingly receives the sufferings of the body, and not naturally
and hypostatically; for while the body suffers naturally, its partner
suffers spiritually, and although it (*sc.* the soul) teaches it (*sc.* the
20 body) the ways of bodily suffering, it is not possible for it (the soul)
to suffer with it (the body) naturally.

And again, on the other hand, if, wherever the Father is, there is
God the Word, and (if) it is not possible that he should be away
from the bosom of his Father, of necessity this man would be
25 required to be without boundary and without (material) density,
like the Father, in order that he might be able to be in natural
union with God the Word. And if not, it would be required of God
[the Word], because of the only begotten within his bosom, to be
contracted to a stature of three cubits, in order that God the Word
30 might be able to effect a union with the man who is from us.

And again, on the other hand, if the hypostasis of the Son is
incarnate and compounded, he does not resemble his Father who
is not incarnate and not compounded, and then our Lord said
falsely: 'Whoever has seen me, has seen the Father.' But if he Joh. 14: 9
35 resembles his Father, and in him we recognize the Father, man is
not united to God the Word hypostatically and naturally, but
willingly and according to order.

28] 'the Word' edd. del.

10] 'collection' (ܩܘܒܫ) shows that the Greek συναγωγή had been introduced into Syriac theological language.

IIId [110] By the same, against the Julianists, who say that God the Word did not receive this common nature which has been transmitted from Adam who transgressed the commandment and was defiled with sin, but (that he received) from the pure (nature) which is free from sins, that which Adam had before he trans- 5 gressed the commandment.

Refutation. Now it is fitting that these new disciples of that new teacher Julian should be asked before all these (things) this: Was the body of our Lord taken from the virgin, or not? If they say that he was not received from the virgin but that he had it with him 10 from heaven, then there was not taken from Adam either this sinful nature of ours, or that new (nature) which (existed) before he transgressed the commandment. But if, being compelled by the truth, they say that he took anything from the virgin, then from David and from Abraham he took it, as the apostles proclaim. And 15 David and Abraham were the descendants of Adam, which is easy

cf. Lk. 3:
23-38

to know from all the scriptures, and in particular from the writing of Luke, who has recounted from the later to the earlier and has shown that Christ is the son of David, the son of Abraham, the son of Sheth, the son of Adam who was from God. How, then, since 20 our Lord was from the fathers in the flesh, has Julian said he is not of our [111] nature?

And again, that sinless nature of Adam, how was it preserved from the beginning until now, that at this time God the Word should have put it on? 25

And again, from where was there for Adam another nature apart from that which he possessed before the transgression of the commandment? From it...that which transgressed the commandment, and became sinful,...all nature was handed down, while moreover not even the nature transgressed the command- 30 ment, but the power of the will.

And again, what compelled him to take a new nature that did not resemble that ancient one? Now, if they say that through his righteousness he will save us – but this would have been easy to do also by means of the angels who did not transgress the 35 commandment. But if they say that these are not corporeal, then what benefit is there from a body which does not resemble us?

And again the books of the Old and New (Testament) testify

1 Cor. 15:
21

that our Lord is from our sinful nature: 'As by man came death, 40

28] illegible in U.
29] illegible in U.

so also by man is the resurrection of the dead', and: 'We are of his cf. Eph. 5: 30
flesh and of his bones.'

And again, how can the head of the body be of (one) nature, and its own limbs of another nature?

5 And again, if our Lord was from another new nature, [112] it would not have been necessary that there should appear in him sweat and hunger, which are the sufferings of mortals which were inflicted on Adam because of the transgression of the commandment.

10 And again, if he was not of sinful nature, what necessity was there for him who was of righteous nature to be justified? And to what purpose was the grace of the Spirit required through which he might be justified? 'He was revealed in the Spirit, and he was cf. 1 Tim. 3: 16
justified in the Spirit', and 'through the eternal Spirit, he offered Heb. 9: 14
15 himself without spot to God'.

And again: it was not by the righteous nature of our Lord that we were justified, but by his will which agreed with the will of his Father, and he subjected the nature to be within the observance of the divine law. 'By this, his will, we are sanctified by the Heb. 10: 10
20 offering of the body of Jesus Christ (that took place) once.'

And again: never in the scriptures has God reckoned nature either sinful or righteous, but the will, and free-will. No one then of those who fear God says human nature is righteous or sinful, but sin and righteousness in the divine scriptures, and with all dis-
25 cerning people, are attributed to the will and to free-will, except (with) those who are the seed of Simon, and who introduce matter into God, saying that sin is deposited in nature, because they also despise nature.

[113] And again, if our Lord was not son of Adam in the nature,
30 why has he been called with the epithets proper to nature, that is: Adam, human being, man, child, infant, new-born babe? And why did he resemble us except in the matter of sin? cf. Heb. 4: 15

But I think that these few things which we have said are sufficient against those bats who teach a new nature, which has no
35 root, and it is not known where it is to be found. For it is easy for anyone who desires to refute their error to take hold of the whole extent of the scriptures, and show concerning the taking of our Lord Jesus, that he is from common nature. Therefore this will be defined here too.

40 Finished is the treatise of Mar Michael Badoqa, may his prayer succour us, Amen.

13] 'Spirit': read 'flesh'? Syr. vg. 'flesh'.

IV*a* Again, chapters of a treatise against those who confess Christ as one nature and hypostasis.

Every nature which exists acquires or has a distinct definition and singular property. If you confess Christ as one nature, what is its distinction, and what is its property? This one nature and one 5 hypostasis which you confess in Christ, is it consubstantial with God the Father, or consubstantial with the blessed Mary? If it is consubstantial with the Father, it is simple and infinite spirit, and [114] nothing was taken from Mary. And if he is consubstantial with Mary, he is an ordinary man. But if he is consubstantial with 10 the Father, and consubstantial with Mary, as the Father and Mary are two natures, so also is Christ two natures. If you confess Christ as one nature and one hypostasis from the godhead and the manhood, of necessity godhead and manhood are parts of this nature and hypostasis; and because the whole exceeds its parts, and the 15 parts are less than the whole, therefore this nature exceeds each one of its parts, and the godhead is less in its being a part than that nature of which it is a part, which is impossible, (namely) that anything could be greater than the godhead. If the nature or the hypostasis, brought together and compounded, is other than the 20 nature and the hypostasis not brought together and not compounded – now the nature of the Father and of the Spirit is not brought together and not compounded, but the nature and the hypostasis of Christ is brought together and compounded from the godhead and the manhood – then the nature and hypostasis of the 25 Son is other than the nature of the Father and the Spirit. If Christ, in his godhead is the maker of his manhood, but in his manhood [115] is made by his godhead, he who makes him and he who is made by him, cannot be one hypostasis.

How can Christ be one hypostasis? Was the one nature or the 30

3] 'acquires or': p. 93, 26 om.
4] 'If you confess...': in the margin, 'This chapter is written in its place below', that is, in VII*b*.
5] 'distinction': p. 94, 2 'definition'.
23/4] 'and the hyp.': p. 94, 23 'or the hyp.'.
30 – p. 67, 1] 'The one nature or one hypostasis, Christ': p. 94, 30 om. (homoioteleuton).

1] IV*a* and *b* are excerpts from the document of 612, where their order is *b, a*, as in VII*b* below. We have to thank Dr Sebastian Brock for the observation that these passages occur twice in our collection.
3 – p. 67, 15] =p. 93, 26 – 95, 12.

one hypostasis, Christ, indeed made one, or was he from before? That which is generated receives in the beginning that it should become. Just as time clave to his beginning, so did creation to his becoming. And if God the Word, together with his body, was made
5 one nature or one hypostasis, (then) he came forth from uncreated nature, and God was his maker. If the nature or hypostasis was constituted from the union, it did not exist before the union. But the nature and hypostasis of the Son existed before the union. Neither the nature nor the hypostasis of the Son arose as a result
10 of the union, but another, as also the natural union of soul and body does not establish the nature of the soul or the body, but the nature of a man. If every hypostasis which exists is a singular ousia, but the hypostasis of Christ one, which is the singular ousia of Christ, and from which common (ousia) is it to be
15 distinguished?

Christ the Son of God, is he God in nature and hypostasis, and IV*b*
man in nature and hypostasis, or not? If he is, see (there are) [116]
two natures and two hypostases without argument; and if (he is)
20 not, which of them is without nature and without hypostasis? But if, while both are preserved in their natures and in their hypostases, one nature and one hypostasis has arisen from them, let them tell us – this one nature and one hypostasis, has it consubstantial (beings) or not? If it has, let them show (us) which is the other
25 hypostasis which is constituted of the godhead and the manhood; and if not, it is alone in its kind, and it is consubstantial with God or with us. Finis.

[117] Again, by the power of the Holy Trinity, we will set down a V
30 few words spoken in the holy scriptures by the Holy Spirit through the tongues of the blessed apostles concerning the dispensation which is in Christ our Lord and our God, that not only before the taking (of the human nature), but also after the taking, the divine scriptures show in every place the difference in property of each
35 one of the natures.
  Now, before the taking: for instance: 'In the beginning was the   Joh. 1: 1
Word, etc.', and that: 'I and my Father are one', and 'He who   Joh. 10: 30
has seen me has seen the Father', and 'Before Abraham should be,   Joh. 14: 9
                                                                  Joh. 8: 58

4] 'God the Word' (= *Syn. Or.*): p. 95, 1 'Christ, God the Word'.
27] rest of p. 116 (text) empty.

17–27] = p. 93, 16–26.

Rom. 9: 5	I am', and 'From them appeared Christ in the flesh who is God
1 Cor. 2: 8	over all', and 'If they had known, they would not have crucified
	the Lord of glory, etc.' About these there is no ambiguity, and they
	are known to all men, i.e. (as concerning the divine nature) before
	the taking; these are spoken only to God or about God.

5

	Those which (belong to the category) 'after the taking' are as
Mt. 1: 1	follows: 'The book of the generation of Jesus Christ.' 'Now the
Mt. 1: 18	birth of Jesus Christ –', and 'you are Christ, the son of the living
Mt. 16: 16	God', and 'Now has Christ risen from the dead', and 'Christ died
1 Cor. 15: 20	
Rom. 5: 8	for us', and 'If therefore we are dead with [118] Christ, we believe
Rom. 6: 8	that we shall live with Christ.' 'For we know that Christ has risen
cf. 1 Cor. 15: 20	from the dead.' 'Now we preach Christ crucified.' 'Because Christ
1 Cor. 1: 23	has died for our sins, as it is written.' 'But if Christ is preached that
1 Cor. 15: 3	he rose from the dead.' 'Remember Jesus Christ who rose from
1 Cor. 15: 12	the dead.'
2 Tim. 2: 8	

10

15

	Now those things which were spoken concerning the prosopon
Mt. 2: 1	of the manhood are as follows: 'When Jesus was born in Bethlehem
cf. Lk. 2: 40	of Judaea'. 'And the child grew and waxed strong in Spirit and
	was filled with wisdom, and the grace of God was upon him.'
Lk. 2: 52	'Jesus grew in stature and in wisdom, and in favour with God and
Mt. 4: 1	men.' 'Then was Jesus led by the Holy Spirit into the wilderness',
Lk. 9: 44	and 'The son of man will be delivered up into the hands of men',
Mk. 9: 9	'Until the son of man shall arise from the dead', 'Father if it be
Mt. 26: 39	possible, let this cup pass from me.' El, El, lemana shebaqtan,
Mt. 27: 46	which means 'My God, my God, why (etc.)?' and 'The son of man
Lk. 22: 22	
Lk. 22: 42	goes where he is assigned', 'Father, if you be willing, let this cup
Lk. 22: 43, 44	pass from me', and 'There appeared to him an angel from heaven
	strengthening him, and being in fear, he was praying earnestly',
Joh. 1: 29	[119] 'Behold the lamb of God', and 'The angels of God as-
Joh. 1: 51	cending and descending to the son of man.' 'See now my soul,
Joh. 12: 27	behold it is troubled', 'O, my Father, deliver me from this hour'
Joh. 12: 49	and 'I of myself have not spoken, but the Father who has sent me,
	he has given commandment what I should say, and what I should
cf. Joh. 17: 3	speak.' 'This is eternal life, that they should know you, that you,
	God, are the Father of truth alone, and him whom you sent, even
Mt. 28: 18	Jesus Christ'. 'All authority has been given to me in heaven and
	in earth.'
Ac. 1: 11	From the Acts of the apostles: 'Men of Galilee, why are you

20

25

30

35

1 ff.] marginal gloss: 'These two sayings do not refer to the prosopon of God
the Word but to the two natures of our Lord. He who wrote (it) made a
mistake.'

20] 'in stature and in wisdom': see above, II p. 46, 23 f.; cp. p. 48, 40.

standing, looking into heaven? This Jesus who was taken up from
you into heaven shall so come in like manner as you have seen
him.' 'Jesus of Nazareth, a man from God was seen with you with   Ac. 2: 22
acts of power and signs and wonders, which God performed in
5 your midst through him.' 'Him who was separated for this purpose   Ac. 2: 23
by the foreknowledge and will of God.' Concerning David: 'For   Ac. 2: 30
he was a prophet, and he knew that God had sworn to him with
oaths, "Of the fruit of your body, shall I set upon your throne".'
'This Jesus has God raised up, and we are his witnesses, and he has   Ac. 2: 32f.
10 been exalted at the right hand of God.' [120] 'Of a truth therefore,   Ac. 2: 36
let all the house of Israel know that God has made this Jesus whom
ye crucified, Lord and Christ', and 'You have killed the prince of   Ac. 3: 15
life whom God raised on the third day.' 'That by the name of Jesus   Ac. 4: 10
Christ of Nazareth whom you crucified whom God raised from the
15 dead.' 'This is the stone which you builders rejected, and it has   Ac. 4: 11f.
become the head of the corner, and there is no salvation through
any other man.' 'The God of our fathers raised Jesus, he whom you   Ac. 5: 30f.
killed, hanging him on a cross. Him has God raised to be prince
and saviour, and he has exalted him on his right hand, etc.' 'The   cf. Ac. 3: 13
20 God of our fathers has glorified his Son Jesus, he whom you killed,
etc.' Concerning Stephen, he says: 'And he being filled with faith   Ac. 7: 55
and the Holy Spirit looked up to heaven and saw the glory of God,
and Jesus standing at the right hand of God.' 'The Spirit of the   Lk. 4: 18
Lord is upon me, therefore he has anointed me, etc.' 'I am Jesus   (Is. 61: 1)
25 of Nazareth whom you are persecuting.' 'Concerning Jesus of   Ac. 9: 5
Nazareth whom God anointed with Spirit and with power.' 'And   Ac. 10: 38, 39
he it was who was going about and healing those who were
afflicted by the evil one because [121] God was with him, and we
are his witnesses.' And. 'Him God raised up on the third day, and   Ac. 10: 40
30 gave him to be seen openly.' 'This is he who was set aside by God   Ac. 10: 42
as judge of the living and the dead.' Concerning David: 'From this   Ac. 13: 23
man's seed God raised up for Israel, as he promised, Jesus, the
saviour.' 'See, we declare to you that the promise which he made   cf. Ac. 13:
to our fathers, behold God has fulfilled for us, their sons, in that he   32, 33
35 raised up Jesus.' 'And so did God raise him from the dead, that he   Ac. 13: 34
should not again see corruption.' 'This one whom God raised did   Ac. 13: 37
not see corruption.'

    From the blessed Paul: 'Paul, the servant of Jesus Christ.'   Rom. 1: 1

9] 'we': Syr. vg. 'we all'.
18] 'Him'² ܠܗ: Syr. vg.+ ܠܗܘ.
24] 'therefore' ܡܛܠܗܢܐ: Syr. vg. ܡܛܠ ܗܕܐ, gr. οὗ ἕνεκεν.
35/6] 'he should' 'see' ܢܚܙܐ: Syr. vg. ܢܚܙܐ ܚܒܠܐ.

Rom. 1: 7	'Peace and grace be with you from God our Father, and from our
Rom. 5: 8	Lord Jesus Christ.' 'Here does God show his love towards us, that
Rom. 5: 14	while we were sinners, Christ died for us.' 'But death reigned from
	Adam to Moses even over those who have not sinned after the
	transgression of Adam, he who was a likeness of him who was to 5
Rom. 5: 15	come.' 'How much therefore will the grace of God, and his gift,
1 Cor. 3:22f.	because of one man, Jesus Christ, abound in many.' 'Everything
1 Cor. 15: 12	is yours, and you are Christ's, and Christ is God's.' [122] 'But if
	Christ is preached that he rose from the dead, how are there those
1 Cor. 15: 15	among you who say there is no resurrection of the dead?' 'Now 10
	we are found to be false witnesses of God, because we have wit-
	nessed against God that he raised Christ, when he did not raise
1 Cor. 15: 21	him', and 'Just as by man came death, so also by man came the
1 Cor. 15: 45	resurrection of the dead.' 'The first Adam became a living soul,
Gal. 1: 4	and the second Adam, a quickening spirit.' 'He who gave himself 15
	for our sins, in order that he might deliver us from this evil world,
	according to the will of God, our Father.' 'For this reason, I also,
Eph. 1:	behold, when I heard of (your) faith in the Lord Jesus Christ, and
15–17	your love towards all the saints I did not cease from giving thanks
	on your behalf and remembering you in my prayers, that the God 20
	of our Lord Jesus Christ, the Father of glory, should give you the
Eph. 1: 19	spirit of wisdom.' 'According to the working of the strength of his
	power which he wrought in Christ, in that he raised him from the
Eph. 5: 5	dead, etc.' 'Because everyone who is a fornicator or unclean per-
	son, etc., has no inheritance in the kingdom of Christ and of God.' 25
Phil. 2: 8, 9	'He humbled himself and became obedient unto death, even the
	death of the cross. Wherefore also God [123] has highly exalted
1 Tim. 2:	him, and given him a name that is above all names.' 'For God is
5, 6	one, and (there is) one mediator between God and men, the man
1 Tim. 5: 21	Jesus Christ, he who gave himself as a ransom for all men.' 'I testify 30
Heb. 2: 6, 7	to you before God and the Lord Jesus Christ.' 'What is man that
(Ps. 8: 5, 6)	you are mindful of him, or the son of man that you visit him? You
	have made him a little lower than the angels, and you have placed
Heb. 2: 9	on his head glory and honour.' 'But we behold him who was a

2/3] 'that while' ܟܕ: Syr. vg. ܟܕ ܐܠܐ.
6] 'How much': Syr. vg. + 'more'.
8] In the lower margin of p. 121 (text) is a gloss (or part of the text?): 'Again
he says: He did not take from the angels, but from the seed of Abraham did he
take. He tasted death apart from God on behalf of all men. He, in whom is
dwelling all the fullness of the godhead bodily...by the veil which ⟨was⟩ his
flesh. Three (kinds of) death: is (there one) by which God died? The death of
animals or of men or of sin?' Quoted in these lines are: Heb. 2: 16, 9; Col. 2: 9;
Heb. 10: 20. 'Three (kinds of) death': cp. above, II*b* p. 60, 14 ff.

little lower than the angels, even Jesus, because of the sufferings of
his death.' 'Therefore, it was right that in all things he should be   Heb. 2: 17
made like unto his brethren, that he might be a merciful and
faithful high priest in things pertaining to God.' 'Wherefore, holy   Heb. 3: 1–3
5 brethren, who have been called by the calling which is from
heaven, see this apostle and high priest of our confession, (even)
Jesus Christ, who was faithful to him who appointed him, like
Moses in all his house. For far greater was his glory than that of
Moses.' 'But one that was tempted in all points like us, except (that   Heb. 4: 15
10 he was without) sin.' 'Also when he was clothed with flesh, he was   Heb. 5: 7
offering up entreaty and mighty request with tears to him who
could [124] save him from death', and 'He was named of God a   Heb. 5: 10
high priest after the likeness of Melchizedek.' 'Now the God of   cf. Heb.
peace, he who raised up from the dead the great shepherd of the   13: 20
15 flock through the blood of the everlasting covenant (διαθήκη),
which is Jesus Christ, our Lord.' 'And he will work in us that   Heb. 13: 21
which is pleasing before him through Jesus Christ, our Lord,
whose is the glory for ever.' 'Because, therefore, we have been   Rom. 5: 1
justified by faith, let us have peace with God through our Lord
20 Jesus Christ.' And: 'By the redemption which is in Jesus Christ   Rom. 3:
this one whom God first made a propitiation through faith in his   24, 25
blood.' 'Heirs of God and co-heirs with Jesus Christ.' 'Nor any   Rom. 8: 17
other creature shall be able to separate us from the love of God   Rom. 8: 39
which is in Jesus Christ', and 'If you shall confess with your mouth   Rom. 10: 9
25 the Lord Jesus, and believe in your heart that God raised him
from the dead, you shall live.' 'For whoever in these things serves   Rom. 14: 18
Christ is pleasing to God.' 'Just as also Christ presented you to the   Rom. 15:
glory of God. But I say that Jesus Christ was a minister of circum-   7, 8
cision for the truth of God.' 'I have therefore pride in Jesus Christ   Rom. 15: 17
30 with God.' 'I praise my God at all times [125] on your behalf for   1 Cor. 1: 4
the grace of God which has been given to us in Jesus Christ.' 'Now   2 Cor. 1: 21
God confirms us with you in Christ.' 'Such trust have we in Christ   2 Cor. 3: 4
towards God.' And: 'We know that he who raised our Lord Jesus   2 Cor. 4: 14
Christ from the dead, etc.' 'But thanks be to God who has given   1 Cor. 15:57
35 us victory through our Lord Jesus Christ.' 'For this reason, through   2 Cor. 1: 20
him we give "Amen" to the glory of God.' 'How much more there-   Rom. 5: 15

2] 'Therefore, it was right' ܗܟܢܐ ܗ̇ܘ ܘܙܕܩ: Syr. vg. ܗܟܢܐ ܗ̇ܘ ܕܘܙܕܩ ܠܗ.
11] 'request with': Syr. vg. 'request with sighing and with'.
17] 'our Lord' deest in Syr. vg.   18] 'ever': Syr. vg.+'and ever. Amen'.
24] 'is in': Syr. vg.+'our Lord'.
31] 'to us': Syr. vg. 'to you'.
33] 'our Lord' deest in Syr. vg.   34] 'from the dead' deest in Syr. vg.

fore the grace of God and the gift shall abound in many because of

Rom. 4: 24 one man, Jesus Christ.' 'Also to us he is about to reckon those
things which we have believed in him who raised our Lord Jesus
Heb. 13: 8 Christ from the dead.' 'Jesus Christ, the same, yesterday, today,
1 Cor. 1:
11–13 and for ever.' 'For they have sent word to me concerning you, my 5
brethren, that there are disputes among you. Now this I say that
there are those of you who say, I am of Paul, and those who say,
I am of Apollos, and those who say, I am of Kephas, and those
who say, I am of Christ. Is Christ divided?'

See, we set down for you, O reader, as you commanded, three 10
ways in which the divine scriptures speak of the dispensation of
Christ which was wrought on our behalf, that is, not only before
the taking (of the human nature), but (also) after the taking: the
first kind – [126] ⟨of⟩ the divine nature only; the second kind –
from the prosopon of the union, that is, the name of Christ; now 15
that third kind – also after the taking and the union: in word
only have the divine scriptures distinguished the two natures,
while they have not confused the properties of the natures – God
forbid! – For Christ, it is said, is consubstantial with us and our
Lord: consubstantial with us in the nature of his manhood, our 20
Lord in the nature of his godhead, and we worship him as one
Christ. – In that he is Christ, he is undivided; the Son in that he is
Son, is undivided. For we do not say 'two Christs' or 'two sons'. –
But the Son is twofold, not in honour, but in the nature, lest we
should seem to be making Christ our Lord into an ordinary man or 25
God divested of manhood. – Our Lord Christ is the same, omni-
potent and man, but not in the same way. For it is not being God

6] 'brethren': Syr. vg.+'from the house of Chloe'.
14] 'of' edd. add.
23] 'say': gr. ἔχομεν.
26/7] 'omnipotent': Severus 'omnipotent God'.
27] 'but': Severus 'the same but'. 'not being': Severus shows our text to have
suffered from an omission by homoioteleuton; he reads: 'not being man, that
he was God and not'.

19] 'For Christ...' here begin some quotations from Nestorius.
19–22] as a whole is unknown; cp. however 20 'consubstantial...manhood'
with Loofs p. 340, 6; and cp. 21 'and we...one' with Loofs p. 263, 15 and
276, 14.
22/3] Sermo 12, Loofs p. 281, 4–6.
24–6] partly unknown; 24–'in the nature': Sermo 12, Loofs p. 281, 8 f.
26 – p. 73, 4] partly unknown; 26 – p. 73, 2 '(he was) man' Sermo 23, Severus,
Ctr. Gramm., III 35, *CSCO* **101** p. 218, 1–7 textus (**102** p. 159, 34 – 160, 5 versio).
Severus has the better text, see first app.

that he was man, but in his Godhead, (he was) God, and in his manhood, (he was) man, and in the two of them, Christ. Christ is the prosopon of the union of the natures. For he is the form of him who took and of him who was taken. – These things are said by
5 the blessed Nestorius in his homilies.

Now this I have said, [127] that there are those who rend sections of the treatise of Mar Narsai and calumniate us by them, as though he was saying that 'lordly manhood' is simple and divested of the godhead – which God forbid – as they who reject
10 the truth suppose. But the blessed Mar Narsai, in these three ways in which the holy scriptures have been set down by the Holy Spirit through the tongues of the blessed apostles, like them he speaks, and with them he agrees, and in their footsteps he walks. And whoever desires to accuse him, accuses and condemns the evan-
15 gelists who were before him. From the blessed Paul: 'Adam, the [I Cor. 15: first man became a living soul, and the last Adam a quickening 45 spirit.' Of Mar Narsai: From the time when the earth conceived Adam, her first-born, in it (*sc.* that time) was formed the second Adam in the earth of her body. – Why does he not censure the
20 blessed Paul with whom the holy Mar Narsai agrees? From the blessed apostle: 'But death reigned from Adam to Moses, even [Rom. 5: 14 over those who had not sinned after the transgression of Adam who was the likeness of him who was to come', namely Christ. Of Mar Narsai: [128] Mary was a human being from the humanity of the
25 family of Adam, and the offspring (born) of her resembled this (Adam) in body and soul. – Now if the first Adam was the likeness of that one who was to come, that is to say, the likeness of Christ, as Paul has said, how can Mar Narsai be condemned, who says that the offspring of Mary resembled her in body and in soul? See
30 only the blessed Paul: 'For this reason it behoved him to be made [Heb. 2: 17 like his fellows in all things,' but 'he who was tempted in all things [Heb. 4: 15 (was) without sin'. Of Mar Narsai: It was not (divine) substance hidden before everybody that Mary bore. She bore a man who entirely resembled his kinsfolk. He was not a spiritual one without
35 a construction fashioned by hands: he was carnal, fashioned by the hands of carnal ones. But if the Word humbled itself and became flesh, why was it necessary for the Spirit to accomplish her con-

31] 'things'²: Syr. vg.+'like us'.

17–19] unidentified.
24–6] unidentified.
32 – p. 74, 1 (or only 32–36?)] unidentified.

Joh. 2: 19
Joh. 2: 21

2 Tim. 2: 8

Lk. 1: 32

1 Cor. 15:
45

1 Cor. 15:
21

cf. Mk. 4:
38f.

ception? – He agrees with the apostle. Of the evangelist: 'Overthrow this temple, and in three days I will raise it up. But he spoke of the temple of his body.' Of Mar Narsai: He is altogether man through the perfection of body and soul. He is also God in that he became a dwelling place for the godhead. – See, has the 5 evangelist called him dwelling and dweller or not? Why is anyone who says the same thing condemned? The blessed Paul: 'Remember Jesus Christ who rose from the dead, he who is of the seed of David.' 'And the Lord God shall give to him the throne of his father David.' Of Mar Narsai: [129] False then is even the promise 10 to David, so that Mary bore not the son of David but the Word? – Whoever says, Son of David means also: from the seed of David. The blessed Paul: 'Adam, the first man, became a living soul, and the second Adam a quickening spirit.' Of Mar Narsai: Mary is the mother of the second Adam, not of the (divine) substance, and like 15 the earth she brought forth, even she, without marriage. The blessed Paul: 'Just as by man came death, so also by man came even the resurrection from the dead.' Of Mar Narsai: That commandment which indicated to the earth that it should bring forth Adam, the same depicted an image in the midst of her limbs in the 20 likeness of Adam. Of Mar Narsai: I say, one prosopon of the Word and the temple that was chosen by him; and I confess one Son, and I proclaim two natures, the glorious and hidden nature of the eternal Word, substance from His father, and our own nature, which he took, according to the promises which he promised; 25 complete in the godhead of him (is he) who was equal with him who begat him, and perfect moreover in his manhood in soul and body of the mortals; two which are in unity, one love and one will; the only begotten Word from the Father and the form of a servant which he took. Now in the mind, [130] the glorious (things) are 30 distinguished from the humble things, and are attributed to the one Lord. Of the two natures which became one, although I have distinguished between the glorious and humble (things) of the natures in my confession, I make no rent, for I confess that one is the Son. It was not possible for mortals to contemplate his nature, 35 and for this reason he took a man so that he might cover his splendour with the man. He slept in the ship, and they awoke him,

3–5] unidentified.
10/11] unidentified.
14–16] unidentified.
18–21] unidentified.
21 – p. 75, 13 (?)] unidentified.

and he arose and rebuked the sea and quietened it. The sleep was
that of mortals, and the silence of the sea was that of the creator.
'Our friend Lazarus is asleep', and 'I am glad I was not there.' Joh. 11: 11,
In his manhood he was not there, in his godhead he was there. 15
5 Whose tears were they but of the body of the family of Adam?
Here, the voice is that of the creator, who called to Lazarus and he
revived. Openly he speaks of these humble (things) concerning
himself, when he says to his disciples: 'I am going to my Father cf. Joh. 20:
and my God.' The suffering and death are of him who suffers who is 17
10 endowed with the suffering in his nature. The resurrection and the life
(are) of the creator who has the Life in his nature. With him from
the beginning was the only begotten Word of the Father, with him
and in him he was dwelling, and not sharing in his humble things.

15 The chapters of Cyril: VI
⟨1.⟩ Whoever does not confess that Emmanuel is in truth God,
[131] and for this reason the holy virgin is God-bearer, for she bare
after the flesh the Word which is from God when he became flesh –
let him be anathema.
20 Refutation and interpretation from the famous fathers in the
church:
First, from Eustathius, archbishop of Antioch, who was great
and praiseworthy in the holy synod of Nicaea. For he said to the
Arians as follows: If God the Word took (his) beginning from the 1
25 birth, in that he passed through the womb of the virgin and was
clothed with the composition of a body, it is established that he
came of a woman. But if the Word is God from the beginning with
the Father, and we say that all came about by him, he came not of cf. Joh. 1: 3
a woman, because he is the cause of all. But from a woman came
30 he who was formed by the Holy Spirit.
From Athanasius, from the homily concerning the virgin, as to
who was he who was of Mary: When the Lord of all, the Word 2
God, sought to renew all, he chose the mother of that body which
he was about to put on, from our race, and in the body which was
35 of her, he renewed all.

16] '1.' edd. add.

15 ff.] Here begins the second of the three refutations of Cyril's anathemata
contained in C (the two others occur in I and XI).
1 = *Eranistes* I **25** col 89 B; Spanneut Nr. 18; from the *Commentary on Prov. 8: 22.*
2 not in the Ps. Athanasian *Sermo in descriptionem sanctae Mariae*, PG 28 col. 944 ff.
The quotation sounds, however, genuine, but some delvings in G. Mueller,
Lexicon Athanasianum, were without success.

Joh. 1: 14   Mar Gregory of Nazianzus: Now that (saying), 'The Word
3   became flesh' is comparable to that (saying) 'He became a curse.'
cf. Gal. 3:   Not as if our Lord was changed into these things! How then? But
13   in that [132] he took these (things) upon himself, because 'he shall
cf. Is. 53:   bear our iniquity and carry our sins'.   5
6, 10

4   Of John (Chrysostom), from the commentary on John: When
Joh. 1: 14   you hear that (saying) 'the Word became flesh', it is not that it
was changed, for that would be absolute blasphemy, but while his
cf. Phil. 2: 7   nature was preserved, he took the form of a servant.

Of the same, against Apollinarius, because (his) admitted   10
5   opinion was that of a change of the divine nature: That (saying)
Joh. 1: 14   'the Word became flesh' – when he (sc. the evangelist) introduces
it, he says, 'and tabernacled with us', that is 'dwelt among us'.
I have not, he asserts, said that God the Word was changed into
Joh. 2: 21   flesh, but that he was dwelling in flesh, this is the same (as) 'he   15
dwelt among us', as he said, 'Now he spoke of the temple of his
body'.

The second chapter of Cyril: Whoever does not confess that the
Word which is from God the Father is united hypostatically to the
flesh, and that Christ is one with his flesh, that is to say, the same   20
one at the same time God and man – let him be anathema.

⟨The orthodox (says)⟩ that anyone who does not confess that
the beginning which is from us was joined unspeakably from the
womb to God the Word, and that Christ is one, who is known in
two complete natures, is far from the truth.   25

6   ⟨Ambrose⟩: From where, O deniers, have you (evidence) that
the body is consubstantial with the godhead [133] of the Word?

2] 'curse' (Gal. 3: 13) Gelasius 'peccatum' (2 Cor. 5: 21).
22] 'The orthodox (says)': edd. suppl., forgotten rubrication.
26] 'Ambrose': edd. suppl., rubric missing.
27] 'body': *Eran.* σῶμα, Ambrosius 'carnem'; 'consubstantial': *Eran.* μιᾶς
φύσεως, Ambr. 'unius naturae'.

3 = Gelasius **37**; *Flor. Greg. Schol.* **68** (Syriac translation different); *ep.* (*101*) *ad
Cledonium* PG 37 col. 189 c.
4 = Gelasius **40**; contained in *Flor. Greg. Schol.* **85** (Syriac translation different);
PG 59 col. 79.
5 cp. PG 59 col. 80 above, but there John 2: 21 is not referred to.
6 has combined the contracted beginning of *Eranistes* II **34** col. 185 c (Ambrosius,
De incarnationis dominicae sacramento c. 6, 49 initium, PL 16 col. 851 A) with the
beginning of *Eran.* II **35** col. 188 A (Ambrosius, *ibid.* c. 6, 52 initium, col.
851 c). Even so, p. 77, 1 'The holy...human body' is not accounted for, and
the rest is translated very freely.

The holy scriptures say that God was in a human body, and our fathers who were at Nicaea have called not the body, but the Son, consubstantial with the Father.

The third chapter of Cyril: Whoever separates the one Christ
5 Our Lord into two hypostases after the union, whilst mingling them in the conjunction alone, which is with authority and command and power, and not rather by a collecting together of the natural union – let him be anathema.

⟨The orthodox⟩: The falsity of this is evident for the following
10 reasons: While it was right for him to say: 'Anyone who divides the one Lord Jesus Christ into prosopa', he said 'hypostases', lest he should openly say 'natures'. Now he boasts himself that he can expound also the kinds of unity which the scripture always passes over in silence, because of their being unutterable and beyond
15 understanding. Nor does he fear to call the union a collecting together of natures, which does not befit the natures, but miraculously has the creator performed it, in that it is beyond word or explanation. But we, what shall we say? Whoever divides our Lord into two prosopa, speaks of him who was begotten of the
20 Father before [134] the worlds as the one, and of him who was (born) of Mary as the other, and (does) not (say) 'One is the Son who is known in the two natures' – because of the unutterable unity, denies the truth. But the Egyptian, in his presumption of the confirmation of this chapter, anathematized first of all Athanasius,
25 and then Gregory of Nyssa. And when he had acted presumptuously towards those things which are incomprehensible, he instructed others in them.

The blessed Paul said, 'Remember Jesus Christ who rose from 2 Tim. 2: 8 the dead, of the seed of David.' But concerning him who was ever-
30 lastingly with the Father, who is before all, Gregory of Nyssa (has written): That God the Word dwelt in human nature, was known 7 openly by the wonders which he performed, and about this we do not dispute; but the 'how' is greater than thought, and we refuse to speak of it.

35 The fourth chapter of Cyril: Whoever distributes among two

2/3] 'body, but the Son, consubstantial': *Eran.* τὴν σάρκα, τὸν δὲ τοῦ θεοῦ λόγον, ἐκ μιᾶς...οὐσίας, Ambr. 'carnem, sed Dei verbum unius substantiae'.
9] 'The orthodox': edd. suppl., rubric missing.
31] 'dwelt': gr. γεγενῆσθαι.
33] 'thought': gr. κατὰ λογισμῶν ἔφοδον.

7 *Or. catechetica magna* c. 11, PG 45 col 44 B.

prosopa or among two hypostases the utterances made about Christ in the gospel or the apostle, or those things spoken about him by the saints, or by him about himself, and applies some of them to man who is deemed to be alone, apart from God the Word, but attributes others of them, as though they were utterances be- 5 fitting [135] the godhead, to the Word which is from God – let him be anathema.

The orthodox: We who are advocates of the truth say against them: Whoever takes the utterances made about our Lord in the gospel or the apostle as referring to two prosopa, and does not 10 believe rather that these are sometimes made concerning the one Son, because of the undivided union and sometimes concerning the two natures because of their 'non-commingling' with each other, so that by this he may know the distinction of the natures, and the union of the sonship, this man is rejecting the truth.   15

8   Of bishop Antiochus: It is not that in one place he is God, and in another place man, but that sometimes these (utterances) suit

Joh. 14: 11   God, while sometimes man, like that saying 'I am in my Father'. Is there perhaps a body in the Father? But he who from everlasting is of the Father, is also in the Father.   20

9   Of Amphilochius: In that you give the sufferings to the body and the miracles to God, very rightly have you confessed.

The fifth chapter of Cyril: Whoever dares to say of Christ that he is God-bearing man, and not rather that he is God in truth, as

Joh. 1: 14   an only son in nature, in that 'the Word became flesh', and shared 25 like us blood and flesh – let him by anathema.

10   [136] Of Basil: The sandal of the godhead is the God-bearing body, through which he came to men.

11   Of Eustathius: Remember Jesus Christ who rose from the dead,

2 Tim. 2: 8   of the seed of David, God-bearing man.   30

12   Of the same: Now when the angels saw that the God-bearing

22] 'very rightly have you confessed': *Eran.* ἀνάγκη καὶ μὴ θέλων δίδως.
28] 'body': *Eran.* and Basil σάρξ.

8 unidentified.
9 contained in *Eranistes* I **49** col. 100B, in Gelasius **27** (p. 100, 21 cum vero passiones – 22 necessario...dabis). The end of the quotation is altered, see first apparatus.
10 end of *Eranistes* I **37** col. 93B; *Hom. in Ps. 59*, PG 29 col. 468B.
11 cp. end of Gelasius **6** (Spanneut Nr. 42) and beginning of Gelasius **7** (Spanneut Nr. 43), evidently contracted.
12 unknown, could easily be the continuation of Gelasius **7**. Both **11** and **12** from *Ctr. Arianos*?

man adhered to the kingdom and was exalted into heaven, with
amazement and with fear were they extolling him, and together
they asked: 'Who is this king of honour?' Ps. 24: 10

The sixth chapter of Cyril: Whoever says that the Word God is
5 the God or Lord of Christ, and does not rather confess that he is
God and man simultaneously, in that 'the Word became flesh', as Joh. 1: 14
it is written, let him be anathema.

The orthodox: Now we say, whoever does not confess that that
form which took and which was taken is one and the same Son
10 known in two perfect natures, in that God the Word took our
nature, and not that he was changed into flesh, as this wise fool
teaches (about the saying) that 'He became flesh', is away from Joh. 1: 14
the truth. That there also he preaches impudently against the
fathers, is evident from those things which have been set down by him.

15 Of Athanasius: The ignorant do not distinguish by which **13**
prosopon prophecy through the Holy Spirit indicates [137]
the body of our Lord, and which is the everlasting prosopon of the
Father, but they suppose one and the same to be God the Word
(who is) impassible and the man, Jesus, (who is) passible. And he cf. Mk. 13:
20 who knows not the day of judgement, he is of Mary; but nothing 32 **13a**
is unknown to him who is of the Father, he who knows everything
before it comes to pass.

Of Ambrose to the emperor Gratian: let us preserve the trans- **14**
formation (*sic!*) of the body and the change (*sic!*) of the godhead,
25 for one Son of God speaks through these two, because there are two
natures in him. But even though the same one is speaking, he does
not speak in one way (only), for you see sometimes the glory of the
godhead, and at other times the sufferings of the man. As God, he
speaks divine (things), because he is the Word, and as man he
30 speaks human (things), because he speaks in our nature.

23/4] 'the transformation of the body and the change of the godhead' is a
wrong translation for διαίρεσιν θεότητος καὶ σαρκός (*Eranistes*).
27] 'speak in one': *Eran.*+πάντοτε ἀλλ' ἑτέρῳ. 'for you see': *Eran.* πρόσεχε
αὐτόν. 'glory of the godhead': *Eran.* δόξαν φθεγγόμενον.
28] 'of the man': *Eran.* ἀνθρώπινα.
30] 'human things': *Eran.* τὰ ταπεινά.
30] 'in our nature': τῇ ἐμῇ ὑποστάσει (Ambrosius: in mea substantia).

13 *Sermo maior de fide* Nr. 40. Some slight deviations from the Greek.
13a=*Flor. Greg. Schol.* **21** (Syriac translation different); *Sermo maior de fide*
Nr. 45. Slightly abbreviated.
14 contained in *Eranistes* II **33** col. 185 BC; *De fide* II 9, PL 16 col. 576 BC; *CSEL*
78, pp. 84, 32 – 85, 38.

15   Theophilus, from 'Against Origen': And the likeness of our nature was not changed by the participation with God into the godhead nor was his godhead transformed into the likeness of our nature, but since he who was from the beginning remained in his own (nature), through it he renewed our nature.   5

The seventh chapter of Cyril: Whoever says that Jesus was diligently made as a man by God the Word, [138] and (that he) put on the glory of the only begotten, as though he was another, apart from him – let him be anathema.

16   Of Athanasius: Just as a great king who enters a great city and 10 abides in one of the houses of the city, by which cause it is counted worthy of much honour, and no one, robbers or enemies, has power over it, because it is counted worthy of much care, because of the honour of that king, so did it happen even to our body, that when our king and our creator came to our land, and dwelt in the 15 nature of our body, forthwith the guile of the devil was powerless against us. For, acting within his own power, our creator formed a body within the womb of the virgin, and formed it as a temple in which he might dwell, so that he might become known through it.

17   Of Joannes from the commentary on Ephesians: From the will 20

1–5] *Eran.* Οὔτε τῆς ἡμετέρας ὁμοιώσεως, πρὸς ἣν κεκοινώνηκεν, εἰς θεότητος φύσιν μεταβαλλομένης, οὔτε τῆς θεότητος αὐτοῦ τρεπομένης εἰς τὴν ἡμετέραν ὁμοίωσιν. Μένει γὰρ ὃ ἦν ἀπ' ἀρχῆς θεός· μένει καὶ τὴν ἡμῶν ἐν ἑαυτῷ παρασκευάζων ὕπαρξιν.

11] 'of the city': gr. ἐν αὐτῇ.

12] 'robbers or enemies': gr. sing.

12/13] 'has power over it': gr. ἐπιβαίνων καταστρέφει.

14] 'the honour of that': gr. τὸν εἰς μίαν αὐτῆς οἰκίαν οἰκήσαντα; 'to our body': gr. ἐπὶ τοῦ πάντων βασιλέως.

15] 'our king and our creator': gr. αὐτοῦ.

15/16] 'in the nature of our body': gr. εἰς ἓν τῶν ὁμοίων σῶμα.

16 'forthwith' – 19] the Syriac first compresses the Greek and is then deviating completely from it.

20 – p. 81, 1] 'will which was his, by which he was fore-ordained': *Eran.* εὐδοκίαν αὐτοῦ, φησὶν, ἣν προέθετο ἐν αὐτῷ, τουτέστιν.

15 = *Eranistes* II **57** col. 197 A. The translation into Syriac is very free and alters the sense in one place; see the first apparatus.

16 *De incarn.* 9, PG 25 col. 112 BC. At the end completely different from the Greek. Our Syriac translation does not follow that of *De incarnatione* in Vat. syr. 104; see Thomson's edition of the latter, *CSCO* **257** p. 12, 10–21 textus (**258** p. 9, 19–30 versio).

17 abbreviation of *Eranistes* II **67** col. 201 B, the difference is at the end; *ad. Eph.*, PG 62 col. 15 lines 12 ff.

which was his, by which he fore-ordained, he was in pains and
longing to speak with us (of) this mystery, (namely) that he would
cause the man to sit above every name.

Of Eustathius: 'Jesus a man who has appeared from God', say
5 the apostles; but God wrought the miracles through him.

The eighth chapter of Cyril: Whoever dares to say that it is right
that the man who was taken should be worshipped with God the
Word, and together with him [139] should be glorified, and
together with him should be considered as God, as if he was one
10 in another – for when there is added this 'together with' it always
gives us to understand this – and does not rather (say that) it is
right in one worship to honour the Emmanuel and let ascend to him
one glory, because 'the Word became flesh', let him be anathema.

Athanasius, from 'Concerning the soul': God the Word wholly
15 clothed himself with the man, and made him in everything a
participant in the honour of his nature, and he constituted the
mediator of the two natures.

The testimony of the blessed Flavian: From that 'The Spirit of
the Lord is upon me', (one concludes that there) is an anointing
20 together with (the fact) that he was anointed. If the body is sharing
the same throne of the honour of him who clothed himself with it,
how much more is the Holy Spirit consubstantial with God the
Word!

The ninth chapter of Cyril: Whoever says concerning our Lord
25 Jesus that he has been glorified by the Spirit, as though he had
made use of a strange power in the power of the Spirit, and that
from him received power against the unclean spirits, and so as to
do signs among men, and does not rather say that the Spirit is his
in a singular manner, through whom he wrought acts of power –
30 let him be anathema.

Marginal references:
cf. Eph. 1:9
cf. Eph. 1: 20f. cf. Phil. 2: 9
18
Ac. 2: 22

Joh. 1: 14
19

20
Lk. 4: 18
(Is. 61: 1)

1/2] 'he was in pains and longing': *Eran.* ὅ ἐπεθύμει, τοῦτο ὤδινεν, ὡς ἄν τις
εἴποι.
2] 'this mystery': *Eran.* τὸ μυστήριον. Ποῖον δὲ τοῦτο;
3] 'every name': *Eran.* ὃ δὴ καὶ γέγονεν.
20/1] 'sharing the same throne' renders ܒܪ ܟܘܪܣܝܐ which is certainly
ὁμόθρονος.

18 partly unknown, contains *Flor. Greg. Schol.* **32** (Syriac translation different).
19 = *Flor. Greg. Schol.* **30** (Syriac translation different), there attributed to
Eustathius of Antioch who is indeed the author of a *De anima*; but in *Flor.
Greg. Schol.* the fragment appears as belonging to the *Commentary on Prov.
8: 22.*
20 unknown.

Ac. 10: 38   Of Peter: 'This Jesus of Nazareth whom [140] God anointed with the Holy Spirit and with power' – now so also have all the doctors of the church taught.

cf. Ac. 10: 38   **21**   Of Flavian: For there has come to you he who was anointed with the Holy Spirit. Now, not anointed is the nature of the Spirit, 5 but the consubstantial one with us.

cf. Rom. 1: 3, 4   **22**   Of Athanasius: Jesus who has been set down as of the seed of David, is Son of God through the Holy Spirit, by the resurrection
cf. 1 Cor. 15: 28   from the dead, which Paul has said, namely that he is the Son who is about to be obedient to the Father. 10

Heb. 3: 1   The tenth chapter of Cyril: The high priest and apostle of our
Eph. 5: 2   faith, Jesus Christ, says divine scripture, and (he) who offered himself for us, a sweet-smelling savour to God the Father. And whoever says therefore that our high priest and our apostle was not the same Word at the time when he became flesh and man in our 15 likeness, but another man who was of a woman, manifestly apart from him: or whoever says that he made an offering on behalf of himself, and not rather on behalf of us, for he who knew no sin was not in need of an offering – let him be anathema.

23   Of Arius, who also calls God the Word high priest: 20

cf. Heb. 9: 11 ff.   The orthodox says: As one who is God and man, Jesus Christ is known in his manhood to be high priest, and [141] he offered sacrifice on our behalf, as man; it was not that he was in need of the cleansing of this sacrifice, for sin and iniquity were not found in his mouth, but the same one received it (*sc.* the sacrifice) 25 with the Father, as God, just as the doctors of the faith have proclaimed.

5] 'Holy' deest in *Eran.*; 'anointed is': *Eran.* πνεύματι δὲ χρίεται; 'of the Spirit': *Eran.* ἀθέατος – however ܠܪܘܚܐ is one of the words put into brackets with a query by the scribe of C, because it was not quite distinct; but since the scribe's errors in guessing are very scarce, the possibility of a fault in the translation remains.

6] 'consubstantial': *Eran.* ὁμογενές.

11] 'high priest and apostle': Syr. vg. *vice versa*.

12/13] 'and (he) who offered himself for us, a sweet-smelling savour to God the Father': Syr. vg. 'and he delivered himself up for us, an offering and a sacrifice to God', gr. καὶ παρέδωκεν ἑαυτὸν ὑπὲρ ἡμῶν προσφορὰν καὶ θυσίαν τῷ θεῷ εἰς ὀσμὴν εὐωδίας.

21 = second half of *Eranistes* I **48** col. 100A; from the same homily as **20**.

22 *Sermo maior de fide* Nr. 42.

23 The text of Arius is lost, no lacuna indicating the loss.

Of Athanasius: When Paul said '...by the apostle and high   Heb. 3: 1
priest of our faith, Jesus, who was faithful to him who made him',   **24**
(he did) not (mean) that he is created who was from the beginning,
for the godhead is not visible, but that that man whom Paul calls
5 the mediator between God and men, gave himself as a ransom   1 Tim. 2: 5
for us.

The eleventh chapter of Cyril: Whoever does not confess that
the body of our Lord is life-giving and belongs singly to the Word
which is from the Father, but as though it was of another man who
10 cleaves to him in honour, or that the indwelling of God only was
in him, and not rather that it was life-giving, as we have said, in
that it belongs singly to the Word who is able to give life to all –
let him be anathema.

This crafty one has openly anathematized not only the blessed
15 Paul, who said 'in whom was pleased to dwell all the fullness of   cf. Col. 1:
the godhead, bodily', but also our saviour himself who before all   19+2: 9
declared his temple [142] to be his body – 'Now he spoke of the   Joh. 2: 21
temple of his body.'

Of Gregory of Nazianzus, from the second treatise (addressed)
20 to Cyril: And concerning the manhood, in a corrupt mind they   **25**
understand that (utterance) 'He was made man' – not that he
was in man, and made him a temple, but they say that he became
and lived like men.

Of Athanasius: The coming of God to the body did not allow   **26**
25 it to become corrupted according to nature, but the dwelling in it
did not permit it to see corruption.   cf. Ac. 2: 31

4] 'that man': gr. and *Flor. Greg. Schol.* 'that lordly man'.
24] 'The coming' in the nominative case, gr. τῇ...ἐπιβάσει; 'of God' gr. τοῦ
λόγου; 'the body' gr. τὸ σῶμα.
24/5] 'allow it to become corrupted': gr. ἐφθείρετο τὸ σῶμα.
25] 'according to nature' ܐ‎ܒ‎ܟ‎ܝ‎ܢ‎ܐ: gr. κατὰ τὴν ἰδίαν φύσιν; 'the dwelling in
it': gr. τὸν ἐνοικοῦντα τοῦ θεοῦ λόγον.
26] 'did not permit it to see': gr. ἐκτὸς ἐγίνετο.

24 = *Flor. Greg. Schol.* **15** (Syriac translation different); = *Sermo maior de fide*
No. 63, 1–9. Both **24** and *Flor. Greg. Schol.* **15** abbreviate the Ps. Athanasian text,
but in different ways. In the first apparatus above, an important variant
reading only is noted.
25 not found.
26 end of *Eranistes* III **33** col. 296 B; = *Sermo maior de fide* No. 9; *De incarn.* 20, 4,
PG 25 col. 132 B. The Syriac translation does not follow that of Vat. syr. 104,
see Thomson's edition of the latter, *CSCO* **257** p. 27, 2–5 textus (**258** p. 20, 4–6
versio).

The twelfth chapter of Cyril: Whoever does not confess that God the Word suffered in the flesh and was crucified in the flesh, and tasted death in the flesh, and became the first begotten of the dead because he is alive and gives life – let him be anathema. 5

The orthodox: Now who is this laying down a new law? He says in this chapter: Whoever does not confess that God the Word suffered in the flesh, and was crucified in the flesh. – What prophet or what apostle taught him to confess these things that he should support these things about God, because not even concerning our 10 soul is there anyone who would say that it dies. Who of the evangelists has calumniated the life-giving nature by suffering and death? Or who of the preachers of the church has preached that God suffered in the flesh? For if it is right for [143] Christ to be believed in those (things) which he teaches about himself, he 15 teaches us who it is in whom he suffers, and who it is in whom he prevails over all. For to the Jews who requested a sign, he said:

Joh. 2: 19 'Destroy this temple, and in three days, etc.' Now that he has named our beginning a temple, even though this new teacher does not wish (it), the testimony of John suffices (to show), which said, 20

Joh. 2: 21 Now he spoke of the temple of his body. But he does not proclaim according to this presumption that the Word through flesh tasted death, but that the body which was from the Jews, was dissolved

Joh. 1: 1 through the power of God in which he rose. And again: 'In the beginning was the Word, etc.', and this he said concerning the 25 only begotten only. And when he came to the words of the crucifixion, the exalted (things) concerning God he left aside, and

Joh. 19: 30 was speaking those things which befit the dispensation: 'When Jesus received the vinegar, he said, Behold, it is finished, and he

Mt. 27: 50 bowed his head, and gave up his spirit.' And Matthew: 'Jesus 30

Lk. 23: 46 cried, and gave up his spirit.' And Luke: 'Jesus cried with a loud voice and said: My Father, in your hands I place my spirit.' And

Mk. 15: 37 Mark: 'He let loose a loud cry and delivered up his spirit.' And the

Mt. 28: 5, 6 angel to the women: 'Fear not, for I know that you seek Jesus who was crucified. He is not here, he is risen, [144] as he said.' Is there 35 from these things which he proclaimed (evidence) anywhere that

18] 'Destroy': see above, I p. 8, 5; cp. II p. 44, 31; VII p. 92, 18.
33] 'He let loose a loud cry and delivered up his spirit' ܟܪܘܡ ܐܠܗ ܘܩܥܐ: Syr. vg. ܟܪܘ ܘܠܥܐ, Philox. ܐܦܗ ܗ ܠܩܗܥܐ ܘܩܪܐ ܠܒܘܡ, gr. ἀφεὶς φωνὴν μεγάλην ἐξέπνευσε. Our text and Philox. are two independent forms of translating the Greek more literally than Syr. vg.

the Word suffered in the flesh? But it is just the opposite. For Peter
and Paul say: 'Christ suffered on our behalf', and 'Christ died',   1 Pet. 2: 21
and 'the God of our fathers raised up Jesus', 'Christ died for our   cf. Rom. 5 : 6
sins.' And the rest of the arguments written down above from the   Ac. 5 : 30
5 evangelists and the rest of the apostles – nothing of the sufferings   1 Cor. 15 : 3
have they imputed to God the Word.

Now we will collect together the testimonies of our fathers, that
by them, on behalf of our Lord, we may refute those who teach in
opposition to him.

10   The testimony of the blessed Clement, third bishop of Rome,   cf. Phil. 4: 3
whom the apostle mentions: Because of the love of our Lord   **27**
Christ for us, his blood he gave for us by the will of God, and his
body for our bodies, and his soul for our souls. As it is (a matter of   **27a**
fact) that he in truth should be tempted, so also is it reasonable   cf. Heb. 4:
15 that he should be glorified. He who was suffering in the flesh, was   15
without suffering in the spirit, that through the flesh might be
seen the sickness of man, but that through strength God might be
known.

Of Eustathius: If 'in Christ dwells all the fullness of the god-   Col. 2 : 9
20 head', there is one who dwells, and another who is inhabited, [145]   **28**
and it is not right that we should attribute suffering and death to
the divine nature, but these suit him who was taken.

Of the same: The life cannot die, but rather brings to life the   **29**
dead. Now a well of life from God was that man who died and rose
25 and intercedes for us, he whom God the Word took for the sake of
our race.

Of Basil: 'God made this Jesus both Lord and Christ.' This   Ac. 2 : 36
    30

2] 'and "Christ died"': is this perhaps a gloss by somebody who had the
Syr. vg. form of 1 Pet. 2. 21 in mind? Syr. vg. 'also Christ died on our behalf'.
24] 'from God': gr. ἐκ πατρὸς θεότητι; 'and': gr. μᾶλλον δὲ καί.
24] 'rose': gr.+ἐκ νεκρῶν. 25] 'us': gr.+ὁ ἐκ παρθένου Μαρίας; 'God the
Word': gr. ἡ τοῦ λόγου θεότης.
25/6] 'for the sake of our race': gr. δι' ἡμᾶς.

27 I Clement 49, 6.
27a not found.
28 unknown. Cp. Spanneut Nr. 41, 47 (Gelasius **5**, **45**).
29 abbreviates *Eranistes* III **29** col. 293A; not Eustathius is quoted, but Ps.
Athanasius, *Sermo maior de fide* Nr. 2 (3), 2–6.
30 second half of Gelasius **21** (p. 99, 14 dominum...); end of *Eranistes* III **39**
col. 297B; in both cases the biblical quotation is longer than ours; **30** contains
Flor. Greg. Schol. **33** (Syriac translation different); *Adv. Eunomium* II, PG 29
col. 577A.

saying which as with a finger indicates the visible man in the sight of all men he used openly.

31   Of Gregory of Nyssa: And which form was beaten at the time of suffering, and which form aforetime was glorified, is therefore manifest even if we do not interpret them.   5

cf. Heb. 10:   Of Cyril, bishop of Jerusalem: And because the veil of his body
20   **32**   suffered dishonour, the veil of the type of his body was rent.
Mt. 27: 51
    33   Of Amphilochius, bishop of Iconium, from the commentary on the gospel: Do not join sufferings to the non-suffering. For he is God and man, O heretic; the miracles (are) God's, the sufferings   10 man's.

34   Of Damasus, bishop of Rome: Whoever says that in the suffering of the cross, the Son of God, God, endured suffering, and not the body together with the soul – he who put on that which is [146] the form of a servant which he took – let him be anathema.   15

1] 'which as with a finger indicates': gr. δεικτικῇ; 'the visible man': gr. (μονονουχὶ Basil) πρὸς τὸ ἀντρώπινον καὶ ὁρώμενον.

1/2] 'in the sight of all men he used openly': gr. πᾶσι προδήλως ἀπερειδόμενος.

3] 'And' deest in gr.; 'at the time': gr. ἐπί.

5] 'them': gr. τῷ λόγῳ.

9] 'sufferings': gr. + τῆς σαρκός; 'non-suffering': gr. + λόγῳ.

9] 'he is': gr. εἰμι.

10/11] 'the miracles...man's': gr. θεὸς, ὡς ἐγγυᾶται τὰ θαύματα, ἄνθρωπος ὡς μαρτυρεῖ τὰ παθήματα.

12] 'Whoever': gr. Εἴ τις.

13] 'Of God, God': Eran. τοῦ θεοῦ καὶ θεός, Damasus 'Dei Deus'; 'suffering'²: gr. πόνον.

14/15] 'he who put on that which is the form of a servant which he took': Eran. ἣν ἐνεδύσατο ἡ τοῦ δούλου μορφή, ἣν ἑαυτῷ ἔλαβε, Damasus 'qua induerat formam servi, quam sibi acceperat'.

31 overlaps with the end of Gelasius **24** (p. 99, 35 quae forma...); =end of *Eranistes* III **48** col. 301 A; *Adv. Eunomium, vulgo lib.* v, PG 45 col. 705 C, *lib.* III 3, 66 ed. Jaeger (ed. secunda 1960, vol. 2 p. 131, 6–8).
32 not found.
33 beginning of Gelasius **28** (– p. 100, 30 testantur passiones); beginning of *Eranistes* III **52** col. 304A. In Holl's edition of the whole sermon (K. Holl. *Amphilochius von Ikonium in seinem Verhaeltnis zu den grossen Kappadoziern*, Tuebingen and Leipzig 1904, pp. 91–102), pp. 100, 32 – 101, 1. **33** abbreviates the text.
34 nearly= Gelasius **56**; = *Eranistes* III **36** col. 296D; *Flor. of 612* **15** gives the text in abbreviated form (Syriac translation different); *ep. 4 ad Paulinum*, anathema 14, PL 13 col. 362A. **34** omits the last clause before the anathema.

Of Ambrose: The body suffered, the Word was free from   **35**
sufferings. And if the soul does not die, how then its creator!

Of Flavian: For the Word was without suffering, but he whom   **36**
God the Word put on suffered.

5 Of Gelasius, bishop of Caesarea in Palestine: He who was of   **37**
Mary endured sufferings, but no one can inflict sufferings on him
who was begotten of the Father before the ages.

Of Epiphanius, bishop of Byzantium: They slew the man of our   **38**
Lord, but not the Word.

10 Of John: Ask the heretic: Does God fear, does he suffer? And if   **39**
he answers: Yes, count him as Satan.

Of Severianus, bishop of Gabala, from the treatise on the Seals: **40**
The Jews strove with him who was seen without perceiving him
who was not seen. They crucified the body without slaying the
15 godhead.

Of the same: God delivered up his Son for the deliverance of all.   **41**
The lamb, but not the godhead, was sacrificed. Even though the cf. Rom.
body suffered, the shame was counted as God's, like a man who 8: 32
dishonours the purple of a king.

1] 'body': *Eran.* σάρξ = Ambrosius; 'Word': *Eran.* θεότης = Ambrosius.

2] 'sufferings': *Eran.* θανάτου = Ambrosius; 'does not die': *Eran.* ἀποκτανθῆ-
ναι οὐ δύναται = Ambrosius; 'its creator': *Eran.* ἡ θεότης θανάτῳ ὑποπεσεῖν
δύναται, Ambrosius 'divinitas potest'. 'its creator' ܣܘܪܝܐ is one of the words
marked by the scribe as difficult to read.

6] 'Mary': gr. + τεχθὲν...σῶμα; 'sufferings': gr. πάντα ταῦτα.

8] 'Byzantium' *sic*! Obviously 'Konstantia' (Salamis) has been mistaken by
some Syriac writer for 'Konstantinou' (*sc.* polis) and the other name of this
city has been given instead. The patriarch Epiphanius of Constantinople
(PG 86 1) is too late for inclusion in our florilegium.

12] 'Severianus': ms. 'Severus'.

14] 'the body': gr. τὴν σάρκα.

---

35 two sentences (the first and the third) of *Eranistes* III **38** col. 297 A; *De fide* II
7, PL 16 col. 571 B. *CSEL* **78** p. 76, 36. 37 f.
36 unknown.
37 contained in *Eranistes* III **59** col. 305 AB.
38 unidentified.
39 contained in *Eranistes* III **63** col. 305 D–308 A, here abbreviated; in Chrysostom not yet identified.
40 = first half of *Eranistes* III **65** col. 308 C; PG 63 col. 543–4.
41 unidentified.

Our faith:

We believe and confess one eternal nature known in three equal hypostases, of the Father, the Son, and the Holy Spirit, infinite and [147] unchangeable. The son of God, God the Word, because of his great love for us, took from our race a complete man, and 5 united him with him (in) an incomprehensible union, and beyond speech and explanation, from the beginning of his being formed in cf. Mt. 2: 1 the virginal womb of the blessed saint Mary, ever-virgin. And he cf. Lk. 2: 52 was born and continued to grow, and progressed in stature and in Lk. 4: 2 wisdom, and hungered and was thirsty and weary, and feared, and 10 Mt. 25: 35 raised the dead, and cleansed the lepers, and opened (the eyes of) Joh. 4: 6 the blind, and suffered, and died, the same one Lord Christ, Heb. 5: 7 yesterday, today, and for ever, perfect God and perfect man, Mt. 11: 5 passible and impassible, mortal and immortal. Now when the Joh. 11: 37 Jews overthrew the temple of his body, he in three days raised it 15 Heb. 2: 18, up, as he said, and affirmed to his disciples concerning the resur- 5: 8 rection of his body, and he is on the right hand of God and makes Rom. 5: 6 supplication on our behalf, and he is about to come at the last Heb. 13: 8 time, to judge the dead and the living. 'Pursue peace and holiness cf. Joh. 2: 21 with all men, without which no man can see our Lord', who in his 20 Rom. 8: 34 grace and mercy will bring us to that faith which is a revelation of cf. 1 Pet. those (things) which are invisible.
4: 5
Heb. 12: 14
cf. Heb.
11: 1

VIIa [150] Again, the creed of the bishops of Persia which Kosroes requested from them. 25

The faith which was composed by the bishops of the land of the Persians together with the doctors and the brethren of the ⟨bishop's palace⟩ who were with them in the royal court, against the Severians, and all the theopaschites, when they were required to show the truth of their faith in a reply to the Severians; which they 30 brought forward boldly and courageously without fear before Kosroes, son of Hormizd, king of Persia; on account of this (faith) the holy Mar Giwargis, confessor, presbyter, hermit and martyr, was crucified, and he sealed it (*sc.* his faith) with his blood; together with other symbols (of belief): 35

We believe in one divine nature, everlasting, without beginning, living and quickening all, powerful, creating all powers, wise,

22] pp. 148 and 149 (text) are empty.
27/8] 'bishop's palace': edd. conj.

26–35] cp. lemma in *Syn. Or.* p. 580, Braun p. 307.
36 – p. 93, 10] French translation *Syn. Or.* pp. 582–4, German Braun pp. 309–14, 2.

imparting all wisdom, simple spirit, infinite, incomprehensible, not compounded and without parts, incorporeal, both invisible and immutable, impassible and immortal; nor is it possible, whether by itself, or by another, or with another, that suffering
5 or change should enter in unto it; but it is perfect in its essence and in everything which belongs to it, nor [151] is it possible for it to receive any addition or subtraction, it being by itself substance, and God over all; he who is known and confessed in three holy hypostases, equal in nature and equal in glory, Father, Son and
10 Holy Spirit, the nature threefold (in) hypostases essentially, and the hypostases singular (in) nature everlastingly without (their possessing) any distinction between themselves, with the exception of the diverse properties of their hypostases, fatherhood, sonship and procession (*sc.* of the Holy Spirit); but for the rest, in every way
15 that the nature in common is confessed, in the same way also each one of the hypostases, singly, is confessed without diminution; and because the Father is impassible and unchangeable, so also is the Son and the Spirit confessed with him (to be) as he is without suffering and change, and just as the Father is believed to be
20 infinite and without parts, so also is confessed Son and Spirit to be without limits and composition; three hypostases, perfect in every-thing, in one godhead, one power which cannot be weakened, one knowledge which cannot be turned aside, one will which cannot be bent, one authority which cannot be annulled; it is he who
25 created the worlds in his goodness, and rules all by the indication [152] of his will. He who since the beginning has instructed in a concise manner the human race in accordance with the extent of the infantine state of its knowledge with knowledge concerning his godhead, and in intervening times by diverse visions and various
30 likenesses revealed himself to the saints (and) by various laws

1] 'wisdom': *Syn. Or.* plur.
2] 'both': *Syn. Or.* om.
3] 'and'¹: *Syn. Or.* om.
5] 'or': *Syn. Or.* 'and'.
9] 'equal...glory': *Syn. Or.* om.
11] 'everlastingly': *Syn. Or.* 'everlasting'.
17] 'is'²: *Syn. Or.* 'are'.
20] 'is': *Syn. Or.* 'are'.
22] 'one'²: *Syn. Or.* 'in one'.
25] 'worlds': *Syn. Or.* sing.
25] 'all': *Syn. Or.* 'it'.
28] 'infantine state of its': *Syn. Or.* 'greatness of his'.

corrected and instructed mankind as an increase of their know-
cf. Heb. 1: 2 ledge; and to whose incomprehensible wisdom in the last times it
seemed good to reveal and declare to rational beings the wondrous
mystery of his glorious Trinity; and in order that he might raise
our nature to honour, and that he might sow in us the true hope of 5
the resurrection from the dead, and the new and incorruptible life
which for ever receives no change, according to his foreknowledge
and his will from everlasting; on this account, for us men, and for
our salvation, the Son of God, God the Word, without departing
cf. Joh. 1: 10 from being with him who begat him, came into the world while he 10
was in the world, and the world came into being through him.
And because created natures were not able to behold the glorious
nature of his godhead, in an extraordinary manner out of the
nature of the house of Adam did he fashion for him a holy temple,
a perfect man, from the blessed virgin Mary, who [153] was made 15
perfect in the natural order without (there being) the participation
of a husband; and he put him on and united him with himself,
and in him he revealed himself to the world and spoke with men,
according to the utterance of the holy angel to the mother of our
Lk. 1: 35 saviour: 'The Holy Spirit shall come, and the power of the most 20
high shall overshadow you; for this reason, he that is born of you
is a holy one, and shall be called Son of God.' By the fact of his
saying 'He shall be called Son of God', he has taught us concerning the wondrous conjunction of the union, without separation, which from the commencement of his being formed, existed 25
between the human nature that was taken, and God the Word
who took it, so that henceforth we know as one prosopon our Lord,
Jesus Christ, the Son of God; who is born before the worlds, without beginning, of the Father in the nature of his godhead, and
cf. Heb. 1: 2 born, in the last times, of the holy virgin, the son of David, in the 30
nature of his manhood, as God had earlier promised to the blessed
Ps. 132: 11 David: 'Of the fruit of your womb shall I set upon your throne.'
cf. Ac. 2: 30 And after the issue of these things, the blessed Paul expounded the

1] 'as': *Syn. Or.* + 'for'.
3/4] 'wondrous mystery': *Syn. Or.* plur.
5] 'us': *Syn. Or.* 'it'; 'hope': *Syn. Or.* 'seed'.
9] 'God'[2]: *Syn. Or.* om.
18] 'and spoke with men': *Syn. Or.* om.
20] 'shall come' ‏ܐܬܐ‎: Syr. vg. ‏ܬܐܬܐ‎.
21] 'of you' ‏ܡܢܟܝ‎; the mss. evidence of Syr. vg. is divided between
‏ܡܢܟܝ‎ and ‏ܡܢܟ‎; the difference recurs in the printed editions.
22/3] 'By the fact...Son of God'] *Syn. Or.* om. (homoioteleuton).
24] 'of': *Syn. Or.* 'and'.

promise, saying to the Jews concerning David: 'From the seed of Ac. 13: 23
this man, God has raised up, as he promised, Jesus, (to be) saviour.'
And again, to the Philippians, [154] he wrote thus: 'Think within cf. Phil. 2:
yourselves that which also Jesus Christ (thought) who, though he 5-7
5 was in the form of God, assumed the form of a servant.' For whom
else would he be calling 'the form of God' but Christ in his godhead, and whom else again would he be naming 'the form of a
servant' but Christ in his manhood? And the former, he said, took,
while the latter was taken. Therefore it is not possible to confuse
10 the properties of the natures, for it is impossible that he who took
should be he who was taken or that he who was taken should be
the taker. For that God the Word should be revealed in the man
whom he took, and (that) the human nature which was taken
should appear to creation in the order of him who took it and (that)
15 at the same time in his undivided union should be confessed the
one Son of God, Christ, this we have learned and do maintain.
But that the godhead should be changed into the manhood, and
that the manhood should be transmuted into the nature of the
godhead is impossible. For the (divine) substance cannot fall under
20 the necessity of change and suffering, because if the godhead under-
went change, there would no longer be a revelation but a corruption of godhead, and if again the manhood departed from its
nature, there would no longer be salvation, but an extinction of
the manhood. And for this reason we believe in our hearts [155] cf. Rom.
25 and confess with our lips one Lord Jesus Christ, Son of the living 10: 9
God, whose godhead is not hidden, nor his manhood concealed,
but he is perfect God and perfect man. But when we call Christ
perfect God we do not name the Trinity, but one of the hypostases
of the Trinity, (namely) God the Word. And when again we give
30 the appellation of man to Christ, we are not naming all men, but
that one hypostasis which was manifestly taken for our salvation
into the union with God the Word. For this reason our Lord Jesus

2] 'raised up': Syr. vg. + 'for Israel'.
6] 'in': *Syn. Or.* + 'the nature of'.
13] 'whom he took': *Syn. Or.* 'with whom he clothed himself'; 'the human':
Syn. Or. 'his human'; 'which was taken': *Syn. Or.* om.
14] 'him who took it': *Syn. Or.* 'his manhood'.
15] 'at the same time': *Syn. Or.* om. 'his' *Syn. Or.* 'the'; 'confessed': *Syn. Or.* om.
16] 'this': *Syn. Or.* 'as'.
17] 'and' *Syn. Or.* 'or'.
25] 'the living': *Syn. Or.* om.
30] 'of': *Syn. Or.* + 'complete'.
32] 'God': *Syn. Or.* om.

Christ, who was born in his godhead of his Father everlastingly, is (also) he who, in the last times, was born for us of the virgin in his manhood. And while he remained in his godhead without deficiency and change, in his manhood after his birth, he was also circumcised and grew, in accordance with the witness of the blessed evangelist: 'Jesus grew in stature and in wisdom, and in favour with God and men.' And he observed the law, and was baptized in Jordan by John, and then he began to preach [156] the new covenant. Whilst by the power of his godhead, he was working wonders, the cleansing of lepers, the giving of sight to the blind, the banishment of demons, the raising of the dead, yet in the nature of his manhood, he hungered, and thirsted, and ate, and drank, and was wearied, and slept; and last of all, for our sakes he delivered himself to death, and was crucified and suffered and died without his godhead (either) departing from him, or suffering. And his body was wrapped in a linen cloth, and he was placed in a tomb, and after three days he rose by the power of his godhead, as he had foretold to the Jews: 'Destroy this temple and in three days I will raise it up.' And the evangelist has expounded this utterance, saying: 'For he was speaking of the temple of his body.' And after he arose, he lived on earth with his disciples for forty days, and showed them his hands and his feet, saying: 'Touch me and know that a spirit has not flesh and bones as you have seen that I have', so that by word and by deeds he might assure them of his resurrection, and that by the assurance of his resurrection, he might confirm in us the hope of our resurrection. And after forty days, he ascended into heaven, in the sight of his disciples as they watched him, [157] and a cloud received him, and he was hidden from their eyes according to the testimony of scripture. And we confess that he will come from heaven with the power and glory of his angels in order to effect the resurrection of the whole race of men, and judgement and examination of all rational beings, as the angels said to the apostles at the time of his ascension:

Margin references:
cf. Heb. 1: 2
Lk. 2: 52
Joh. 2: 19
Joh. 2: 21
Lk. 24: 39
cf. Ac. 1: 3, 9f.

Line numbers: 5, 10, 15, 20, 25, 30

2] 'of the': *Syn. Or.* + 'holy'.
3/4] 'deficiency': *Syn. Or.* + 'and suffering'.
5/6] 'blessed evangelist': *Syn. Or.* 'evangelist Luke'.
9] 'Whilst': *Syn. Or.* 'And whilst'.
12] 'hungered and thirsted': *Syn. Or.* 'thirsted, hungered'.
14] 'to death': *Syn. Or.* om.
18] 'Destroy': see above, I p. 8, 5; cp. II p. 44, 31; VI p. 84, 18.
19] 'I will raise it up': see above I p. 8, 5 f.; cp. II 44, 32.
20] 'utterance': *Syn. Or.* om.; 'For he': *Syn. Or.* 'But he'.
22] 'and showed': *Syn. Or.* 'showing'.

'This Jesus who has been taken up from you into heaven shall so   Ac. 1: 11
come as you have seen him ascend into heaven.' And by this they
have manifestly taught us that even when he was taken up into
heaven, the hypostasis of the manhood was not annulled or
5 changed but is preserved in indivisible union with the godhead in
that exalted glory in which he will be seen in his final revelation
from heaven for the shame of those who crucified him and for the
joy and pride of those who believe in him, to whom, with his
Father and the Holy Spirit be glory and honour for ever and ever,
10 Amen.

Controversial chapters which the fathers drew up and affixed to   VIIb
the creed.
   Against those who ⟨confess Christ⟩ as one nature and one hypo-
15 stasis.
   Christ, the Son of God – is he God in nature and hypostasis, and
man in nature and hypostasis, or not? If he is, see (there are) two
natures and two hypostases without argument; and if (he is) not,
which [158] of them is without nature and without hypostasis?
20 But if, while both are preserved in their natures and in their
hypostases, one nature or one hypostasis has arisen from them, let
them tell us – this one nature and one hypostasis, has it consubstantial (beings) or not? If it has, let them show (us) which is
the other hypostasis which is constituted of the godhead and the
25 manhood; and if not, it is alone in its kind, and is not consubstantial with God or with us. Every nature which exists has a

3] 'when': *Syn. Or.* 'this (*sc.* saying)'.
4] 'of the': *Syn. Or.* 'of his'. 'not...or': *Syn. Or.* 'neither...nor'.
5] 'with the'. *Syn. Or.* 'with his'.
9/10] 'for...Amen': *Syn. Or.* 'for ever'.
14] 'confess Christ': *Syn. Or.*
18] 'without': *Syn. Or.*+'doubt and without'.
21/2] 'let them...hypostasis': *Syn. Or.* om. (homoioteleuton).
26 'Every nature' – p. 94, 2 'property'] is not in *Syn. Or.* p. 587, evidently lost
in the course of the erroneous transposition of the original ch. I to the end of this
series.
26] 'has': p. 66, 3 'acquires or has'.

14/15] French translation *Syn. Or.* p. 586, 4 f. For Chabot's rather confusing
translation of ܩܢܘܡܐ with 'personne' see *ibid.* n. 2; Braun, too, says 'Person'
for ܩܢܘܡܐ; German transl. Braun p. 315 below.
16–26] 'with us': French *Syn. Or.* p. 587, 8–15 (VIII + IX); German Braun
p. 317 (No. 8+9); = IVb, above, p. 67, 17–27.
26 – p. 95, 12] = IVa, above, p. 66, 3–67, 15.

distinct definition and a singular property. If you confess Christ as one nature, what is its definition, and what is its property?

This one nature and one hypostasis which you confess in Christ, is it consubstantial with God the Father, or consubstantial with the blessed Mary? If it is consubstantial with the Father, it is simple and infinite spirit, and nothing was taken from Mary. And if he is consubstantial with Mary, he is an ordinary man. But if he is consubstantial with the Father and consubstantial with Mary, as the Father and Mary are two natures, so also Christ is two natures.

If you confess Christ as one nature and one hypostasis from the godhead and the manhood, of necessity godhead and manhood are parts of this nature and hypostasis. [159] And because the whole exceeds its parts, and the parts are less than the whole, therefore this nature exceeds each one of its parts, and the godhead is less in its being a part than that nature of which it is a part, which is impossible, (namely) that anything could be greater than godhead.

If the nature or the hypostasis, brought together and compounded, is other than the nature and the hypostasis not brought together and not compounded – now the nature of the Father and of the Spirit is not brought together and not compounded, but the nature or the hypostasis of Christ is brought together and compounded from the godhead and the manhood – then the nature and the hypostasis of the Son is other than the nature of the Father and of the Spirit.

If Christ in his godhead is the maker of his manhood, but in his manhood is made by his godhead, he who makes him, and he who is made by him, cannot be one hypostasis. How is Christ one hypostasis?

Was he indeed made one, or was he one from before? That which is generated receives in the beginning that it should become. Just as time clave to his beginning, so did creation to his becoming.

2] 'definition': p. 66, 5, 'distinction'.
13] 'And because': *Syn. Or.* 'Because'.   14] 'its': *Syn. Or.* 'the'.
19] 'or the': *Syn. Or.* 'and the'.
23] 'or the hyp.': p. 66, 23 f. 'and the hyp.'
24/5] 'nature and the hypostasis': *Syn. Or. vice versa.*
31] 'Was he indeed made': *Syn. Or.* (=p. 66, 30 f.) 'Was the one nature or one hypostasis, Christ, made and created' (p. 67, 1 'indeed made').

3 – p. 95, 12] French *Syn. Or.* pp. 586, 6 – 587, 7 (II–VII); German Braun pp. 316–17 (Nos. 2–7).

[160] And if Christ, God the Word, together with his body, was made one nature or one hypostasis, he came forth from uncreated nature, and God was his maker, if the nature or the hypostasis which was constituted from the union did not exist before the union. But the nature and the hypostasis of the Son existed before the union. Neither the nature nor the hypostasis of the Son arose as a result of the union, but another, as also the natural union of soul and body does not establish the nature of the soul or of the body, but the nature of a man.

If every hypostasis which exists is a singular ousia, but the hypostasis of Christ is one, which is the singular ousia in Christ, and from what common (ousia) is it to be distinguished?

Against those who falsely accuse us as if we were confessing quaternity in the place of Trinity in the adorable and royal godhead.

If the Trinity of equal nature is confessed, how is he who is not of the nature of the Trinity, counted with the Trinity as a fourth?

And if the Trinity is confessed as godhead, how can godhead be numbered with manhood so that they are four?

If the hypostases of the Trinity are everlastingly confessed, how is a temporal hypostasis [161] counted together with an eternal one as a fourth?

And further they shall say to us: Was the body which was from Mary changed in its nature from the nature of the Trinity or not? If it was not changed, it was consubstantial with the Father and the Spirit. If, however, it was changed we ask: As the body was changed in its nature, was it thus changed in its hypostasis from the hypostases of the Trinity, or not? But if it was not changed, see, precise quaternity is confessed by you. If it was changed, how when you speak of a change of the body from the Trinity, do you not speak of quaternity while we speak of it as quaternity?

If the man who was from us, because he was united to God the Word, made an addition within the Trinity, God the Word also, because he was united to the man who was from us made an

1] 'Christ': *Syn. Or.* (=p. 67, 4) om.

7] 'also': *Syn. Or.* + 'from' (then translate 'result' and not 'establish' in l. 8).

10] 'is': *Syn. Or.* 'possesses'.   10/11] 'but the...one': *Syn. Or.* om.

14] 'adorable and royal': *Syn. Or.* om.

18] 'And if': *Syn. Or.* 'If'.

13 – p. 97, 2] French *Syn. Or.* pp. 590–1, 8; German pp. 320 below – 322 middle.

addition in the enumeration of men. But if it is not possible that God should be added with men in enumeration, neither is it possible for man to be added to the hypostases of the Trinity in number.

If God the Word is complete in his hypostasis everlastingly, but 5 exalted the manhood which he took to his hypostasis – how did he not make an addition in his hypostasis?

If there was added to the hypostasis of the Word that which had never been in it, how [162] does the hypostasis of the Word not surpass that of the Father and the Spirit? If the hypostasis of the 10 Word surpassed that of the Father and the Spirit, how has the Trinity continued in its equality which is from everlasting? Since with one name and one prosopon of the Son at the same time we know the godhead and the manhood of Christ because of his union, by what necessity are we compelled to fall into the confession of 15 quaternity?

Against those who insult us with the duality of sons.

Whoever does not speak of the manhood of the Son of God without the godhead of our Lord separately, but with the god-head unitedly – from whence is he compelled to speak of two 20 sons?

If in the union of God the Word with the body which was born from Mary, we are not compelled to say two sons who are born of the blessed Mary, how in the union of the manhood with God the Word can we be compelled to say two sons who were (born) of 25 God the Father? If we were saying that just as God the Word was born according to nature from the Father, so was the manhood born according to nature from the Father, we would justly have been accused of (the confession of) duality of sons. For where there are two sons, they are brothers. But if there is no one who has 30 commenced to say thus, [163] that in accordance with nature the manhood was born of the Father, or after the fashion of a brother to God the Word, but that it (*sc.* manhood) is with him one Son in

---

3] 'Trinity': *Syn. Or.* 'godhead'.

10/11] 'If the...Spirit': *Syn. Or.* om. (homoioteleuton).

13] 'one name and one prosopon': *Syn. Or.* 'the prosopon of one name'.

14] 'of his': *Syn. Or.* 'of the'.

17] 'insult': *Syn. Or.* 'accuse'.

18] 'Whoever': *Syn. Or.* 'Because one'.

23] 'Mary': *Syn. Or.* 'the blessed Mary'.

23 'two sons' – 25 'to say'] *Syn. Or.* om. (homoioteleuton).

30/1] 'who has commenced to say thus': read with *Syn. Or.* 'who is so mad to say'.

the union with the Word in the sonship of the Word – how is he reckoned in duality of sons with God the Word?

Against those who ask us: Is the holy virgin God-bearer, or bearer of an ordinary man?

5　The truth of (the matter) that the virgin gave birth without marriage we learn from the holy scriptures. In the same way also, we may learn from the scriptures who it was who was born. 'The ⟨Mt. 1: 1⟩ book of the generation of Jesus Christ, the son of David, the son of Abraham.' And: 'The birth of Jesus Christ was as follows.' And: ⟨Mt. 1: 18⟩

10　'There is born to you today a saviour, who is the Lord Christ, in ⟨Lk. 2: 11⟩ the city of David.' And: 'When Jesus was born in Bethlehem of ⟨Mt. 2: 1⟩ Judah', and many (texts) like these. He therefore who bare-facedly calls the holy virgin God-bearer – where will he flee (to avoid) the impiety of those who renounce the manhood of our

15　Lord Christ? And he who calls the virgin bearer of man in an ordinary fashion, how shall he not be placed on an equality with those who deny the godhead of Christ? [164] If in the invocation of the holy name of Christ there is to be understood his godhead and his manhood together, (then) he who confesses the holy virgin

20　to be Christ-bearer, in one confession of truth has overthrown and brought to an end the two impieties – the denial of his godhead and the denial of his manhood.

　　If Christ is true God and true man, and in that he is God, he is without beginning from the Father, and in that he is man, he took

25　the beginning from the virgin, how did she not bear him who began from her, and did she bear that everlasting one who was not from her so that he should be?

　　If, in that he is God, Christ is born of the Father everlastingly, and in that he is God, he is born of the virgin in time, twice is he

---

3] 'us': *Syn. Or.* om.
4] 'ordinary': *Syn. Or.* om.
7] 'who was born': *Syn. Or.* 'whom she bore'.
14/15] 'our Lord': *Syn. Or.* om.
18] 'holy': *Syn. Or.* om.
19] 'holy': *Syn. Or.* om.
21] 'the two': *Syn. Or.* 'all'.
23] 'and true man': *Syn. Or.* om. (homoioteleuton). 'and'²: *Syn. Or.* om.
24] 'from': *Syn. Or.* 'and from'.
26] 'from her': *Syn. Or.*+'to be'.
29] 'in time': *Syn. Or.* 'in another way'.

3 – p. 98, 27] French *Syn. Or.* pp. 588, 28–589; German Braun pp. 319–20 below.

found to be born in that he is God, but in that he is man, not even once.

If the virgin bore him who was formed within her by the Spirit, and for this reason bore God, then the Holy Spirit forms God. But if it is not possible for God the Word to be formed by God the Holy 5 Spirit, how can the virgin be God-bearer?

If without his godhead, Christ is not God, yet in his godhead [165] was not born of the virgin, how can the virgin be God-bearer?

If because Christ is God (and) for this reason the virgin is God- 10 bearer, how much more because Christ is man, should the virgin be called man-bearer.

But if he who calls the virgin bearer of ⟨man⟩ – calls Christ an ordinary man, also he who names the virgin God-bearer, speaks of Christ as God divested of manhood. Because he who is confessed as 15

cf. Lk 2: 52 born of the virgin, of necessity is the same who was circumcised and has grown in stature and wisdom and grace, and was crucified and suffered and died, according to the witness of scripture, (therefore) not for the honour of Christ or of his bearer are the heretics naming the holy virgin God-bearer, but in order that they might 20 find the opportunity to attribute all this weakness to God.

If there is no God who has a God, also there is no God who is more than God; but it is said of Christ by the prophet and the

Heb. 1: 9
(Ps. 45: 8) apostle expounds it: 'For this reason God your God has anointed you with the oil of gladness more than your fellows' – who is the 25 God of God the Word who has anointed him, or those [166] his fellows above whom he has been anointed?

Against those who say: God suffered in the flesh and died in the flesh.

If, as the soul is united to the body naturally, so is the godhead 30 of Christ united to his manhood naturally, (then) just as the soul

3] 'Spirit': *Syn. Or.* 'holy Spirit'.
4] 'then': *Syn. Or.* + 'also'.
4/5] 'But if it is not': p. 11, 27 'How is it'.
13] 'man': edd. add., *Syn. Or.* has it.
18/19] '(therefore)': p. 12, 6 f. 'Wherefore it is clear that it is'.
20] 'holy': *Syn. Or.* (=p. 12, 8) om.
21] 'weakness': *Syn. Or.* (=p. 12, 9) + 'and (these) sufferings'.
26] 'who': p. 12, 14 + 'with the oil'.

4/5 'But if – 27] quoted by Shahdost (Ic), above pp. 11, 27 – 12, 15 and app.
28 – p. 100, 19] French *Syn. Or.* pp. 587, 16 – 588, 27; German Braun pp. 317–19 above.

is enclosed within the body in a finite manner, and does not see or hear or do anything, except through the senses of the body, and moreover is troubled and distressed and fears with the body, so also is the godhead enclosed in the body in a finite manner, and is
5 in need of it for the completion of its actions, endures in it all its sufferings with trouble and fear and distress; and if these things have happened to the godhead, it has gone forth from its impassible nature. But if it is free from these things, how was it united naturally? And if it was not united naturally, how did it establish
10 one nature with the body and suffer? If the soul therefore suffers because it is naturally passible, how is it possible that God the Word who is impassible according to nature, should suffer in the body?

If the soul, which as a creature is immortal, cannot die in the
15 body, how can God the Word, who is substantially immortal, [167] die in the body?

If in Christ our Lord there is immortal life everlastingly, and immortal life temporarily, how can he not be two natures, one which is living everlastingly, and one which received immortal life
20 temporarily?

If in a natural and hypostatic union, the godhead of our Lord was united to his manhood, as his soul was united to his body, how, when the godhead was with the body, did it not live and rise, and when his soul returned to his body, did it live and rise? One of the
25 two (is right) – either the godhead is weaker than the soul, or the godhead was not united naturally to the structure of the nature, but willingly and personally for the provision of the dispensation.

If because the soul is united to the body naturally, a man cannot die as long as his unity is preserved, how, if the union of the god-
30 hood and the manhood of Christ is a natural one, when the union of Christ was not separated, did Christ die?

If (he was) one hypostasis when he was dying, he had need of another to raise him up. But (if) the hypostasis of Christ is one, how was he saying of his body: [168] 'I will raise it up'?   Joh. 2: 19

2] 'hear or do': *Syn. Or. vice versa.*   10] 'suffers': *Syn. Or.* + 'with the body'.
17/18] 'everlastingly, and immortal life': *Syn. Or.* om. (homoioteleuton).
18] 'temporarily': *Syn. Or.* 'in another way'. 'he': *Syn. Or.* 'Christ'.
19] 'one': *Syn. Or.* 'another'. 'immortal': *Syn. Or.* om.
23] 'with the body': *Syn. Or.* 'with it in the grave'.
26] 'naturally': *Syn. Or.* 'closely'.   34] 'was he': *Syn. Or.* 'was Christ'.

14] – p. 100, 2] quoted by Shahdost (*Id*), above pp. 34, 31–35, 16.

If death is the deprivation of life, how is it possible that the life of God should be deprived?

If everybody who is naturally impassible, cannot suffer in anything – now God is impassible by nature – it was not possible that he should suffer in the body. 5

If the death of a man means that his soul goes forth from his body, because also the soul of our Lord went forth from his body – who is it who died, the manhood compounded of soul and body, or the godhead which is without composition?

If the body for this reason dies, when his soul departs, by which 10 it is alive – but the godhead is not alive by the life of the soul – how, by the departure of the soul is God said to die?

If on all accounts he is other in the nature and in the hypostasis, the needy (other) than the supplier of necessity, the perfected (different) from him who perfects, the resurrected from him who 15 raises, each and all of the above being said in the scriptures concerning Christ, how is it possible for all these things which are in opposition to each other to be wrought in one hypostasis of Christ by itself?

20

Again, the questions which king Kosroes asked the fathers, the bishops.

First: Have [169] the Nestorians or the Severians deviated from the foundation of the faith which the first doctors made?

Second: And until Nestorius, did one say that Christ is two 25 natures and two hypostases, or not?

Third: Did Mary bear man or God?

The reply to these questions which the bishops and brethren, the monks, who were with them, made:

Because it is (only) when, before all things, the orthodox faith in 30 Christ is known, that it is possible to know who has deviated from the foundation of the faith of the first doctors; now the orthodox faith may be known especially from the holy scriptures which are

8] 'soul and': *Syn. Or.* om.
10] 'when': *Syn. Or.* 'because'.
16] 'each and all': *Syn. Or.* 'all this'.
18] 'of Christ': *Syn. Or.* om.
23] 'Severians': *Syn. Or.* 'monks'.
27] 'Third...': this question is wanting in *Syn. Or.*

21–29] cp. *Syn. Or.* p. 591, 9–12; our text has advantages, see first app.
30 – p. 101, 9] French *Syn. Or.* p. 591, 13–22 'Majesté, une seule'; German Braun pp. 322 below – 323 first word.

themselves the teachers of Christianity, just as also the coming of
Christ and his dispensation for us is known exactly and clearly from
the scriptures, (therefore) we write down briefly first, what the
holy scriptures have taught concerning Christ, and afterwards
5 what the doctors who were before Nestorius have said from the
doctrines of the scriptures.

The holy scriptures then teach us thus concerning Christ our
Lord: that he is complete God and complete man in one sonship,
and in one lordship, and one

10 [170] Again, chapters of disputations which are made in brief VIII
against those heretics who confess the unity of composition in
Christ, by Rabban Ḥenanisho' the monk, sister's son to Mar
Elijah who founded the monastery in Assyria.

15 If the creator was compounded, he is no different from creation,
and if he is different from creation, he cannot be compounded.
Anyone who receives composition is in need of one who compounds, and he who compounds all has no compounder. He who
is above all boundary is free from composition, and he who is
20 bound by composition, is bound under a boundary. If the Word
was compounded, he was cut off from his Father, and if he is in his
Father, he is not receiving composition. He who is subjected to
composition, is subjected also to sufferings, and he who is subjected
to sufferings, is yoked to necessity. Every hypostasis which is com-
25 pounded, has one life, and Christ, our Lord, is alive in two lives.
An hypostasis which is renewed is wholly renewed, and God
renews all, he does not renew himself. He who grows old, is the one
who is renewed; the splendour which is from the Father is far cf. Heb. 1:
removed from growing old. The form which was renewed is 9

5/6] 'from the doctrines of': *Syn. Or.* 'in the doctrine from'.
9] copyist's note on lacuna: 'From here ten leaves, that is a quire, have
fallen from the exemplar.'
11 – p. 105, 28] For this part of VIII there is a second ms. testimony in B. B is
for the greatest part illegible, being destroyed by the ink. Variant readings are
therefore only to be gathered from the beginning and the end of the parallel
(and some lines in between).
17] 'is in need': B 'is necessarily in need'.
20] 'boundary': B+'perforce'.

11–14] The lemma in B reads: 'Again, treatise made by Ḥenanisho' the monk,
sister's son to Mar Elijah, and again in the disputative way against Isaiah
Taḥalaya; that is an accusation against the Chalcedonians. Our Lord, help my
sin in all ways.'

visible in all of us – and how can we be changed into the form of
the Word? The form of God took the form of a servant, and [171]
two forms do not perfect one hypostasis. He who was born of Mary
was of the Holy Spirit – and was not a substantial hypostasis
formed anew. He who was formed within the womb, is he the
forming Word? And was not the Word forming his hypostasis?
Did he establish both of them in the way of composition? Now he
is both of them in the way of dwelling. If he indeed took the seed
of Abraham – see the hypostasis that was taken, and see the
hypostasis which took. The birth from the Father is hypostasis like
the Father, and the birth from Mary is hypostasis like her. The
creator of all has no creator, and he who was faithful to him who
made him is hypostasis like Moses. The first Adam did not keep
the law and he who kept the law was hypostasis like Adam. He
who is substantially powerful is substance from the Father and he
who received power is a perfect hypostasis. He who is consubstantial with the Father does not serve the sanctuary, the minister
of the sanctuary is hypostasis like Aaron. God the Word does not
resemble Melchizedek; he who resembles Melchizedek is hypostasis like him. He who is perfect according to nature is not made
perfect through sufferings, and he who was made perfect through
sufferings was hypostasis like his fellows. He who is different in his
properties, is different in his natures, [172] and he who is different
in his natures is also separate in his hypostases. He who has no
hypostasis is an accident in the ousia, and an accident in ousia
would not 'grow in wisdom'. He who stands by himself, the same
receives accidents, and an accident cannot stand within an accident. He who *was* Son is not *called* Son; he who was *called* Son was
not from everlasting. He who paid for our guilt is consubstantial
with us, and he who has no hypostasis, does not pay for guilt. He
who created Satan did not make war with him, and he who con-
quered Satan is hypostasis, of the same race as ourselves. If an
hypostasis is more than no hypostasis, Adam is more than Christ in
the flesh. But if Christ is surpassing without measure, he possesses
hypostasis fully in his manhood. Eternal substance does not
receive death, and nature without hypostasis is not lifted up on the
cross. He who rose in three days, fell under death, and he who fell
under death is not the creator of all. He who ascended upon the
clouds shall in like manner come, and the hypostasis of the Word
does not go and come. He who is perfect in his knowledge, is
perfect by his nature, and he who received knowledge, was newly

cf. Phil. 2: 7

cf. Heb. 3: 2

cf. Heb. 7: 15

cf. Lk. 2: 52

cf. Ac. 1: 9

2] 'servant': B+'who speaks (is) apostolic' (*sic*).

perfected. The knowledge which was of itself proclaims a hypostasis, and the knowledge which is in need [173] is hypostasis like it;
two rational beings in two hypostases, the giver and the receiver in
one Lord Jesus Christ. If the manhood of our Lord which was
5 from us, had no hypostasis, to whom would perfect knowledge
have been given? The man partook of the almighty power, and if
he possessed no hypostasis, with what did he receive it?

It is nonsense to speak of nature without hypostasis, like a father
without a son, for which there is no occasion. If the Word is united
10 with the Father and the body, and with the Father is simple, and
with the body is compounded, he is divided against himself, so that
he does not exist as one. If the body by itself is without hypostasis,
it does not accept an hypostasis from him who is apart from it.
And if the Word was compounded with the body in the womb, in
15 what is the Word better than the soul? 'Behold, my servant deals   Is. 52: 13
wisely', said Isaiah, and the Word which was from God was not a
servant. The parts of a composition relate to something, and he
who is not related to anything, with what is he compounded? If
the world consists of two parts, he through whom it was renewed
20 is not of three parts. If the Word was renewing the whole world,
how could the Word be renewing itself? If out of three parts, two
were renewed, the compounded hypostasis was divided against
itself. If the body could not [174] be extended (together) with the
Word, how could the Word be compounded with the body? If
25 because of our need the Word was united to us, the satisfying of
our need is not his own composition. If through his commandment
alone he spoke, and everything came about, how in the renewing
of all did he compound himself? If three parts compound one
hypostasis, its parts are equal in the species of composition, and as
30 two are bound in the sufferings of each other, (so) also the third
part is enclosed in it. And as the soul was saddened by the sufferings
of its fellow, it was necessary that the Word also should be grieved.
But if the Word was free from all of them, more than from all of
them (he was free) from composition.
35 If the hypostasis which was perfected did not belong to our
manhood, how did he resemble his fellows in everything? If God   cf. Heb. 2:
the Word was of the hypostasis of high priest, the Word was   17
ministering as priest to the two hypostases that remained. If the
hypostasis of high priest is of three parts, he is foreign to all men
40 and different in his hypostasis. If our own head is not consubstantial with us, how is it said: 'He shall be first in everything'?   cf. Col. 1:
If we, his limbs, are perfect hypostases, how can our head be   18

cf. Heb. 2: 7 lacking in this? If that hypostasis which suffered was less than the angels, how lower without measure was he than the substance? If [175] the life of him who created life is one, how did the Word suffer, while his Father did not suffer? If every hypostasis that exists is equal to that which is consubstantial with it, how can the hypostasis of the Word be foreign to his father? If the birth which is from the Father is beyond the ages, how is it possible that he should be compounded within time? If all nature that exists abides within its own definition, how can the (divine) substance depart from his own? If the nature of the earthly one remained as he was, how has his creator compounded his simplicity? If he who was exalted remained in his nature, how can he who exalted him be changed? If the nature of the manhood did not possess an hypostasis belonging to itself how can he be consubstantial with his mother? If the hypostasis of the Word was perforce compounded, how can he be consubstantial with his father? If the body was not compounded with his sacrament (i.e. the bread), how can the (divine) substance be compounded with body? If every image that exists consists of the likenesses which it bears, how can the Word have been compounded with its image? If God has a body hypostatically, God is not different in this from man. Now if the hypostasis of the Word is spirit like his Father, how can he possess limbs hypostatically? If it be the case that the Word possesses a bodily hypostasis, everything corporeal is his by nature. If every hypostasis that exists possesses the definition of its nature, [176] how can the hypostasis of the Word be foreign to its nature?

If every nature that exists has an hypostasis of its own, how have you deprived the body of this? If everything that in fact came into being is foreign to the (divine) substance, how can the Word possess a body hypostatically? If everything which is compounded is foreign to that which is simple, the Word possesses (the body only as) a temple; foreign (is the Word) to the body which was from Mary. If simplicity is foreign to the body, to a greater degree is composition foreign to the (divine) substance. If the body which

cf. Heb. 1: 9 was from Mary has no hypostasis, whom did the Spirit anoint more
(Ps. 45: 8) than his fellows? If the manhood from us has no hypostasis, who

cf. Nu. 24: was glorified with the glory from the Father? If the hypostasis is
17, cf. Dan. taken away from the star out of Jacob, who was brought near to
7: 13 the ancient of days? If the rod which is from Jesse possessed no
cf. Is. 11: 1 hypostasis, who is the prophet who arose in the likeness of Moses?
cf. Dt. 18:
15 (cited If there is no union where there is no distinction – when there are
Ac. 3: 22,
7: 37)

not two hypostases, in what is there distinction? If there is no union when there are two hypostases neither is there union when there are two natures.

If it is not a man that became man by man, how did he become man by one who was not man? If everyone who is man, is man from man, how does a man from man not possess hypostasis? If the Word has not joined himself to a man from man, the man who is spoken of in Christ was a phantom. [177] If he who was not (divine) substance was made God by the (divine) substance, then also he who was not man was by man made man. If there was no (divine) substance who was perfect in its hypostasis, he who was man, by what means was he made God? If he who was from our race was not perfect in his hypostasis, he who was God, by what means was he made man? If the Word did not take a complete man, from whence is our Lord perfect man?

If he from Mary was less than man, how is it written that Jesus was man? If he who was of our nature was not perfect in his constitution, how was he perfected so as to be man? If the hypostasis of man was perfected in the Word, he was neither man nor God. If not every hypostasis that exists is emptied, how can one hypostasis possess two natures? If all natures are constituted in hypostases, how can this one exist without hypostasis? If the hypostases excel the species, how is our beginning inferior to that which is great? If the hypostases are comprehended by our senses, how do we touch and see him who is not hypostasis? If an ousia is called common for the two, how can the body which was from Mary be in common? If, after the union, the Son is one hypostasis, union is equivalent to disunion. [178] If the staying on of the natures does not annul the union, then the non-preservation of the hypostases takes away the union.

If since the natures have been compounded into the hypostasis,

7/8] 'the man who is spoken of in Christ': B 'Jesus from our race'.
10] 'by man': B om.
15] 'from whence is our Lord perfect man?': B 'then Jesus in his hypostasis is not complete'.
17/18] 'his constitution': B 'the ousia'.
20] 'emptied': B 'cut off' (or the like).
23–5] 'If the hypostases...who is not hypostasis': B om.
27/8] 'to disunion': B ends here.
28 ff.] marginal note in the exemplar: 'An addition which we found in another manuscript.'

30 – p. 106, 2] The first half of this sentence is no doubt meant as an irrealis; it is used as the first member for a conclusion *a minore ad maius*.

they have established union, since the hypostases were united into the prosopon, they have confirmed the union. If every nature which exists is revealed in its hypostases, the hypostasis which was seen is of the nature of our manhood. If the hypostasis of the Word put on a body, and not the whole Trinity, then also one man was 5 taken from Mary, and not all men. If Jesus, who was from Mary, was not distinct in his hypostasis, he would not have been known to be of the order of men. If every hypostasis that exists is counted with that which is of his kind, it is fitting that he who was born of Mary and circumcised, should be counted with his consubstantial 10 (beings). If every nature which exists is reckoned with its own

hypostases, he who was bound in swaddling clothes, and grew in wisdom and in stature, was not of the nature of the Trinity. And if he was not of the Trinity, how is it possible that we should introduce quaternity? And if the Trinity is simple and infinite, 15 and Jesus who was from Mary compounded of body and soul, and is finite in his hypostasis, how is it possible [179] that he should be reckoned with the Trinity? If the nature is everlastingly (divine) substance, how is a temporary (being) reckoned with the (divine) substance? If the (divine) substance is perfect and complete 20 nature, how can it receive an addition? And if it is not possible for the complete one to receive an addition, how have the Word and the man established one hypostasis? If the Word and the man have established one hypostasis, the uncompounded Father is half a hypostasis. 25

Finished is the addition which we found afterwards in another manuscript.

IX Again, various chapters and diverse questions of the holy Nestorius. 30

1 First chapter: What distinction is there between nature and hypostasis?

'Nature' means what is common, as one might say 'all mankind'. But 'hypostasis' is what each one of us is. Now what each one of us is, signifies that (which is) in accordance with that which is 35

29 ff.] For the whole of IX there is R as a second ms. testimony. Three chapters are also contained in V and edited from it; for them *vide ad locum.*

35 – p. 107, 1] 'which is deposited and set in motion': Liddell–Scott refer *s.v.* κινέω B (= Passive) to Plato's *Sophistes* 250 B, etc. In the discussion of στάσις 'rest' and κίνησις 'motion' in their relation to Being (249 A ff.) there occurs the following statement about Being which could be the key to the difficult clause of our text: κατὰ τὴν αὐτοῦ φύσιν ἄρα τὸ ὂν οὔτε ἕστηκεν οὔτε κινεῖται (250 C). This was

deposited and set in motion. Now the same (person) is nature and hypostasis, because the former is, as I have said, that which is common, while the latter, in that it signifies (the individual, gives) the cognition of each one of us. This, together with many other
5 things, the blessed Theodore, also, speaks of in the 18th book against Eunomius, [180] as follows: Prosopon is used in a twofold way; for either it signifies the hypostasis, and that which each one of us is, or it is conferred upon honour, greatness and worship; for example: 'Paul' and 'Peter' signify the hypostasis and the
10 prosopon of each one of them, but the prosopon of our Lord Christ means honour, greatness and worship. For because God the Word was revealed in manhood, he was causing the glory of his hypostasis to cleave to the visible one; and for this reason, 'prosopon of Christ' declares it (*sc.* the prosopon) to be (a prosopon) of honour,
15 not of the ousia of the two natures. [For the honour is neither cf. Phil. 2: 9 nature nor hypostasis, but an elevation to great dignity which is awarded as a due for the cause of the revelation.] What purple garments or royal apparel are for the king is for God the Word the beginning which was taken from us without separation, alienation
20 or distance in worship. Therefore, as it is not by nature that a king has purple robes, so also neither is it by nature that God the Word has flesh. For anyone who affirms God the Word to have flesh by nature (predicates that) he has something foreign to the divine substance by undergoing an alteration [181] by the addition of a
25 nature. But if he has not flesh by nature, how does Apollinarius say that the same one is in part consubstantial with the Father in his godhead, and the same (in part) consubstantial with us in the

15–17] ancient gloss to the text of Theodore.
19] 'alienation : R 'alteration'.

evidently taken later as a statement about 'nature'. If rest and motion do not belong to the nature as common, then they must belong to the single, the individual, i.e. to the hypostasis in our case. It makes good sense then for ܣܩܘ̈ܡ to be used for a form of ἑστάναι though it looks grotesque in translation; but ܣܩܘ has always the connotation of 'standing up', 'rising', therefore of motion. The author refers so casually to the Platonic terms and takes their shifted emphasis so much for granted that he must rely on a source where they were used already in the same way.
4 – p. 108, 3] German translation *Muséon* **71** (1958), pp. 99–101 and *Zeitschrift für Kirchengeschichte* **72** (1961), pp. 263 f. In the English translation given here we have corrected the last sentence of the German translation; the corrected form is already used by A. Grillmeier, *Christ in Christian Tradition*, London 1965, pp. 352 f.

flesh, so that he may make him composite? For he who is thus divided into natures becomes and is found (to be) something composite, by nature.

2   Second: What distinction is there between composition, mixture, 5 and union?

Composition is one thing, mixture is another, and yet another thing is the union. Now mixture is an indistinguishable participation of natures, just as bread is fashioned from wheat and barley. Composition is a participation of natures as parts, so that it is 10 known in its differences, like soul and body, and like a coat which is mixed and woven from wool and flax, of which the parts are seen, and the external connection of their nature is shown, because from it it has a composition. For that which is from one and the other is alien to the two of them (together), and even if it should 15 desire to be the two of them and not one of them, it remains (as it is). But the union is the conjunction of the perfect natures who are known in the one prosopon, and they participate [182] in the worship and in the honour, and in the greatness of the one prosopon. 20

3   Third: How it befits us to understand the hypostasis and the prosopon.

Hypostasis and prosopon are one and the same (when) applied successively to men. For the prosopon of Paul is the same as the 25 hypostasis of Paul – the prosopon of Peter is the same as the hypostasis of Peter. But when we apply prosopon to our Lord Christ, that is: to the two natures of the godhead and of the manhood, it is not one compounded hypostasis that is referred to in the ordinary way, but it (*sc.* the prosopon) signifies honour and 30 greatness and worship. Because he who was taken, namely the human nature in which God was unceasingly revealed, (who) put on the glory of God, and in the order of the prosopon of the only begotten appeared to creation, is the one prosopon, of honour. For although the manhood possesses an hypostasis of its own – as 35 indeed it does, nevertheless, this hypostasis is the temple of its inhabitant, and the revelation of him who takes it, and the indicator of God; and there is no time when it is seen by itself, so that its own prosopon, without godhead, should appear to the

24 – p. 109, 33] in German translation *Muséon* **71** (1958), pp. 101 f.
31–4] 'Because...honour': the syntactic construction is corrected over against the German translation, *ibid.* p. 101, 7–11 'Denn...Ehre'.

beholders. For even if the hypostasis of that which was taken is complete ⟨...⟩, but in the ranks of hypostases is it found by the beholders. But everything that there is, [183] is exalted with him who takes it, like apparel with him who puts it on, and like purple
5 with a king, and like an image with its archetype. Every one of them belongs not to that which it is in itself, but to him with whom it is exalted. If he who was taken were a thing by itself or were bare, or simple, or separate from him who takes him, they would be called two prosopa and two sons. Now, this one in that he is
10 exalted with God the Word in the union as the prosopon of the godhead is revealed through the form of a servant. For if two natures in mortals make one hypostasis, O Apollinarius, then one nature makes one half of an hypostasis – which does not happen with God; and if two hypostases are two prosopa, they make also
15 two sons. But if you say that the natures partake of each other according to nature, and one compounded hypostasis came into being from the two of them, then this hypostasis is something other than it was aforetime, in that it is compounded instead of simple, and from consubstantiality with the Father it has become com-
20 pletely estranged. If the substance of the Father remained in its simplicity, but that of the Son became compounded – whoever says this [184] introduces a distinction into the substance, and the dispensation in our manhood would be a depreciation of its dispenser. Now if anyone speaks of a hypostasis of the two natures,
25 of the consubstantial (one) with the Father in his godhead, and (of) the consubstantial (one) with us in his manhood, all the more has he who says such things, asserted a composition. For any nature, having an hypostasis divided amongst several natures, and having kinship with them, is a compounded thing, and foreign to every
30 thing by nature – which matters, when we think them in relation to God, are full of impiety. For it is right to say that he who was consubstantial with the Father took inseparably for his revelation him who was consubstantial with us. And it is not that the same one was the two of them, or that with those who are other in the
35 natures, he was in part consubstantial, as one might speak of a garment as having kinship with the wool or with the flax of which it consists; for although it is divisible into the two of them, never-theless, from the two of them it is different, and according to know-

2] lacuna edd. conj.

1–3] 'For...beholders' has been omitted by homoioteleuton in the German translation, *ibid.* p. 101; its place is after 'hätte', p. 101, 15.

ledge one sees (that). But if, in (the case of) these things here (mentioned), the bringing together by craftsmanship has effected a distinction, what are we going to say when there is fulfilled naturally the story which is told about him (*sc.* Jesus Christ)?

4   Fourth: Concerning this: – that the prosopon of Christ is one, that is: the divine nature [185] and the human nature – in these demonstrations:

When anyone says 'city', he refers both to the inhabitants and to the habitation, and they are two hypostases, but one is the prosopon of the city. And also, in the same way, a house is named after him who dwells in it, and from (the fact that it is) his dwelling place; and the prosopon now is one, but the hypostases are two, without partaking with each other in composition. So also do we understand in the case of a martyr and a martyr-chapel: namely two hypostases, the building and the martyr who is honoured in it, but it is the one prosopon of the martyr which is known.

5   Fifth: How the Son is confessed in a twofold manner.

The Son is spoken of in the divine scriptures in a double manner – in hypostasis, as relating to God the Word, and in honour, as relating to him who was taken, for in the honour of the union which he has with God the Word, he is called Son. He is not (Son) because of himself nor in himself, nor through grace, like those who are baptized – these being sons through grace. The sonship therefore of the godhead and of the manhood is not one in a composition of one hypostasis, but in honour. If we say that as in the composition of an hypostasis is there the form of a servant, who was taken, [186] and of him who takes (united together), he who was taken would be found to be (derived) from the Father, if (it is) not by union or by conjunction (that) he is called Son.

6   Concerning the nature and the hypostasis.

With the grammarians (the terms) 'true' and 'named' are used. The 'true' (thing) then is that which signifies the nature;

24] 'nor': R 'and (not)'.
27] 'of one': R 'in one'.

34 – p. 111, 1] 'true' and 'named': The edd. have to thank G. C. Stead for the following comment on this passage: 'The writer seems to have confused the distinction between the real and the merely nominal with that between the general and the particular, or common nouns and proper nouns. προσηγορικός can mean

that which is the hypostasis, is 'named'; that which signifies the common ousia, is the nature.

Against those who say that sin is natural.　　　　　　　　　　　7

5　　Ask thus: Does God sin, or does he not? Does he sin in creating? Does he sin in ordaining laws? Does he sin in judging? They answer: No. If then he does not sin in creating, he was not appointing man to be a vessel of natural sin. And if, again, he was not sinning in ordaining laws, he was not thus ordaining those
10　against which nature is (set). And if he does not sin in inflicting punishment, he was not punishing us for those things which we were not able to do.

Concerning this: 'The Word became flesh.'　　　　　　　　　　8

15　　Here (i.e. in this passage) it is thought by many that 'he　Joh. 1: 14
became' is not clear. But the divine substance is known by the confession which is confessed. Now it is clear that the divine substance is incapable of change, transformation or composition. Since you uphold these (things) as (being) the law of the
20　eternal substance, [187] expound, how it befits God, that he 'became', so that the saying does not do violence to his nature. But in relation to the substance do you expound the unintelligibility of the saying! Thus were we hearing from the Baptist the (expression) 'generation of vipers', which was spoken about men,　Mt. 3: 7 &
25　and it is evident that this is not assigned to the nature, but to the　par.
mind, and while we adhere to the word, we do not wrong the nature, and we do not say that he speaks literally of vipers. And again: 'Behold the lamb of God'; and immediately we inquire　Joh. 1: 29
the reason why he called our Lord 'lamb'; it is clear that it was on
30　account of the sacrifice, not of the substance, that he thus named him. We agree that he was not an inarticulate sheep, being convinced by the reading of the passage. And, again, he says: 'They　Jer. 5: 8
were horses unrestrained amongst the mares'; he has uttered the

25] 'assigned to': R 'conferred on'.
32/3] 'They were horses unrestrained amongst the mares' ܩܪܒ ܡܪܗܓܝܢ
ܘܗܘ ܒܣܘܣܝܐ: Syr. vg., ܘܗܘ ܣܘܣ̈ܝܐ ܩܝܠ̈ܝ ܩܪܒ ܝܚܝ̈, Sept. ἵπποι θηλυμανεῖς ἐγενήθησαν.

"common", as opp. to κύριος or ὀνοματικός, "proper"; but also, apparently, "nominal", as opp. to κύριος or ἀληθής, "real". So the "true", which "signifies the nature" can hardly represent κύριος, since κύριον ὄνομα is a *proper* noun; but "named" might represent ὀνοματικός.'

saying about the depravity of men, not about nature. And again,
about Zedekiah: 'He became a lion, and learned to plunder' – the
evil will, and not a change of his nature, received reproof. So also
the (passage): 'He gave them power to become sons of God', does
it now signify the same nature, or the reception of the adoption of
sons? So also this: 'The Word became flesh', is assigned to the
dispensation, [188] and does not signify either a transformation of
the nature, or a composition. Now the dispensation of God is the
taking of the flesh, apt for the divine revelation, no necessity being
laid upon it that it should submit to God without his nature, but 10
(it was something) which is indicating the invisible one in visible
flesh, whilst in the appearance of the equality of honour it was
leading and bringing near the spectator to the invisible one. 'The
Word became flesh.' Now what is this: 'He became'? He (*sc.* the
evangelist) has completed it by saying: 'and dwelt among us', 15
that is to say, he was occupying our nature, making his revelation
in our flesh. Take to yourself Paul as witness to the matter: 'He
who was the form of God, took upon himself the form of a servant.'
And again: 'He did not take (it) from angels, but he took (it)
from the seed of Abraham.' Thus the apostle understood 'he 20
became' as 'he took'; so also this: 'Christ purchased us from the
curse of the law, and himself became a curse on our behalf' –
instead of saying that he took the curse. And again: 'Him who
knew no sin he made to be sin for our sakes', now that is: he
prepared him to take our sins – as it is said: 'He will take our sins.' 25
Also the custom is known that somebody is called (with such a
title) as we would say that so-and-so became a Comes, that is a
general, [189] in that he received honour, and not in that he was
changed; and that so-and-so became a prefect, and not because
his nature was changed, but due to the fact that he received 30
authority. So 'he became flesh' (indicates that) the Word took the
flesh, and so was revealed. And so is to be expounded the (saying):
'Adam, Adam, where are you'? and: 'Where is Abel your

Marginal references (left column):
Ezek. 19: 3
Joh. 1: 12
Joh. 1: 14
Joh. 1: 14
cf. Phil. 2: 6, 7
cf. Heb. 2: 16
Gal. 3: 13
2 Cor. 5: 21
cf. 1 Joh. 3: 5
cf. Joh. 1: 14
cf. Gen. 3: 9; Gen. 4: 9

2] 'to plunder' ܠܡܒܙ: Syr. vg. ܠܡܒܙ, Sept ἁρπάзειν.

9/10] 'necessity being laid': R uses another verb of the same meaning.

19/20] 'He did not take (it) from angels, but he took (it) from the seed of
Abraham' = gr.; Syr. vg. 'Not over angels did death have power, but over the
seed of Abraham.'

24] 'for our sakes' = gr.; Syr. vg. 'for your sakes'; 'now that is': R om.

30] 'changed': R has another verb with the same meaning.

31] 'So "he"': R 'So also "the Word"'.

32] 'was so revealed': R 'was revealed in him'.

brother?' and: 'Where have you laid Lazarus?' and: 'How many   cf. Joh. 11:
loaves have you?' and: 'Who touched me?' The inquiry is not an   34; Mt. 15:
ignorant rebuke, but the supplying of facts for the conversion of   34; Mk.5:31
hearers. Let sayings therefore be measured with their causes, and
5 let not the divine nature be insulted with words which do not fit it.

About this: 'The Holy Spirit shall come, and the power of the   9
most high shall overshadow you.'   cf. Lk. 1: 35

   Now, what does this intend, (namely) that 'the Holy Spirit shall
10 come', as it were from another locality, and contained in a place?
And now – who comes, but previously was not present in this way?
What is this also that 'he shall overshadow you'? And look, a
shadow signifies the coming of a body, and is the indication of a
body. But when the divine nature is incorporeal, and infinite, how
15 is there a place to which it 'shall come'? How again is to be understood the further (statement) that 'he shall overshadow you',
since [190] this is also solved in the (same) context? What then is
the understanding of 'he shall come' and 'he shall overshadow'?
They say: the Holy Spirit shall show in you the working and the
20 power of his creative activity, and shall form in your womb fruit
higher than nature, in which all creation shall be receiving a
renewal. – But, they ask, who is it that was born? We reply: He
who was born: did he come out (after) having been in the womb;
or was he born while (already) outside it? It is evident that he who
25 was within was born (to be) without. But God is within the womb
and outside it, and in heaven and on earth and everywhere. How
is it therefore that he who is everywhere receives birth so that his
beginning should be from the womb? Now if you inquire who it is
that was born, I give you in answer the utterance of the angel,
30 'Christ the Lord is born to you today in the city of David.' Now   cf. Lk. 2: 11
(the name) 'Christ' is the indicator of the divine dispensation of
which the dispenser dwelt within him. – But, they say, God was
born. I ask: Well now, was God born that which he was, or so as
to become that which he had not been? If he was born that which
35 he was, that is, invisible and incorporeal, and infinite, God without
a body was born; therefore he who was born was the invisible, [191]
and incorporeal one. But if you say that he became that which he

2] 'Who touched' ܘܡܢܘ ܗܘ ܗܢܐ: Syr. vg. ܘܡܢܘ ܗܢܐ
7] 'shall come' ܢܐܬܐ: see above, VII p. 90, 20.
17] 'since this is also solved': R. 'when it is measured'.
19] 'working and': R 'working of'.
26/7] 'How', 'he is everywhere': R. om. (haplography).

had not been, and (so) was born, then that which was born is not God. If he who is without change is God, he who is not that is not God. And it is not the same that he should become Son when he was not God. You say: God, by becoming something which he had not been, was born; therefore, according to what you say, it was 5 not God that was born, for you have changed his nature into gross flesh. And about the suffering he asks in the same way: Did he suffer in that which he was, or in becoming that which he had not been? If in that which he was – God suffered, then the invisible and incorporeal one suffered; if in becoming what he had not been, 10 then he who was not God in nature suffered, according to your blasphemy, O heretic. For you have first altered the unalterable nature, and have then brought it nigh unto suffering, and have subjected the impassible and immortal substance to a double suffering. But, he says, the impassible suffered in accordance with 15 his will. – Then his will changed his nature, in that it was found to be more powerful than his nature, [192] his will striving with his nature. But, he says, he willed to suffer. – He willed therefore that he should not be God, for impassibility belongs to God only. But, he says, when the Son became man and was born, on this 20 account he suffered. – He became estranged then from the substance, and (so) was born. Now the same thing is said again. Moreover, concerning the suffering, this is the word of truth: God the Word took human nature, and, in the order of his likeness and of his image, he displayed it, and in it he provided and directed 25 our (affairs) – not because he was in need of salvation. And if, as though in good faith, they ask us: Who was it that was born? we reply: The temple of God the Word while God the Word was dwelling in it. Howbeit, the indwelling of God the Word was not a participation in the beginning of birth, even though it was the 30 glory of the birth, nor did he share the sufferings, even though it was the glory of the suffering. Again they ask: Who was it who was born? We answer: The dispensation of God the Word. – And: who was he who suffered? We reply again: The dispensation of God the Word. Do not thou therefore make answer to them from 35 the nature of him that was taken; and do not say merely that a man was born, and that a man suffered, but concerning the honour of him who suffered, speak with them thus: [193] Of what fashion are the dispensation of God the Word, and the temple of

2] 'God, he': R 'God, and he'.
9] 'was – God': R 'was for himself'.
14] 'impassible': R 'passible'.

God the Word? For they are dispensations ⟨indicating⟩ the honour of God. Just as about a picture of a king, we do not say that (it is) pigments, tablets, linen, and the craftsmanship of the artist's hand, but the image of royalty, for from where it has honour from there
5 also does it receive its appellation; so also we understand about the beginning which is from us, which was taken by God the Word, that its honour is higher than all the world, and is elevated to the heavenly throne of the divine substance. Thus also is the Eucharist which is given from the altar – in no ordinary manner
10 do we call it that which is in the nature, but body and blood; for when we understand to what honour it has passed in its consecration, it is from there that we seize upon the attribute of its appellation. Therefore we are misunderstood, when they say that thus there are two sons, and that there are four prosopa (sc. in Trinity) –
15 that would be manifestly absurd. For (several) purple robes are not counted in the case of a king, because one is the worship, nor does the image of a king cut royalty in two, nor does the armour with which he is armed [194] divide the soldier, nor is the dispensation made distinct in counting from him who dispenses, but there
20 is one honour, one authority, and one worship, in the visible temple of the revealed invisible one. The blessed Paul openly proclaims the passible nature when he says: 'For he was crucified cf. 2 Cor. through weakness, yet he lives through the power of God.' After he 13: 4 had reckoned weakness to be of the mortal flesh, he proclaimed
25 concerning the power of the divine substance.

Concerning the union of the Son. 10

We ask: Is the Son of God one or two? Is he God or man? Is he created or was he uncreated? Was he consubstantial with the
30 Father, or was he foreign to him? Is he what he was, or, according to what you say, that which he became? Was the flesh which he took foreign to the nature who took it, or was it consubstantial with him who took it? They say: It was foreign to the nature of him who took it. The flesh then is an ousia on its own. And further,
35 according to your dictum, that which is foreign to the substance of the Son is consubstantial with it (sc. with the flesh). Therefore

1] 'indicating': R filling up a lacuna in our ms.
5] 'also'¹: R om.
18/19] 'is'², 'made distinct': R om.
20/21] 'worship, in the visible temple': R 'visible worship of honour'.
23] 'through the power' ܚܝܠܐ ܡܢ: Syr. vg. ܒܚܝܠܐ, gr. ἐκ δυνάμεως.
27] '10': R. om.

it (the flesh) is foreign to the divine substance. The nature of that which was taken is common, even though he was not an ordinary man. When therefore we make the confession of [195] the Son, we confess that he is consubstantial with his Father, and further that it was God who took of the seed of Abraham. But we say also of 5 him who was taken, that he was by himself alone, and not of a man in the way that every (other) man is. For it was not for a small dispensation that he took on this (flesh), but in order that through it he might effect his revelation, always in proportion to the greatness of this dispensation. No one can sufficiently wonder at it. 10

cf. Heb. 2: 16

11   That we do not say there are two sons, but one Son.

Whenever you make confession of the Son to them, first accuse them by the arguments which you are presenting against those who say there are two sons, whilst not denying that you do confess 15 one Son. For Apollinarius and the Egyptian make false accusation, and spread the rumour of (the confession of) two sons with reference to these who confess one Son – who being consubstantial with the Father, took the form of a servant, not for the perfection of his substance but for his dispensation. 20

12   Concerning the manhood of our Lord.

God the Word is the only begotten of the Father. Now he who was taken was the temple of God the Word, which was separated out for this, and it became the perfect living man. And from the 25 beginning of its being formed, [196] there was within it always he who was dwelling in it, being revealed according to the need of our affairs in the dispensation on our behalf. Now God was being revealed, not by becoming visible, nor by being created, nor again by having a share in the visible and created one, but in that he 30 came to the knowledge of the rational (beings) through the visible and created one which was taken for this (reason), because he (*sc.* the man) that is seen, is seen as (being) him who took him, being glorified with his glory, and worshipped with his worship, not as one who is thus (glorified and worshipped) in (his own human) 35 nature.

cf. 1 Cor. 15: 45 (Gen. 2: 7)

13   In what manner and on what grounds do we worship the form of a servant without introducing four prosopa into the Trinity?

We worship him who was taken with the worship of the only 40

5] 'took of the seed of Abraham': see above, ch. 8 p. 112, 19 f.
38] 'In what manner and' R om.

begotten, so that that which is incapable of being taken is incapable of being worshipped, and that no created nature will
receive divine worship. But we fulfil in the one worship of the only
begotten both (things), just as also the prophets were worshipping
5 the parts that were visible to them as God, the while, as from a
shadow, they were learning the truth of the matter. Now the
enemies of the truth say of us that we speak of a fourfold hypostasis
with reference to the Trinity, and that [197] we offer divine
worship to one to whom it is not due, because we do not confess
10 with them the confusion of the two natures which is said by them.
But they have erred because they introduce all creation into the
Trinity, assigning to the only begotten, by means of composition
with created (things), participation of the flesh, and they offer
divine worship to the created nature contrary to what is due to it.

15
Concerning those (things) given by God to the created nature.   14

All those (things) which belong to God, such as are of his
honour, and not of his substance, he is bestowing and giving; that
is: that he is called God (belongs) to the honour, that he is Lord,
20 to the greatness and to the worship – all these (things) belong to
him who was taken; and that he should be called God, because of
God who is in him, and that he should be called Lord, and should
be named Son. But for the cause exists also the honour, that is: he
who cannot be reckoned as anything, but is sent to (be) with
25 another, is not the honoured nature, but its honour is in him who
takes it. That he is man (belongs) to the nature, that he is Christ
(belongs) to the honour, and signifies him who was anointed. Now
he who anoints is included in this appellation, as in the same way
his being the temple indicates [198] him who dwells (in it), (and)
30 as also that which is taken indicates him who takes it.

Concerning the physical and the metaphorical.   15

Those things which are spoken of in a physical sense with regard
to God are to be taken metaphorically when applied to ourselves –
35 as, for instance, references to God, king and judge; and those
things which have a physical application to us are to be spoken of
metaphorically when applied to God, like his ascending and   cf. Eph. 4:
descending, that he is visible, etc. For it is said that God descended   9, 10
that he should raise us up to him – not that he should change his
40 substance.

1/2] 'so that that which is incapable of being taken is incapable of being
worshipped': R 'that which is incapable of being taken is worshipped'.

16 Concerning baptism.

cf. Joh. 3: 5   We say that baptism is water and Spirit, because he who was baptized was visible and invisible. For this reason also, baptism is completed with water which can be seen, and with Spirit which cannot be seen. 5

17 Against him who asks: Who is it that walked upon the water?

cf. Mt. 14: 25   We reply that it was the feet that were walking, and the material body, through the strength that dwells therein. (It is) this that is (a cause) of wonder. For if God were walking on water, that is not 10 astonishing, as also (it would not be were he walking) on air. And cf. Joh. 20: 19, 26 this again, that the material body entered through closed doors, this too is a marvel. [199] But if the divine nature entered, it would not be remarkable if I kept silent, for it is infinite.

18 Concerning this: 'My God, my God, why have you forsaken me?' 15

Mt. 27: 46   What then (is this)? Does he speak truth or does he lie? If he truly says he is left alone, where then is the infinity of God? And if he is not left alone, he has therefore lied. What then do we say? (We say) that he turned aside in order that his temple should 20 suffer, just as he allowed it to hunger, so that the dispensation might be fulfilled.

19 Again, concerning the crucifixion.

    Moreover, we ask: Was he crucified willingly or not? If they 25 say: Willingly, we reply: Therefore, by doing his will, the Jews were worthy of the kingdom. But if they say: Unwillingly, there is

7] 'Against': V 'Again the same. Against'; 'water'= Syr. vg., gr. θάλασσαν, Philox. 'sea'.
11] 'on' R om.
13/14] 'it would not be remarkable': V 'it would have been nothing at all'.
16] 'Concerning this': V 'Again the same. They ask: It is written:'.
17] 'What then (is this)': V 'What is this'.
17/18] 'he truly says': V om.
18/19] 'And if...not': V 'If not'.
20/21] 'his temple should suffer': V has a corrupt reading.
21] 'just as he allowed it to hunger': Loofs' translation of this line in *Nestoriana* p. 219, 16 f. is erroneous, due to his misreading of one word in V.

7–14] German translation of V, Loofs pp. 218, 20 – 219, 9.
16–22] German translation of V, Loofs p. 219, 10–17, with a fault at the end, see first app.

no place for this. So then the will did not take precedence, but he took upon himself something which was expedient for men.

Against those who say that the Father made the Son. 20

5 To him who says that the Father made the Son so that he is called his offspring, we reply: Certainly. But we say that the Son also made the Father so that he is called Father. For if there were no Son, neither would there be a Father, but they are the cause of each other.

10

Against him who asks whether the substance was born or not. 21

They ask: One is the substance of the Father, Son and Holy Spirit. [200] What (is it) therefore, was the substance born or not? We answer that the substance bore the hypostasis, for (it was) not 15 the substance (that) was born, but the hypostasis.

Against those who wish to divide the nature of the Trinity. 22

They say that those whose deeds are distinct (from each other), are also different natures, that is: the Father begat, the Son was 20 born, while the Holy Spirit was not (either) one of them; wherefore they are foreign in the nature. Now we say that this is a falsehood. For see, Adam was formed from the earth, Eve was from a rib, but Abel was born. Well then – was the nature of these one or was it divided?

25

Against those who by reason of the order of number subordinate 23 the Son and the Spirit.

They say that those who are enumerated last are lower than those who are before them. We answer that this is a falsehood. It is 30 said: 'Faith, hope, and love, but the greatest of these is love'; 1 Cor. 13:13 again: 'I have planted, Apollos watered, but God gave the in- 1 Cor. 3:6 crease', and again: 'I am the vine, you are the branches'; but 'My Joh. 15:5 / Joh. 15:1 Father is the husbandman'; and that: 'I and my Father are one'; Joh. 10:30 and again: 'The grace of our Lord Jesus Christ, and the love of 2 Cor. 13: 35 God the Father, and the communion of the Holy Spirit [201] be 14 with us all'.

15] 'was born': R 'bore'.
21] 'Now': R om.
31] 'but God' ⤳? ‪ܠܐܗܐ‬: Syr. vg. ‪ܠܐܗܐ ܗܝ‬
32/3] 'My Father is' ⤳? ‪ܐܒܝ‬: Syr. vg. ‪ܗܘ ܐܒܝ‬.
33] 'my Father' = Syr. vg., gr. ὁ πατήρ.
35] 'the Father' deest in Syr. vg. et gr.
36] 'us all': Syr. vg. 'you all'.

24   Against the followers of Arius.

Thus ask him who is (one) of the followers of Arius: Is God one or many? He says to thee: He is one. Ask him moreover: Is he one or divided in the substance? If they are different in the nature, then it is heathenism.   5

25   Again, against the followers of Arius.

cf. 1 Cor. 8: 6   The Arian asks: Is God, from whom all is, one? We reply: These are the (things) all of which are from him – the heavens and the

cf. Col. 1: 16   earth, and those things which are contained in them, in their 10 entirety. And again: one is the Lord, through whom everything is. We ask: Are those (things) which are through the Son of one kind, and those things which are from the Father of another or are they the same? He answers you: The same. Therefore, those things which the Father made, the same also (did) the Son (make). But, 15 they say, the Father commanded, and the Son made. Therefore

Is. 44: 24   the Father did not make. And see, it is written that he said: 'I have

Jer. 10: 11   stretched out the heavens by myself', and again: 'The gods which did not make heaven and earth shall perish'.
    20

26   Against the heretic who causes God to suffer and puts him to death.

Those who assembled at Nicaea repudiate the multitude of the gods of heathendom in that they have said: We believe in one God. They repudiate also [202] that which the followers of Arius say, (namely) that the Son is foreign in substance, in that they (the 25 orthodox) speak of the Son as consubstantial with his Father. They reject Judaism in that they have said: Father. Do you state your profession of faith!

27   Against the Arians.   30

We say: Because we say that God is one, we confess that the substance is one. But you who say that the Father and the Son are not alike, speak of something which is not in the substance dividing that which (belongs) to one God amongst two gods, and speak of a divided substance in which there are prosopa which are not from 35 one and the same substance.

28   Against those who say that Christ is God alone.

And see, God is the Trinity; is therefore Christ the Trinity? But

38] 'Against those who say': V 'They say'.

38] Lemma to chapters 28, 17, 18 according to V, in Loofs p. 218 app., in German translation; the latter part of that Lemma is taken from the Lemma to 28. 39 – p. 121, 4] German translation of V, Loofs p. 218, 13–19.

if Christ is God alone, the Father not being Christ, (then) they are different in nature. So that (the right thing to say is that) 'Christ' is the name, not of the substance but of the dispensation. And Christ is God, but God is not Christ.

5
Against him who makes God to suffer. 29

Establish before all else and declare yourself: on which side are you? Are you a heathen? You say: No. Therefore you flee from the distinction of gods. You do not belong to Judaism? [203] Then 10 you repudiate the principle of the one hypostasis. You are not a follower of Arius? Then you reject (the belief) that the Son is foreign to the (divine) substance. The Father therefore did not suffer. But, as you say, the Son suffered. Where is the equality of the nature? But, you say, in the flesh he suffered; namely God 15 suffered. Then the flesh was more powerful than God, in that it shewed the impassible to be passible!

Against him who asks whether the Son did suffer or did not suffer. 30

It is asked of us by them: Did the Son suffer, or did he not? We 20 answer: Son is a name. Tell me, therefore what the substance of the Son is, and I will tell you whether he suffered or did not suffer.

About this: 'The Father who sent me is greater than I.' 31

We reply: If he was greater than him, the Son was not consub- cf. Joh. 14: 25 stantial with the Father. For those things which are consubstantial 28 are a counterpart of each other. But after these things, tell me: In what is he greater? Well now – in time? But he is the creator of time. But if not this – in stature? But that substance is without measure and without parts.

30
On this: that the Father was not born in substance. 32

We ask: Is God simple and not compounded, and undivided and alone in his kind, or not? They say: He is. Therefore in substance he is unborn. Therefore that which is of God is not sub-35 stance, because he is undivided and not of different parts. And

8] 'say': R om.
13] 'as you say, the Son suffered. Where': R 'as (you) say, if then Son suffered, where'.
14] 'nature': R 'substance'.
14/15] 'namely God suffered. Then the flesh': R 'and if God suffered, then the flesh also'. Read R.
35] 'of different': R 'different'.

again: because he is God, [204] is he not born, or because he is not born is he God? God, they say, in substance. Therefore, if God is substance, he who is born is not substance, and if he who is not born is God, the Son is not God. But if the Son is God, then he is not born, and that which is of God is not therefore substance which is not born.

33   On this: that the hypostases of the Trinity are not distinct in the will, or in the nature.

He who was taken is outside of the substance of the Son, but not (outside) of the sonship. Therefore, the two natures are called one Son. That which is of God, is common to the substance; but that which is of the Father, (signifies) who he (*sc.* the Father) is, and that which is of the Holy Spirit, signifies who he (*sc.* the Spirit) is. But not in the same way that they are distinct in the hypostases are the prosopa of the Trinity distinct in the nature, or in power, or in will, or in creativeness, or in operation. For everything which has come into being, and is said to exist, came into being from the Father, the Son, and the Holy Spirit equally, and (so it is that) it exists, and becomes, and is provided for. Even if the narrative of the scriptures is (in the form of) a discrimination of divine deeds, accounting them to be, at one time, of the Father, at another, of the Son, and at another, of the Holy Spirit, notwithstanding their being in common, all of them belong equally to God. [205] For whenever we name the name of God alone, we designate the Trinity, but if we wish to speak of one of the hypostases, or prosopa, we make use of the addition of 'Father', 'Son', or 'Holy Spirit'. Then we are able to understand which hypostasis the word (*sc.* 'God') speaks about and (whom it) designates.

34   That the human nature that was taken is perfect.

Call him Son who is incorporeal, and name him God alone, without the manhood which he took from the seed of Abraham and of David. And now that he is perfect who was taken (is corroborated by) the following witnesses: 'For David was a prophet', said the blessed Paul, 'and he knew that God had made oaths with him that of the fruit of his loin would he raise up Christ in the flesh. And he foresaw and spoke concerning his resurrection that his

cf. Heb. 2: 16

cf. Ac. 2: 30, 31

16/17] 'or in power, or in will': R 'and..., and...'.
28] 'Then': R 'And then'.
36] 'Paul': *sic*, marginal note 'Peter', at which Jenks remarks: 'note of Daniel'. That is the name of the copyist which appears here for the first time.

soul was not left in Sheol, neither did his body see corruption.'
Flesh and soul then – is he not (therefore) a perfect man? And
again: 'Into your hands I commend my spirit', he did not say: Lk. 23: 46
'I lay down', but 'I commend', because of the preparation for the
5 resurrection.

Of the order of divine revelations. [206]   35

⟨The Son⟩ interprets ⟨the visible revelations as a type of the
dispensation⟩; the Son is putting honour upon (material) things, as
10 for instance that (saying): 'Heaven is the throne', and that: 'The   cf. Is. 66: 1
earth is the footstool beneath his feet.' The fire he has shown (to be)   Ac. 7: 49
an apparition, the clouds (to be) the ascending and the descending,   Mt. 5: 34f.
but the form of a servant to be him whose (i.e. the Word's) form it   cf. Ex. 3: 2
was. Just as he shows the visible one, so does he also speak about   Ac. 2: 3
15 him; and so also is he spoken about by others.   Ac. 1: 9–11
                                                                       Phil. 2: 7

Concerning virtue.   36

Virtue is difficult and hard in that it is hindered by the inclination (to sin) from knowing what is seemly for it, and, in accordance
20 with it, completing its course. Now the nature, being free in its
reason, does not ever do that which is unfitting, when it uses (it,
sc. reason) in accordance with nature; for it has from God helping
strength at all times. The more its reasoning looks towards God
and towards virtue, in accordance with that the honour is exalted
25 above all. For that which is of good will is above judgement.
Finished are the chapters of the holy Mar Nestorius.

[207] From Mar Babai the Great.   X
Every nature is known and revealed in the hypostases which are
30 beneath it, and every hypostasis is a demonstrator and upholder of
the nature from which it is. And every prosopon in the hypostasis
is fixed and made distinct (as to what) it is. And no nature can be
known without an hypostasis and no hypostasis can stand without
a nature, and no prosopon can be distinguished without the

4] 'I commend' ܡܓܥܠ܏ܢܐ is used by Ephrem in his *Commentary on the
Diatessaron*, see our note, *New Testament Studies* **13** (1967), pp. 290 f. 'I lay down'
ܣܐܡ ܐܢܐ is the expression used by Syr. vg.
8/9] 'The Son', 'the visible revelations as a type of the dispensation': om.
already in U, supplied from R.
26] 'Nestorius': R + 'and to God be glory and to the wretched one who wrote
(it) remissions of sins'. The rest of p. 206 (text) is empty.

hypostasis. Take the hypostasis and show us the prosopon! Take away the nature and show us the hypostasis! Because nature is common and invisible, it is known in its own hypostases. And just as the nature of the Trinity is common to the three hypostases, so the nature of men is common to all the hypostases of men. And if 5 we say of the two natures that they were united in one prosopon, not declaring expressly two hypostases with them, we are saying that the whole nature of the Trinity was united, Father, Son and Holy Spirit, and that the whole nature of men was united, Jesus, Judas and Simon. This is (a matter) of wickedness and blasphemy, 10 in that prosopon cannot be the same as nature, because it (*sc.* nature) is common; but it (the prosopon) is fixed and distinguished in hypostasis, as in the visible, so in the known (things), so that the Father is not the Son, nor is Gabriel Michael, nor Peter John. For the difference between these is in prosopa, [208] not in hypostases 15 and not in the equality of the natures.

For concerning one of the hypostases of the Trinity, that is God the Word, the scriptures say and proclaim that he took from us the man Jesus as one hypostasis, and joined and united it to himself, and made it with him one prosopon of sonship. For 'the Word', 20 it is said, 'became flesh', and: 'God sent his Son and he was (born) of a woman.' And see 'the Word' and 'the Son' and the 'form of God', is not the whole nature of the Trinity, but one of the hypostases in it, God the Word, I say. 'No man has seen God at any time; the only begotten Son who is in the bosom of his Father, 25 he has declared (him)', and: 'God so loved the world as to give his only begotten Son', and: 'Father glorify your Son that your Son may glorify you' – and that is not the whole Trinity. Because of all this, we do not say that Father, Son and Holy Spirit were united with all the hypostases of human nature. For even if one is the will 30 and the power and the authority and the lordship of the whole nature of the Trinity, nevertheless the apostles in their writings proclaim that the union into the prosopon of the Son took place in a distinct manner. In the same way also (is it understood) in relation to the nature of men, for even though all our nature was raised 35 and uplifted from the corruption of mortality, nevertheless one form of a servant was taken, one hypostasis, the man Jesus, was united, according to the word of the angel to the blessed Mary: 'The Holy Spirit shall come, and the power [209] of the most high

Joh. 1: 14
Gal. 4: 4

Joh. 1: 18

Joh. 3: 16
Joh. 17: 1

Lk. 1: 35

13] 'known (things)' must mean νοητά.
25] 'Son': Syr. vg. 'God', Syr. vt. 'Son'.
39] 'shall come': see above, VII p. 90, 20, cp. IX p. 113, 7.

shall overshadow you. Therefore, he who shall be born of you is holy, and shall be called the Son of the most high', that is: by his union with the Son of the most high is he the one Son of the most high. And see, Mary did not bear the common nature without
5 hypostasis, nor many hypostases, but she bore one hypostasis, the man Jesus, he who is also Son of the most high in the union of the one prosopon. Therefore it is known and evident that it is impossible for us to say that the two natures were united to one prosopon without our confessing and declaring with them two hypostases.
10 There are also (instances) where the fathers make use of (the expressions) 'two natures, one prosopon', not denying and demolishing the hypostasis, for see, in many places where it is necessary, they declare with the natures also the hypostases. For the fathers were persuaded that there is no nature which has no
15 hypostasis, and they knew that when they were setting down 'prosopon', they were declaring a hypostasis, because it is impossible for prosopon to stand without hypostasis, so that it (sc. the prosopon) is seen to be fixed in it for its differentiation. And they were discerning accurately that it is not possible for prosopon to be
20 the same as the common nature, because it (the common nature) encloses all the hypostases that are in it. But as we say two natures from the testimonies of the scriptures, so also, two hypostases from the same natures have we learnt, as we have shown above. And therefore everybody who does not declare and confess two natures preserving
25 their properties, which are their hypostases, in one prosopon of Christ, the Son of God, he is foreign to the church and denies the truth.

[211] Again, the kephalaia of Cyril.   XI

Chapter I. Whoever does not confess that Emmanuel is in truth
30 God, and for this reason the virgin is God-bearer, for she bare after the flesh the Word which is from God the Father when he became flesh – let him be anathema.

II. Whoever does not confess that the Word which is from God the Father is united hypostatically to the flesh, and that Christ is
35 one with his flesh, that is to say, the same one at the same time God and man – let him be anathema.

26] p. 210 (text) is empty. Copyist's note: 'I suppose nothing remained on this page, for it was left in the exemplar, not because (something) was lacking there, but because it (just) pleased the scribe.'

28 ff.] This is the third and last appearance of Cyril's anathemata with a refutation in C; the others are in I (pp. 31 ff.) and VI.

III. Whoever makes distinctions concerning the one Christ, into hypostases after the union, whilst mingling them in the conjunction alone, which is with authority and command and power, and not rather by a collecting together of the natural union – let him be anathema. 5

IV. Whoever distributes among two prosopa or among two hypostases the utterances made about Christ in the scripture of the gospel or of the apostle, or those things spoken about him in the writing of the gospel or of the apostle, or those things spoken about him by the saints, or by him about himself, and applies some 10 of them to man who is deemed to be alone, apart from God the Word, but others of them, as though they were utterances [212] befitting the godhead, to the Word which is from God the Father – let him be anathema.

Joh. 1 : 14

V. Whoever says of Christ that he is God-bearing man, and not 15 rather that he is God in truth, as an only Son in nature, in that 'the Word became flesh', and shared like us blood and flesh – let him be anathema.

Joh. 1 : 14

VI. Whoever says that the Word of God the Father is the God or Lord of Christ, and does not rather confess that he is God and 20 man simultaneously, in that 'the Word became flesh', as it is written – let him be anathema.

VII. Whoever says that Jesus was energized as a man by God the Word, and says that he took the glory of the only begotten on himself as though he was another, apart from him – let him be 25 anathema.

VIII. Whoever dares to say that it is right that the man who was taken should be worshipped and glorified with God the Word, and together with him should be considered as God, as if he was one in another – for when there is added this 'together with', it 30 always gives us to understand this – and does not rather in one [213] worship honour the Emmanuel, and let ascend to him one glory, because 'the Word became flesh' – let him be anathema.

Joh. 1 : 14

IX. Whoever says concerning our one Lord Jesus Christ that he has been glorified by the Spirit, as though he had made use of 35 a strange power in the power of the Spirit, and from him received power against the unclean spirits, and so as to do signs among men, and does not rather say that the Spirit is his in a singular manner, through whom he wrought the divine miracles – let him be anathema. 40

Heb. 3 : 1

X. The high priest and apostle of our faith, Jesus Christ, says

41] 'The high priest and apostle': Syr. vg. *vice versa*, cp. VI p. 82, 11.

divine scripture, and (he) who offered himself for us, a sweet- Eph. 5: 2
smelling savour to God the Father. And whoever says therefore
that the high priest and our apostle was not the Word, God, at the
time when he became flesh and man in our likeness, but another
5 man who was of a woman, manifestly apart from him: or whoever
says that he made an offering on behalf of himself, and not rather
on behalf of us, for he who knew no sin was not in need of an
offering – [214] let him be anathema.

XI. Whoever does not confess that the body of our Lord Christ
10 is life-giving and belongs singly to the Word which is from God
the Father, but as though it was another man who cleaves to him
in honour, or that the indwelling of God only was in him, and not
rather that it was life-giving, as we have said, in that it belongs
singly to the Word who is able to save all – let him be anathema.

15 XII. Whoever does not confess that God the Word suffered in
the flesh, and was crucified in the flesh, and tasted death in the
flesh, and became the first-begotten of the dead, because he is
alive and gives life – let him be anathema.

Again, the theses of Mar Nestorius.

20 I. Whoever does not say of the Holy Trinity that it is equal in
substance, and that the everlasting God is one, incorporeal and
infinite, wholly impassible and unchangeable, who is the cause and
the creator of all, who is known in the three hypostases of Father,
Son and Holy Spirit, in which three hypostatic prosopa and in
25 their peculiarity consists [215] the measure of his eternity and of
his substance, and of the fullness of his nature – denies the truth.

2. Whoever says that God the Word was ever changed out of
his nature, for whatever cause soever, or in any way whatsoever,
and does not say that he was conjoined to his Father at all times,
30 while all is filled by him and there is absolutely none of the

1/2] 'and (he) who...God the Father'; see above, VI p. 82, 12 f.
19 – p. 130, 3] preserved also in V.
21] 'one': V+'and'.
22] 'wholly impassible and unchangeable': V, 2 3 1 4
24] 'in'¹: V 'and in'.
25] 'peculiarity': V 'union'.
27] 'out of': V 'in'.

19 – p. 130, 3] in Latin translation after V in Assemani, *Bibl. Orient.* III 2,
pp. cic–ccii, reproduced by Loofs pp. 220–3; the Lemma in V (Latin in
Assemani) gives a good idea of the contents: 'Again,' (om. by Assemani)
'section which is in twelve chapters said about God and about his dispensation
in the flesh by Nestorius the patriarch about the orthodox faith.'

127

beings which could, without his power, live and exist – denies the truth.

3. Whoever does not say that the Son is equal to the Father and to the Holy Spirit, denies the truth.

4. Whoever says that he, the Son, who is equal to the Father, became not equal, that is: man, and thus suffered, and does not rather say that he took a man, and when he suffered, he was conjoined to him in the union, while he remained impassible – denies the truth.

5. Whoever shall say of the Holy Spirit, that he is a minister, or a servant, or second (in dignity), and, to put it briefly, unequal to the Father and the Son, denies the truth.

6. Whoever deletes and removes the three hypostases of cognition of the Holy Trinity, that of the Father, the Son and the Holy Spirit, and while he uses their three names, [216] establishes one hypostasis in his mind, and does not wish to understand the distinction of the prosopa, resembling in these things Sabellius – denies the truth.

7. Whoever dares to divide the simple and infinite, inseparable and indivisible nature of the one godhead of Father, Son and Holy Spirit, or to say that there are three ousias diverse from each other, resembling in these things Arius – denies the truth.

8. Whoever does not confess of him, who is always, and exists at all times, and did not begin, and cease to be, that he took man for his revelation, but says that he became man, resembling in these matters Apollinarius, and that he was born, and was helped, and that he suffered, and arose, and ascended, and was placed equal with the throne which is on the right hand of God, and that he took away what he had previously given to the holy temple which he had taken through it (*sc.* the temple), also to us, because of whom, and for the salvation of whom, it was taken – denies the truth.

9. Whoever shall say of him, who once was taken for the revelation of God the Word, that after the utterance of the angel, and that from the beginning of his being formed through the Holy Spirit within the womb [217] of the virgin, he was at any time deprived of the indwelling of the godhead, either from the beginning of his being formed, or after the beginning, so that he

13] 'Whoever': V + 'says that he'.
19] 'infinite': V + 'and'.
26] 'helped': read with V 'circumcised'.
27/8] 'placed equal': V 'confessed', Assemani 'meruisse'.

might be thought to have been taken twice; or (if) anyone shall say that the Son or the Lord which was taken was other than him who took him, so that they should be thought of as two; or, if he is not saying this, he shall say that a part of the Son was he who was
5 taken, or (if he says) none of these (things), yet will not say that he is the temple of God, and the indivisible image, and that he who was taken participates in honour and renown with him who was the taker, because of the perpetual manifestation in him, the natures being preserved evidently, without corruption, together
10 with the peculiarities of each one of them – denies the truth.

10. Whoever shall speak of Christ, our Lord, as an ordinary man, after the utterance of the angel, that he became changed, whether in the twinkling of an eye, or for an instant, or in whatsoever way it might be, or that we should speak of him as a man
15 only, in whom God was very well pleased, and that from Mary alone was the beginning of his substance, and (that) in name empty, and devoid of understanding, he is honoured with the [218] natural sonship and with the lordship together with God the Word, resembling in these things Paul of Samosata and Photinus
20 the Galatian; and (who) will not rather confess that he is God and man, and that each one of them is preserved in his hypostasis with the indivisible union – denies the truth.

11. Whoever shall say of the animated flesh of the intelligent soul which God the Word, the only begotten Son of the Father,
25 took from the beginning of his being formed, to be revealed in him unceasingly, that it is less in authority than him who took it, and does not confess that it is the same (authority) as he (has), and that he performs in the gift to men, and to all creation, the same power – denies the truth.

30 12. He who does not confess of the man who was taken – I refer to the temple of the Word – whom the apostle names the mediator between God and man, that he is Son and Lord and king, and, to put it briefly, powerful over all, that is to say, (over) angels and

cf. 1 Tim. 2: 5
cf. Rom. 8: 38; Col. 1: 16

1] 'or (if)': V 'or if'.
5] 'none': V 'one'.
15] 'Mary': V 'something'.
18/19] 'the Word': V om.
24] 'God': V om.
28] 'gift': V plur.
30] 'I refer': V 'we refer'.
31] 'of the Word': V 'of God the Word'.
33] 'angels': V + 'men'.

archangels and powers and dominions, and which means at the same time all invisible powers, or rather visible and invisible, because of the divine communion in him – denies the truth.

They are ended.

5

XIIa [219] Again, from the sermons against Bar Daisan, of Mar Ephrem.

There is one being who knows himself and sees himself. He reposes in himself, and from himself sets forth. Glory to his name. This is a being, who by his will is in every place, who is hidden and 10 revealed, is manifest and secret, is above and below. Mingling and condescending by his grace, with the lowly ones, and higher and more exalted, in accordance with his glory than the exalted ones. That which is swift does not surpass his swiftness, and the tardy does not outlast his patience for he is before all, and is after all, 15 and is in the midst of all. He resembles the sea since all created things move in him; as the water cleaves to the fishes in all their fast movements, so does God cleave to all creatures. And as the fishes are clothed with water throughout all their hours, so is the creator clothed with all which has been fashioned, from great to 20 small. And as the fishes are hidden in the waters, so is there hidden in God height and depth, far and near, and those who dwell therein. And as the water meets the fish wherever it goes, so does God meet everyone who walks; and as the water accompanies the 25 fish in all its ways, God accompanies and beholds everyone in all his deeds. Men do not alight from the earth, which is their carriage, and no [220] one removes himself from the just one who is his escort. The good one is woven together with all his possessions on all sides, as the soul is woven together with the body, and light 30 with the eyes. No man can flee from his soul, which is with him, nor anyone hide himself from the good one, who cleaves to him. Just as the waters surround the fish, and they touch them, so do all natures touch God. He is mingled with the air, and with your

1] 'and powers and dominions': V om.   2] 'all': V 'about all'.
3] 'in him': V om.   12] 'and higher': IM 'higher'.

Nr. XIIa: English translation after I by A. S. Duncan Jones, *Journ. Theol. Studies* 5 (1904), p. 551 (p. 552 translates the continuation of the text in I which our ms. does not give). Jones' translation is used here with slight corrections. Latin translation after M by I. E. Rahmani, *Studia Syriaca* I, Scharfeh (Liban), 1904, pp. 9 f. (pp. 10 f. translates the continuation which M has in agreement with I). I and M are here always the editions, not the mss. themselves.

breathing he enters into you. He is mingled with the light, also in your seeing he penetrates into the eyes. He is intermingled with your spirit, and within you searches you out, how you are. In your soul he dwells, and nothing that is within your heart is hidden
5 from him. As the mind precedes the body to all places, so also he previously searches out your soul, whilst as yet you do not search out him. And just as the thought greatly anticipates the deed, so also does his thought know beforehand what you will think. Compared with his subtleness, your soul is flesh, and your spirit a body,
10 he who created you is soul of your soul, and spirit of your spirit. He is far removed from all, and mingled with all, and manifest to all, wonder and amazement which is unsearchable and unspeakable. He is the being whose substance on man can inquire into. He is power, whose depth is inexpressible. Neither among
15 visible things nor among hidden things is there that which corresponds to him. This is he who created and formed from nothing everything that exists; to whom be glory for ever and ever, Amen and Amen.

20 [221] Again, from the holy Mar Ephrem.   XII*b*
God is not far from us, but inwardly does he dwell in our minds. Now, no one of us is near to his soul as God is near to him. The head of each one of us is far from his feet, but God is in the head and in the feet. And in every place is he near and is there, and
25 nowhere is he imprisoned. Whoever in his love resembles Christ is a confessor, and he whose reflection at all times gives heed to God,

---

12/13] 'wonder and amazement which is unsearchable and unspeakable': IM 'great wonder and hidden amazement which is unsearchable'.
17/18] 'to whom...Amen': not in I or M, which continue the text as follows (cf. p. 552, Duncan Jones; pp. 10 f., Rahmani): 'God said, "Let there be light." Lo! it is created. He made darkness, and it became night. Observe! It is made. Fire in stones, water in rocks, The Being created them. There is one Power who raised them from nothing. Behold, even to-day, fire is not in a storehouse in the earth. For lo! it is continually created by means of flints. It is the Being who ordains its existence by means of him who holds it. When He wishes He lights it, when He wishes He quenches it by way of appeal against the obstinate. In a great grove by the rubbing of a stick fire is kindled. The flame devours, it grows strong, at last sinks down. If fire and water are Beings and not creatures, then before the earth (was), where were their roots hid? Whoso would destroy his life, opens his mouth to speak concerning everything. Whoso hateth himself, and would not circumscribe God, holds it great impiety that one should think himself overwise. And if he thinks he has said the last things he has reached heathenism. Oh, Bardaisan, whose mind is liquid like his name!'

his soul is filled with the desire for confessorship, and he bears the suffering of patience. The visible sun is equal for everyone also, but if a man does not open his door, it has no opportunity to enter. But if a man will not open his door, the sun is not lacking, nevertheless it does not illuminate the house. When we fast, we are not 5 giving anything to God, but we acquire profit for ourselves. The dog which stands at the table of its master and eats that which is left over, wags its tail so as to coax, because of its lack of verbal entreaty; but the men whom God has deemed worthy of speech do not confess him, not even with their food. The light with its rays 10 darkens the eyes; not that its abundance is darkness, but because the weakness of sight is not sufficient for it. Now the light comes and everything is seen as it is. Whenever now the mind is enlightened by God, everything stays behind (and) below – business, motion, [222] labour, space. For the wing is not as swift as the 15 thought, for the latter cannot be withholden by anything, when it passes the sun and rends the heavens, and is not persuaded to stay with the angels, nor is it possible that its course should stand still until it arrives at that dwelling-place of the (divine) substance, and beholds that glorious image. Come let us all wonder, because also 20 the angels above wonder at this, how we all are immortal, because of him who was in glory, and was made man for our sakes; to whom be glory for ever and ever, Amen.

XIIc Again, from the holy Mar Ephrem, in the fourth tone.   25
   He who forsakes thought for God, God afflicts him in everything. And if you have care for God, he has taken away the burden of all your care. And if your care is as to how you shall live, on two sides have you come to harm, for you are not sufficient for yourself, nor have you waited for him who is sufficient. That we do not 30 care for one thing only, gives us care for that which is detrimental to us. If you care for many things, none of them will be accomplished. And the righteous one who cares for one thing, that (one thing) cares for his many things.

                                                                            35

XIId Again, from the holy one.
   If the king abide in your house, it is honour to your gate. How much then is your soul honoured if the Lord of all, [God], abides in you! Do not think of him at one time, and neglect him at

38] 'God' del. metri causa.

36 ff.] Cp. *Exhortatio ad monachos*, ed. Lamy vol. IV, pp. 209 f.

another time, but [223] should you not by night and by day seek work with him? And if you grow weary standing, sit awhile and meditate upon him. For the whole time when God will not come into your mind not only is lost, but is reckoned as harm for you.

5 He who disposes himself for God is before his (God's) eyes in his repentance. Repent therefore, O sinner, and seek mercy for your guilt, lest suddenly shall come the thief, and steal your life. 'For you know not the time', said our Lord to his disciples, 'when he who gives life to all shall come, lest he come suddenly, and find

10 you sleeping.' 'Be watchful, and diligent in prayer, lest you enter into temptation.'

cf. Mk. 13: 35–7
cf. 1 Tim. 6: 13
cf. Mk. 14: 38

2 f.] cp. Isaac of Nineveh, *De perfectione religiosa*, ed. Bedjan, p. 138, 1 f., English transl. Wensinck, *Isaac of Nineveh's Mystical Treatises*, Amsterdam 1923, p. 94.

INDEX OF BIBLICAL QUOTATIONS

INDEX OF OTHER QUOTATIONS

† This quotation was discovered too late to take it into account in vol. I and in the
introduction to vol. II; for the same reason the parallel passages have not been collated.

† This series of quotations was discovered too late to take it into account in vol. I and in the introduction to vol. II; for the same reason the parallel passages have not been collated and reference is made to Chabot's translation only.

INDEX OF SUBJECTS

N.B. Cyril's anathemata (Ps.), Ephrem's sermons and the well-known patristic quotations have not been indexed; nor are listed the standard terms of Nestorian polemics or apologetics (one hypostasis, hypostatic union, compound or composite hypostasis, one nature, god-bearer, the suffering of the divine nature, two sons, etc.), since the only possible reference to them could be '*passim*'.

Arians 75, 24

Chalcedonians 13, 21
christology, terms of
  (the relation of) water and Spirit in *baptism* (as analogy to the relation of) the visible and invisible in the baptized Christ 118, 2ff.
  (union of Word and man in Christ) not in the way of *composition*, but in the way of *dwelling* 102, 7f.
  conjunction (corr. *synapheia*) 10, 15f., 20f.; 11, 19ff.; 31, 29 (exact c.); 45, 9f.; 57, 20f.; 90, 24f.; 108, 17f.; 110, 31
  (the relation of) the *eucharistic bread* and the natural body of Christ (as christological analogy) 51, 20ff.; 52, 8ff.; 104, 16ff.; 115, 8ff.
  familiarity (corr. *oikeiosis*) 26, 5; 53, 11. 12
  God-bearing man (corr. *theophoros anthropos*) 78, 31f. (unknown quot. of Eustathius)
  honour (authority, worship, glory, greatness, dignity, good pleasure [corr. *eudokia*]) 46, 7ff. (equality of h. etc.); 47, 17. 25f. (the prosopon of God the Word is h. etc.) 33ff. (in glory and in great dignity which is in good pleasure); 49, 38ff. (united in good pleasure); 50, 1 (exalted good pleasure); 4. 18ff.; 107, 8 ('prosopon' conferred upon honour etc. – Theod. of Mopsuestia) 10f.; 108, 34; 110, 21ff.; 112, 12; 114, 38; 115, 20f.; 116, 34ff.; 117, 26f.; 129, 6ff.
  Christ, our Lord, is alive in two *lives* 101, 25
  lordly man (corr. *kyriakos anthropos*) 45, 32; 48, 31; 73, 8 (l. manhood)
  nature, hypostasis, prosopon (general definitions) 9, 17ff. (hyp. indicative of the common nat.); 93, 26ff. =66, 3f. (every nat. has a distinct definition); 95, 10=67, 12f. (every

hyp....a singular ousia); 102, 3 (two forms do not perfect one hyp.). 24f. (who has no hyp. is an accident in the ousia); 103, 8; 104, 4f., 8f., 25f., 28; 105, 21; 106, 2f., 33ff.; 107, 6ff. (pros. used in a twofold way – either signifies hyp....or it is conferred upon honour etc. – Theod. of M.). 9f.; 108, 24f.; 123, 29ff. (nat. – hyp. – pros.); 125, 16f. (impossible for pros. to stand without hyp.)
  two natures, two hypostases, one prosopon in Christ 20, 11f. (true faith of the two nat. and the two hyp.); 29, 41; 31, 5f.; 37, 33f., 38f.; 38, 13f.; 43, 40; 44, 20f.; 47, 6f.; 50, 29; 51, 38ff.; 104, 42ff.; 105, 28f.; 110, 13 (the pros. is one, but the hyp. are two)
  two natures, two hypostases and their *properties preserved or distinguished* in the one prosopon 10, 16f., 30f.; 22, 12; 28, 17f.; 31, 30f.; 37, 41f.; 44, 6ff.; 67, 21, 32ff.; 72, 16ff.; 74, 30ff.; 91, 9ff.; 93, 4ff.; 125, 24ff. (the nat. preserving their properties which are their hyp. in one pros.); 129, 20f.
  ordinary man (corr. *psilos anthropos*) – always refuted 12, 1; 21, 21; 26, 9; 38, 27f.; 47, 22; 53, 5; 66, 10; 72, 25 (unknown quot. of Nestorius); 97, 4; 98, 14; 116, 2f.; 129, 11f.
  two prosopa, 'own' prosopon 30, 16ff.; 31, 26; 46, 4ff.; 47, 17ff., 28f., 38f.; 68, 16; two prosopa refuted: 77, 10, 19; 78, 10; 109, 14f.
  prosopon of union, union of one prosopon etc. 10, 22f.; 11, 21; 22, 16; 30, 1f., 3f.; 37, 39; 47, 23ff., 37f.; 50, 2; 52, 7f.; 72, 15; 73, 2f.; 96, 12ff.; 124, 18ff.; 125, 6f.
  revelation 45, 33 ([the human nature] the temple for his rev. *sc.* of God the Word); 47, 7f., 18, 30ff.; 58, 18f. (rev. in the flesh and not coming into

INDEX OF NAMES

142